CATALINA ISLAND

MURDERS

An Artist's Tale

Sally Jordan

Sally Jordan Fine Art

Catalina Island Murders. Copyright 2025 Sally J. Jordan

ISBN 979-8-9916880-2-4

First Edition 2025

Front cover provided by

Sally Jordan

PUBLISHER NOTE

I dedicate this book to my husband Peter and my son Chris.
Special thanks to Andre Padilla and Judy Monaghan and Kate Joyce.

ALSO BY SALLY JORDAN

All That Glitters: A Fashion Designer's Tale

Table of Contents

Saturday

Chapter 1: Leaving San Diego

On a beautiful Saturday morning in September, thirteen passengers from San Diego arrived at the Dana Point loading dock and boarded the Catalina Express. The voyagers were headed for the shores of Avalon Bay on Catalina Island expecting to attend or participate in a much-anticipated art festival held annually on the island. The mood was lively and upbeat, the passengers expecting their journey to carry them to the pleasures of Catalina Island. None were aware that some of them would never return home again, for unbeknownst to those passengers, a rendezvous with death awaited them. All thirteen would become either suspects or victims of the Catalina Island murders of 1999.

It all began when I, Annabel Adams and my friend and painting partner, David Ainsworth, were heading to Catalina early in the morning for the weeklong festival. I had been accepted as one of the participating artists in the event.

"I'm so sorry I'm late, David. I didn't wake up when my alarm went off even though it was buzzing for a half hour."

"It's okay, Annabel, you're usually punctual. You're forgiven this once, but let's get going or we'll miss the boat!" David insisted.

We were rushing to catch the Catalina Express which would be leaving at 9:30 a.m. Though David tried to be polite, I could tell he was annoyed so I hurried as I stowed my suitcase and art gear in the trunk of his old green Honda. I then settled back in the seat and relaxed as David pulled away and raced to get onto the Interstate 5. We were headed for Dana Point where the sleek, blue and white catamaran would ferry us to Catalina Island and the annual plein aire art festival. Plein aire refers to the nineteenth century style of painting outdoors on location which was a central feature of French Impressionism. The Plein Aire Painters of California are modern day impressionists and PAPOC is the name of our painting organization.

David and I are members of the San Diego chapter of plein aire artists and have been members of PAPOC for the past two years. In our organization there are two classifications of artists, Signature Artists who are the top level, and Artist Members who are considered less accomplished. I was a Signature Member of the organization, but most of the San Diego artists who painted with us were Artist Members which included my friend David. He wanted very much to improve his standing because only the Signature Members were invited to paint in the best shows.

The Plein Aire Festival on Catalina Island for which we were heading was one of our finest events, and even the Signature Member artists had to be juried into the show. It was a real "feather in my cap" to be included, especially since I was only twenty-four years old, and likely the youngest artist in the show. I was thrilled to be included with forty of the finest artists from all over California who would be gathering to paint the scenic beauty of the Island.

Though Monday morning was the official starting day and time, the Catalina Art Committee gave permission to artists who arrived a day early on Saturday to begin painting Sunday. Before we began, we first needed to get our canvas boards stamped on the back with the date and signed by a committee member. That would be advantageous to the artists because it allowed us to paint for six days instead of five, meaning we would have more paintings to exhibit and sell at the show. At 9:00 on the following Saturday morning, we were to bring our two best framed paintings to be displayed on easels provided for us by the committee. Then a reputable judge would select and place ribbons on the award-winning paintings. Later that afternoon we could bring more painting to be shown, and the Avalon Casino would be open to the public for the art exhibition and sale.

Because my friend David wasn't a Signature Member of PAPOC, he wasn't invited to paint with artists who were official entrants, but that didn't deter David. Regardless of other people's opinions, he decided to accompany me and paint along with the rest of the juried artists despite their likely objections. We both understood that his presence would perturb some of the other Signature Members and cause trouble, but as far as David was concerned, it was a free country, and no Signature Member artist, committee member, or judge owned Catalina Island, and it was his decision to accompany me.

David was a maverick who didn't conform to arbitrary rules created by self-serving individuals who had no relevant connection to him. His quirky personality was one of the reasons I liked David so much; he was his own man. Because of his eccentric personality, he was considered "persona non grata" by some San Diego painters and was shunned by the most powerful women in the organization, namely, Hillary Applegate and her cronies, Karla Streicher and Nancy Hall.

Karla and Nancy had a lot of clout, but it was Hillary who was the "queen bee" and driving force of the San Diego chapter of the club. It was Hillary who held the official title of Chairperson of San Diego PAPOC. Karla and Nancy were her two "first lieutenants" who usually carried out Hillary's directives. Karla and Hillary were talented artists who rightfully deserved the Signature Member designation, but Nancy did not. Never-the-less, she was a Signature Member only because Nancy did as she was told. Karla, on the other hand, was headstrong and frequently challenged Hillary's authority. The three women were in their late forties, egotistical, and each wanted to be regarded as the best artist in the club.

A situation in the club arose with another artist, Sybil Halifax, who many silently considered to be the most talented of all the San Diego painters. Hillary took no quarter with anyone in the organization who could artistically outshine her. "Mirror, mirror on the wall, who's the best artist of us all" was her mindset and continual question. But recently the mirror's answer was Sybil Halifax.

For Hillary, that was intolerable. A noticeable change took place in her treatment of Sybil over several months when she finally came to the realization that Sybil truly was the better artist. Unfortunately, Sybil was an emotionally fragile woman who suffered from bouts of depression which could be triggered by difficult situations that occurred in life.

Her downfall began after a dispute regarding a month-long exhibition in a La Jolla art gallery that Hillary had arranged for our group. One would think that Hillary was attempting to promote the plein aire artists with whom she painted, but that was not the case. The truth was, she wanted the upper echelons of PAPOC to see her, the head of the San Diego chapter, as an important addition to the California plein aire painters hoping to raise her status in the entire organization which included artists from all California.

In addition, since she believed her work was by far superior to the other San Diego artists, she was expecting to have her paintings prominently displayed showcasing her work above the rest of us. To her dismay, all the artists, including Hillary, were only allowed to exhibit one painting in the gallery. She was not pleased.

After the exhibition concluded, the gallery owner asked four artists, Hillary, Karla, Sybil and me, to bring a dozen paintings for her to examine. She would then decide if our work was of a high enough caliber to be exhibited permanently in her gallery. After making her selection, she created a display of our paintings, but to Hillary and Karla's dismay, almost half of the paintings on the wall were Sybil's. I had the next largest amount, and Hillary and Karla were a distant third and forth.

That was devastating to Hillary and her relationship with Sybil went downhill from then on. Hillary, Karla, and Nancy shunned and colluded against Sybil deliberately excluding her from information about the locations of our plein aire events.

Eventually, Hillary made up an arbitrary excuse and told Sybil that she was no longer welcome to paint with the group anymore. That caused Sybil to sink into a deep depression and last month, we learned that Sybil had committed suicide. The situation was a shock to us and had been foremost on the minds of many members of our organization.

"Did you hear about the celebration of life service for Sybil?" David asked as we sped along the freeway.

"I did, I heard about it after it had already taken place. For some reason Hillary didn't inform me. I certainly would have liked to have paid my respects to Sybil. She was a wonderful friend,"

"I heard the place was packed," David said.

"I was told there were almost two hundred people there, not surprising because she was so well liked."

"She was too sensitive for this world, and though her death was tragic, it wasn't a shock to me. I heard that Sybil recently learned that her boyfriend was dying. There was too much heartbreak in her life," David speculated.

"Yes, Sybil had secretly been corresponding with a man in prison for about a year. She told me he had recently been released, and she had to keep the relationship with her lover, Fred, a secret. Sybil knew her family wouldn't approve of him and their whirlwind romance. David, I told her that it wasn't wise to get involved with someone who had a track record of making bad or violent choices. You don't want to introduce malevolent forces not only into your life, but the ones you love as well. The likelihood of any relationship working out is doubtful, but with someone who has been in prison, the odds of failure would be much greater. Wasting time with him didn't make sense. I predicted that she was walking down a dead-end street."

"I can't understand that fascination some women have with bad boys," David said shaking his head.

"I've tried to figure it out, but I don't get it either. It was almost as if she was deliberately bringing bad energy into her life. That situation, plus being blackballed from PAPOC, caused her to descend into a severe depression. I was told she put a gun in her mouth and pulled the trigger." I cringed as I relayed the awful news to David.

"It doesn't seem right. Such a beautiful life shouldn't come to such a tragic end."

"It's so sad! What a waste of a great talent, but more importantly, what a waste of a wonderful person. I'm really going to miss Sybil, David. I think she was the kindest person I ever met."

"You could see it in her paintings. Her handling of color was miraculous." What she could do with paint and a brush was truly magical," David replied.

"She was so generous to me, giving me so much information about creating quality art. She took me under her wing and pointed out things in my paintings that I didn't see. She taught me so much and I credit her with being responsible for my rapid advancement in our painting group. I never would have been accepted as a Signature Member artist if it wasn't for Sybil."

"You underestimate your talent, Annabel. You're better than Hillary, and so much better than all the others."

"Ooo, don't let her hear you say that, David, or I'll be blackballed too, especially since I had more paintings exhibited than she did at the La Jolla gallery. But thank you for the compliment."

"I hear you, Annabel. When you started out, you were a beginner and under the radar, but you've improved a lot and progressed over the past couple of years. Hillary is cold and ruthless and would do anything to prove that she is the best artist of all thinking she should be revered and put up on a pedestal by everyone."

"I've never met anyone so extremely narcissistic in my life."

"I don't understand her icy personality and it scares me," he said.

"Sociopathic is the word I would choose to describe her. Sybil wasn't the only one that fell on her hit list, she's excommunicated several others with whom she couldn't get along or felt threatened by," I said.

"Hillary has made a lot of enemies and sooner or later, it will come back to bite her, Annabel."

"I agree, I've been next to her painting the same scene she's painting, and she becomes paranoid if anyone is standing behind her and painting. She thinks we have nothing better to do than to copy her. That's so strange! Even if that were true, I would be flattered if someone wanted to copy me," I said with a shrug.

"Well, that's because you're reasonably well adjusted, while most of the rest of us are absolutely barking mad," David responded. We both burst out laughing, understanding there was a great deal of truth in what he had said. To put it politely, artists have a reputation for being eccentric. Many of the artists we knew seemed way out of touch with the reality of their ability and the quality of their work, and though I hated to admit it, even my friend David fell into that category at times. Who knows, maybe I did too and am not aware of it. Hmm... I had better keep that in mind.

"I'll bet that Hillary never even mentions Sybil while we're on the island, Annabel. Most of us would like to pay our respects with at least a moment of silence. Sybil was one of us and should be acknowledged. Life is so unfair!"

"Sometimes it is. But still, even though it was said to be a suicide, I just can't come to terms with it. It just doesn't seem plausible to me. I spoke to her after she was kicked out of PAPOC and after learning about Fred's illness. She was depressed but talked about finding some good galleries to get into. She seemed to be handling it reasonably well, but what do I know?"

"Sybil was a fighter, and I saw her battle through her depression on other occasions," David said.

"Yes, sometimes she'd arrive with all her gear and told me she was struggling. She'd apologize for her mood and tell me she needed to be quiet for a few hours. Later, she was relatively alright after she completed her painting."

"I saw that too, Annabel."

"I know how much she loved her mother and daughter. She talked about them all the time. I have a hard time believing that she would cause such grief to her family. That wasn't like her; she simply was not that selfish," I said still unable to make sense of it all.

"This is a terrible thing to say, but I honestly think Hillary is glad Sybil's gone. I'm sure of it. Now she's rid of someone who could knock her down off that 'queen of the mountain' position she thinks she holds," David said.

"Do you know what bothers me? Nancy Hall is a mediocre artist at best, but Hillary got her accepted as a Signature Member artist because she does Hillary's bidding. You're so much better than Nancy, and you can't get accepted by that group to save your life. It's all so political and not based on the quality of one's work, as it should be!"

"As you sow, so shall you reap," David said, his devout Christian background coming to the fore.

It was time to get off the freeway and onto Pacific Coast highway which meant we were getting close to Dana Point. My heart quickened in anticipation, realizing we were almost at our destination. We entered the quaint little seaport village made famous in 1835 when Richard Henry Dana and his crew threw cattle hides off the cliffs of Dana Point to his ships anchored off the beaches below. I loved California with its many miles of beautiful shorelines. I had spent my first nine years in Massachusetts enjoying the seaside there, but the color and look of the ocean was often gray, or a cold, icy blue, so different from California's warm sparkling shades of turquoise, azure, and cobalt. I'm so glad my parents decided to pack up and make the move to The Golden State.

"We're almost to the parking lot and the boat dock. I'm looking forward to being back with you on Catalina Island again," I said.

"We surely had a wonderful trip the last time we were there. Who knows what great adventures we'll encounter this time." David was excited.

I was so glad to have my good friend and companion with me. Though it was easy for me to make friends, I liked having someone I knew well to rely on in case of trouble. David was older than I and though he was eccentric, he was wise in so many ways. I felt much more secure when he was with me. Unlike many artists, I'm most definitely not a loner; I enjoy being around people and interacting with them.

"Catalina is a great place to eat, drink, explore and chill out. I checked online and read that it's very safe. We can go anywhere on the island we want, whenever we want without any fear," I explained to David.

"Annabel, don't be so complacent," he warned. "I know you're planning on doing some nocturns, but if you're going to be painting night scenes, I want you to do them in well populated areas. All it takes is one psychopath, and it's over. Promise me you'll give me updates on your locations if we paint separately."

"Okay, I promise... sort of," I said. David put his hands on his hips and gave me a scowl.

"In that case, my dear, it would be wise for me to paint close to you for the entire festival. I've told you on many occasions that you're way too naïve and much too trusting. That coupled with being headstrong, obstinate, and at times rebellious is not a good combination and can get you into serious trouble."

"I'm so glad you're my friend, David. You're like a big brother to me. We've been able to go all over the place in the west, and I wouldn't have gone there and done those things if it weren't for you."

"Me too. It's great having a little buddy who is so upbeat and cheerful. I'm such an old grump and you brighten my days. It's also wonderful to share a room and split the expense of the hotel for our week-long stay. I couldn't have afforded this otherwise. Who knows, we each might even find romance with someone we meet on the island this time. After all, it is called the island of romance."

"Right, right! But as far as romance goes, I'm going to be way too busy for that. I'm going to be trying to win awards. The Best of Show award win pays $15,000, second place pays $10,000, and third place pays $5,000. People's Choice, Artist's Choice, and the two Honorable Mentions each pay $1,000. I would love to have any one of those simply to help pay expenses. Even though the prize money is great, what I really want most of all, is the acclaim and recognition for my work that comes with the awards. You know how hard I work, and how hard I try. It's not really about the money.

"That's what we all want," David said while shaking his head and looking downcast.

"I wish you had a chance too." David struggled financially. Because of Hillary, Karla, and Nancy, I knew they would never let him advance to Signature Member artist status, so he had no hope of winning any decent prize money. He was just too poor and nonconforming for their sensibilities and too noncompliant with their directives. All three of them were spoiled, rich, country club women. All three of them had married successful, wealthy husbands, who Karla and Nancy divorced and were now collecting sizable alimony checks. None of them had ever done a lick of work or understood what it meant to have to choose between food, gas, or the next car payment. David and I supported ourselves and needed to keep painting sales in mind.

For the opening of the exhibition next Saturday, only two paintings would be allowed in the judging, but after the award-winning paintings were selected and ribbons attached, we could add more paintings to our designated area and replace paintings as they sold. The easels had two extra hooks, one at the very top of the easel and one under the shelf near the bottom on which additional paintings could be hung. With two easels, that would allow the artists to display a total of six paintings at once if none of them were too large. Sunday was more informal, and we could figure out a way to display all that we had painted throughout the week. Though it wasn't allowed, I had seen some artists (some very famous) bring a box of old paintings they had previously done to sell at a discount rate. Even though there were strict instructions forbidding the sale of previously painted art, a few of them got away with selling some of their nice work, but not quite gallery quality at a discounted rate. Because of that practice, they made a lot more money at the show. I think the organizers turned a blind eye, wanting the prestige of having those famous artists in their show. I was too much of a newcomer to try to pull that off. Maybe I would give it a try next year and see if I could get away with it. Honestly, I think it was to everyone's benefit, since the artists gave half the proceeds to the art festival.

Chapter 2: The Catalina Express

"We're here!" I said as we pulled into the parking lot near the loading dock, found a space, and then unloaded our suitcases and art equipment.

We had figured out a system using a rolling cart that would allow us to pack our easels, oil paints, and enough frames that we would need for the eight-day long event. Toting everything was a real balancing act, but with practice, we had gotten reasonably capable at maneuvering all our effects. David looked at his watch and winced because an accident on the freeway had caused another delay.

"Come on, hurry up! We don't want to miss the boat," David called out. He was a stickler for punctuality and organization. I was more relaxed.

"Okay, okay, I'm ready, let's go. Gee whiz!" I responded.

We raced toward the Dana Point Wharf bumpety bumping along the walkway to the location of the kiosk where we purchased tickets. Because we were almost late, we ended up at the back of the line behind the other passengers. The boat ride, as I remembered, would take us about an hour to get to the island. After dock workers stored our gear below deck in the luggage compartment, we walked up the boarding ramp and onto the Catalina Express. I loved being out on the ocean and had been looking forward to this boat ride. To me it was a thrill that heralded the beginning of my first major artistic achievement.

"Ta da! We made it!" I sang, lifting my arms feeling so full of high spirits in anticipation of the event. I had hoped and dreamed of being one of the participating artists while attending the festival as an observer over the past several years.

David just smiled and affectionately huffed at my childish exuberance. We decided to stay on the lower deck of the boat where there were many available seats for us to sit and relax out of the sun and wind of the upper deck. I remembered it could get uncomfortably cold and windy up there. We found our seats, settled in.

"It's not very crowded on this level. A lot of people like being outside," David said as he looked around.

"I see several artists who will be in the show, David. Hi guys," I said as I waved to Randy Creighton, Michael Mitchell, and Saul Katten, the three super star artists of the festival. All of them were exceptionally talented and would probably take home most of the awards. I didn't begrudge them their winning streaks, they were all nice, fun-loving guys who had been kind and respectful to me, even when I was just starting out, often producing some truly awful paintings. The judge of the show was known for favoring the male artists which would also add to their chances of winning. Although there were many gifted women plein aire artists, it was still a man's art world in 1999. I had seen or been in shows where all the prizes went unfairly to only the men. But women were speaking up and there was some movement in the award selections. I was undeterred, for I could see things were improving for the women.

I tried to analyze the difference in male and female painting but for the most part, there wasn't a lot. I noticed that men focused more on architecture, cars, and boats, while women seemed to be attracted to color, frequently including flowers or something colorful in their paintings. The term "value" is an art term which refers to the lightness or darkness of a color or shade. Artists who control their values are generally considered more favorably than those who rely on color. Color is generally seen as superficial while value is structural and the building blocks of fine art. Art is always evolving and though I agree with that concept in theory, all anyone needs to do is look at the art of Vincent van Gogh and the power of his use of color to see that old viewpoint blown out of the water.

There is a little-known fact that roughly twelve percent of women have a fourth color cone in their vision while most people have only three cones. Women with the fourth cone are called tetrachromats and see more colors than the general population. That might explain the excessive preoccupation some women seem to have with color.

"Look to your left," I said. "There are Hillary, Karla, and Nancy... wave, David." David groaned and turned away from them, ignoring my advice. I put on a fake smile as I waved, knowing it was in our best interest to be reasonably cordial to the old bats. Though I tried to help my friend be more diplomatic, the truth was, I admired and respected him for refusing to capitulate to their domination. There was nothing phony or insincere about David, but he paid a high price for his integrity.

Then two nicely dressed women sat down next to David and me as they greeted us. For a moment I thought I recognized them, but then realized they were strangers.

"Is this your first trip to Catalina?" I asked, attempting to make conversation.

"No, we've been here before. I'm Charlotte Fitzsimmons, and this is my granddaughter, Alice Smith.

"So nice to meet you. I'm Annabel Adams, and this is my friend David Ainsworth. We're both going to be painting on the island. Are you going there for the art show?" I asked.

"Yes, we certainly are. We're both art collectors and each of us own many wonderful paintings. I've heard your name before, and I look forward to seeing some of your work, Annabel," Charlotte remarked. Alice then joined the conversation and said,

"If for some reason you get injured, have a headache, or stomachache, my grandmother was a registered nurse for many years and keeps all kinds of medicines to cure whatever ails you. She's a true angel of mercy."

"How nice, David and I will keep that in mind, but hopefully we'll be able to stay healthy." Charlotte looked to be about sixty-five or seventy, and she walked with a cane. Her knee was swollen so I assumed she was probably in some pain. That might have explained why she had so many medicines at hand, and after all, she was a nurse.

"At what hotel will you be staying?" David asked. I smiled at him pleased that he was attempting to be more social.

"We're at the Glenmore Plaza Hotel, the oldest hotel on the island. Alice is sharing a room with someone named Karla Streicher on the third floor. I'll be alone on the second floor because of my knee. The only room still available on the second floor had just one full size bed so we couldn't share a room together."

"That's where we're staying too. We stayed at the Glenmore the last time we were here, and we love it. Have you stayed at the Glenmore Hotel before?" I asked.

"I have," Alice said. "It seems I always end up on the third floor. There are so many stairs to climb since the hotel has no elevators, but I don't mind. I can always use the exercise."

"You seem very fit Alice, what is it you do to stay in such good shape?" I asked. Alice was very tall, probably over six feet, and quite athletic looking from what I could see.

"I was in the navy. The training was rigorous back then. Now I lift weights and run several miles each day. I guess staying in shape has become a habit, but I do like how I feel when I stay with my routine."

"Wow, I'm impressed!" I said looking at David. He nodded in agreement. I've read that people who run have endorphins and stay more emotionally well-adjusted as well as physically fit."

"Yes, that's true. When I get lax and miss a few days, I feel sluggish and off kilter. I recommend some form of exercise to everyone," Alice said looking at her grandmother, who looked down, diverting her gaze.

An older couple who was sitting in front of us turned around to join in the conversation. They introduced themselves as Miriam and Asher Bloomberg.

"The reason we're here is for the art festival. We're serious collectors and love plein aire art. Most importantly, we're here to celebrate Miriam's sixty-second birthday. We'll be staying at the Hotel Mac Rae. Have any of you stayed there before?" Asher asked.

"No, no," we all answered. None of us had.

"We're staying in our favorite room that looks out over the bay. It has such a great view. We can see the Casino, the Pleasure Pier, and all the beautiful little boats floating in the water. It's so romantic." Miriam said as Asher gave her a kiss on the cheek. "My husband is three years younger than me. I guess that makes me a 'cougar,' she said winking at Asher as she put her arm around her husband. Miriam had a delightful twinkle in her eyes, and at first impression she seemed to be a fun-loving, cheerful sort of person.

"If you're art collectors you should keep an eye on Annabel's work," David interjected. "She's as good as they get."

"Are you Annabel Adams?" Miriam asked looking puzzled.

"Yes, I'm surprised you know my name."

"Oh, my dear, you have quite the reputation as one of the best," Mrs. Bloomberg said. "But I'm surprised you're so young."

"Oh, that's so nice to hear. Thank you for passing along that information. We artists love to feel our work is appreciated." Although I loved being complimented, it made me a little uncomfortable not knowing what to say. I didn't like false modesty, but though I thought I was good, I didn't want to come across as arrogant, so to alleviate my discomfort with the situation, I stood up and said, "I'm going to the bar for a drink. Would any of you like me to bring you back something?" No one wanted anything so I walked over to the snack bar and stood next to a nicely dressed, silver haired gentleman who smiled at me.

"I wonder where the clerk has gone. I hope he comes back soon." I said being friendly.

"I don't know, but I'm sure he'll be back in a minute. I certainly could use some ginger ale right now," he answered.

"Are you having trouble with sea sickness?" I asked.

"I really am. Hello, young lady, I'm Tony Rossi," he said as he offered me his hand. I took it and noticed he had a nice, gentle grip, which was unusual for such a large man.

"Hi, I'm Annabel Adams, it's nice to meet you, Tony. Are you here for the art show?" I asked. Tony got a peculiar look on his face when I mentioned my name. I wondered what he was thinking. I noticed he didn't look well. His skin was pale and had an unhealthy undertone, probably from the sea sickness.

"Oh yes, absolutely. I wouldn't miss this show for the world." Tony was about fifty. He was tall and well-built though slender. It looked to me as if he probably kept fit with some kind of weightlifting regimen.

"You look familiar, have we met before, Tony?" I thought I had seen him somewhere but couldn't place where or when.

"No, I don't think so. I just have one of those sorts of faces, I guess."

By then the attendant had returned and we ordered our drinks.

"Have you been to Catalina before?" I asked.

"No never." he said definitively. "This will be the first and last time I come here so I'm going to make the most of it."

"Where will you be staying?" I asked, ignoring that quizzical remark he just made. While I was standing there, I couldn't help but notice that Tony had an interesting face which was like a pot someone had broken and tried unsuccessfully to glue back together. One of his eyes was lower on his face than the other. His nose had an "s" curve to it. Though his smile was warm and friendly, it was asymmetrical. I couldn't say Tony was good looking, but he had a sweet face that was pleasant and inviting.

"I'll be at the Portofino Hotel." Tony said as the attendant handed us our drinks.

"Oh, I like it there," I said as the attendant handed me my drink. "My friend, David, and I shared a room there once, but this time we're staying at the Glenmore Plaza. Well, I hope you enjoy your stay and have a wonderful time on the island."

"I'm sure it will be a once in a lifetime experience." he said, making another curious comment.

"I better get back to my friends. I'm sure I'll see you again. We're bound to run into each other around Avalon.

"I'm sure we will. It was nice meeting you, Annabel."

It was awfully nice meeting you too, Tony." Poor guy, he seemed so alone and unhappy. But what a nice gentleman.

For a while I sat quietly watching the people milling about. It was amazing what could be learned watching people and their body language. It was obvious to me that, Hillary needed to be the center of attention making grand, exaggerated gestures as she gazed down upon other people. But her face remained strangely expressionless with vacant eyes that resembled two leaden little beads.

Karla was a beautiful woman and like Hillary also needed to be the center of attention. I'm sure she had gotten her way with her looks most of her life, but now she was playing a different game. I observed her folding her arms and rolling her eyes as she interrupted and contradicted Hillary. Karla was smart and sarcastic with a biting edge to her. She could have put Hillary in her place, but she grudgingly capitulated to Hillary because she believed, incorrectly, that she was the superior artist and secretly planned to knock Hillary off her pedestal.

Nancy was not as bright or talented as the other two, and though she put on airs and acted as if she was their equal, she wasn't. I observed as she imitated Hillary's grand gestures and mannerisms. She was even beginning to sound like Hillary using the same phrases. Nancy was a submissive kiss ass, believing it was to her benefit to be included in such an auspicious clique. I neither respected Nancy's artistic ability nor admired her personally for she was lacking in character and good judgement.

While I had been talking to Tony, David had gotten restless and got up and wandered around the outside of the boat hoping to enjoy the ride and appreciate the freshness of the Pacific Ocean air. Wanting to locate my friend, I also went outside and paused for a moment. It was wonderful feeling the sun on my face, and the wind in my hair, but though it was exhilarating, I had to avoid getting too much sun exposure and a likely sunburn. In the distance, there was a faint sound of the seagull's crying which meant we were coming closer to land. To my delight, there were dolphins breaching the water beside the boat. I spotted David and called and motioned to him,

"David, come look at these guys."

"I also saw some swimming behind the boat. Why do you think dolphins do that?" he asked.

"Maybe they're curious, or maybe they get in the wake of the boat and it pulls them along. They certainly are interesting creatures, aren't they? Someday I'd like to swim with them and pet them."

"Yes, that sounds like something I'd like to do too. They're such nice fish," David said.

"No, David, they're not fish, they're mammals, silly boy." I was now laughing at his blunder.

"Of course they are, I was just testing you to see if you knew," David said embarrassed by his faux pas. "I want to tell you what I just heard before you called me over. Hillary and Nancy are also sharing a room on the third floor of the Glenmore. So are Karla and Alice, the tall woman we just met...and so are we."

"How cozy! You and I are going to be right next to those three sweethearts and are going to be seeing a lot of them. I'd change hotels if we could, but everything is booked because of the art show," I said, grimacing.

"We're just going to have to put up with some snarky, condescending remarks, Annabel. You know how I can let people's nasty comments get to me. I'll just have to do my best to ignore them. We're coming into port now. Let's go inside," David said, turning and heading toward our seats.

We gathered up our carry-on things and got ready to disembark. As the three "dragons," Hillary, Karla, and Nancy with their Louis Vuitton handbags and luggage got in line in front of David and me, we watched and listened as they walked down the ramp.

"It looks like Annabel's putting on a little weight," Hillary said snickering to herself.

"I don't think so. It's just those ugly, paint splattered pants she always wears to paint in. You'd think she'd try to dress a little better. She looks like a homeless person most of the time." Karla replied.

"She thinks she's so pretty that she doesn't even have to try. She's always swishing and flipping that long, red hair of hers to get attention," Nancy added.

"Oh, please... it's blond, Nancy, can't you tell the difference. Maybe Annabel should forget about her hair and pay attention to improving her paintings. They could use some work," Karla hissed.

"That'll never happen if she continues hanging around with that no talent, David," Hillary declared. They all cackled in unison. David and I heard everything they said, and though he tried not to show it, David was hurt.

"How mean, David," I said sympathizing with him when they were out of our ear shot. "I guess they didn't realize we were right behind them."

"Are you kidding! Do you think it would have mattered to them even if they did. They're a nasty bunch, the whole lot of them."

"I don't think any of them like each other. Their relationships are based on how they can use one another for their own advancement." David nodded in agreement.

"Let's forget about them and get our equipment. They're starting to unload now," he said wanting to change the subject.

Chapter 3: Avalon Bay Arrival

David and I shuffled through the piles of suitcases, back packs, and belongings the dock workers had unloaded for the Catalina Express passengers until we located each one of our personal effects. We had taken the walk down Pebbly Beach Road with our art equipment pulled by one hand and suitcases pulled by the other hand before, but now we had more than a dozen frames piled on top as well. Thank Goodness plein aire frames were thin. It would be quite a balancing act on the long, bumpy road ahead of us before we got to the right turn onto the smooth sidewalks of Crescent Ave. Thank goodness for bungy cords. The last bit of the journey was the left turn up Sumner Ave to the Glenmore Hotel. The challenging walk would be about a half mile.

"Let's just take it easy, David. There's no point hurting our hands or our backs trying to break a speed record." David was in his forties and had arthritis. I didn't want this trek to aggravate his condition.

"Good thinking. We can even take breaks on the benches along the way, if need be," he said.

"I hope you're not letting the things those 'old bats' said get you down, David. I don't know who they've deceived themselves into thinking they are, but they're nowhere close to who they imagine themselves to be. I hope Randy, Michael, and Saul beat the heck out of them at the art show."

"I'm hoping and praying that you'll be the one to do that. Wouldn't that be poetic justice?" David asked.

"I'll certainly try my best. It's interesting how comments like that compel a person to try harder, isn't it," I asked.

David looked at me and smiled. I knew exactly what that look meant. He didn't need to say a word. We made our way down Pebbly Beach Road without needing a break, but it was just as bumpy as an old European cobblestone road could have been. Shortly after, we made the right turn at the curve onto Crescent Ave, the main street that parallels the length of the Avalon beach front with the beach on the east side of the street, and all the little storefronts on the west side. While we were walking, I noticed a man standing on the corner of Sumner and Crescent Avenues talking to a policeman. The man was tall, wearing a kind of jacket like the East Indian men wear. Even from across the street I could see he was very good looking.

"I wonder who that bronze beauty is over there wearing the tunic. I've seen him before," I said to David nodding my head in the man's direction.

"I met him and talked to him briefly the last time we were here," David said. "He referred to you as the 'pretty girl with the long, blond hair' during the conversation. He was inquisitive asking me a series of questions, and though he tried not to be obvious, I could tell you were the object of his interest."

"Hmm... how intriguing." I said looking in his direction. He was looking at me now and I turned away not wanting to appear noticeably curious. "I want to take some pictures of the Green Pleasure Pier and the boats before we head up Sumner Ave to the Glenmore Hotel. Could you take care of my stuff for about ten or fifteen minutes, David?"

"Of course. Take your time."

There were several angles I wanted to examine hoping to find the very best place to set up my easel as soon as I got my canvases stamped. After leaning down, squatting like a frog with my face practically touching the sand, I heard a voice from behind saying,

"I don't know if I'm looking at a pretzel or a girl. Which is it, Captain?" the man asked.

"If I had to guess, I'd go with a pretzel. How can anyone possibly get into a contorted position like that?" the officer answered in his heavy southern drawl.

"I turned my head and was surprised to see it was the Indian man and the police officer." The two of them were snickering, clearly amused by my twisted position."

"I'm sorry, I thought this was Catalina Island, I must have taken a wrong turn and ended up in the Mississippi Delta," I said making fun of the policeman's southern accent.

"Ooo... she got you good, Captain," the Indian man said wincing.

"I was trying to find an interesting angle from which I could paint this pier," I explained, feeling rather foolish and awkward.

"I doubt if you'll be able to paint anything from that position," the Indian man said still laughing at me.

"I guess not, but it doesn't mean I can't paint it from the photo I just took when I get home to my studio." I said, hoping to dispel the idea that I was a blithering idiot. The man was making fun of me, making quips at my expense. I don't mind being teased by friends, but I don't like being laughed at by strangers. I decided that rather than getting angry, the way to handle the situation was to stay calm and take charge of the situation. I stood up, getting out of my awkward position as quickly as possible. "Hi... I'm Annabel Adams." I held out my hand to greet the two men. They both had impressively firm grips. I made certain mine was equal to the challenge.

"Yes, I know your work and who you are. Nice to finally meet you Annabel, I've seen you here with your boyfriend before. I'm Raj Moghaswammi, and this is the Station Commander, Captain Tom Derringer."

"Raj looked even better up close. He must have been about thirty, had broad shoulders, stood straight and tall, and spoke with the slightest hint of an English accent. His handsome face had fine features with pale hazel, piercing eyes. There was an undeniable magnetism about him, but my first impression was that he was arrogant, and I didn't like him. Still, I couldn't deny, I was curious.

"Are you originally from England," I asked.

"No, I'm not, but my parents both lived there for most of their lives. I'm sure that has something to do with it, plus I've visited relatives there many times. Most people think I sound like a typical American." he answered.

Raj was polished and classy, but on the other hand, Tom Derringer was rough-edged, about forty-five, at least 6' 4" tall, with a huge, shaved head. The captain was dressed in his well pressed khaki uniform displaying a shiny gold badge and some official insignias verifying his authority. Standing close to this thick boned man with an imposing frame was unnerving. His size alone was intimidating, but he spoke with a booming voice that would put the most insolent dissident back on his heels. Strangely enough, it was combined with a disarmingly amusing southern drawl, totally incongruous. Though he wasn't handsome, the man had a formidable presence.

"So nice to meet you both, but David isn't my boyfriend. We're just good friends and painting partners," I said looking to see where David was.

"That's very interesting. The last time you and David were here, he told me you were staying together in the same room," Raj said. The tone of his voice gave evidence of his strong disapproval. How rude and presumptuous of him to bring it up now as we were just meeting. Now I was angry.

"Not that I usually feel it's necessary to explain myself to a total stranger, but I'm going to make an exception this time. For your information we always share a room to cut down on expenses. We're both practical and have worked out a system that allows us some privacy. David is like a brother to me, nothing more, not that's it's anyone's business." I huffed, making it clear that I was annoyed and insulted by his implications.

"Well, I certainly didn't mean to pry into your affairs. Let me make it up to you by buying you and David lunch after you get settled at the Glenmore Hotel?" Mr. Moghaswammi said realizing he had offended me.

"Thank you very much, but that won't be necessary," I said still fuming. MY AFFAIRS? How dare he make those kinds of insinuations to a perfect stranger. He has no say in what I choose to do or with whom I choose to do it.

"It's very necessary as far as I'm concerned. I don't want to start things off on the wrong foot with you. Won't you reconsider?"

"We'd be happy to accept your invitation," David said. He had been listening to the conversation as he joined us. My frugal friend wasn't going to let free lunch go unaccepted, for he was someone who often went without any lunch at all.

"How did you know we we're staying at the Glenmore?" I asked.

"You stayed there the last time you were on the island, and today, you and David were just starting to head up Sumner Ave where the Glenmore is located," Raj said lowering his voice and moving in uncomfortably close to me. I stepped back feeling crowded as he invaded my space.

"How perceptive of you. Do you work here on the island?" I asked as I was now cooling off a bit.

"Raj is a private investigator who's truly a technical genius with the computer," Tom, the police captain answered. Some of my men are so dumb, they couldn't find their butt if they had both hands in their back pockets, but Raj and my sergeant, Jim Monaghan, are my two best men. They're the ones who help me solve most of our crimes... but that's just one of Raj's many talents."

"I know you figured it out already, Annabel, but our police captain is from the south." Once again, Raj moved in closer to me. "He was the captain of a small island off the Georgia coast before he came here." There was something about the way he invaded my space and was looking down that perfect nose at me that made me terribly uncomfortable. "You'll soon get used to the accent and unique way he has of expressing himself. Now, back to lunch, how about it?" Raj asked.

"Well... can we meet you on the terrace of the Busy Bee in about an hour?" I asked. I wasn't sure if I liked this sarcastic man or wanted to spend any time with him. He was too overconfident and conceited, but he was intriguing in a pushy sort of way, so I accepted his invitation.

"Perfect! Let me give you my phone number in case you run into a delay." Raj answered without missing a beat.

"Good idea, but if we can get our things up to the third floor reasonably soon, at least one of us will meet you on time. See you then." My, he's insistent, I thought. And I heard the East Indians were gentle people. I'm not sure I want to feel obligated to him. If I change my mind and want to back out, at least David could join him and bring me back half his lunch.

David and I gathered our things and headed up Sumner Avenue to the hotel. The Glenmore Plaza was a charming Victorian structure painted pale yellow with white trim. We learned that it was built in 1891 and was the oldest hotel on Catalina Island and the second oldest hotel in the state of California. The structure resembled the style of the Hotel del Coronado in San Diego which was built three years earlier. Some of the guests who had stayed at the Glenmore were, Marilyn Monroe, Clark Gable, Charlie Chaplin, and Amelia Earhart. David and I might possibly be occupying one of their rooms. Checking in with the desk clerk went smoothly and with no minor glitches.

"Here we are!" I said. As usual, I was affected by the charm of Avalon with its sparkling blue water and the small white boats in the harbor. The little town seemed to be stuck in some mysterious time warp, but where in time was the question. Some of the iconic structures like the Glenmore Hotel and the Holly House were wooden and built in the Queen Anne style of the late 1880s. The Tuna Club, the oldest fishing club in the USA, was built in 1898. Fortunately, those icons were all loved and cared for, keeping the island's past preserved for the enjoyment of present and future generations of visitors.

Many of the island's most iconic structures were built in the 1920s including the Chimes Tower monument, the Yacht club, the Zane Grey Hotel, and the Casino which was once filled with people in the grand ballroom dancing the night away to the sound of the big bands. Several of the finest examples Art Deco painted murals were still on display at the entrance of the Casino. The remnants of the Art Deco influence could be seen in the architecture throughout the town, especially in the two heavily decorated fountains situated in the middle of the street at both ends of Crescent Ave.

Most of the little shops along Crescent Ave. were reminiscent of the 1950s recalling the post war Main Streets of America. This artist's dream town was a destination for painters and art lovers from all over the country. Everywhere one would turn, there was a painting waiting to materialize. There was a myth that the cove and the island were enchanted, and I couldn't deny that it was one of those unique places where lovers find romance. They were here and all around us.

"Do you have a place where we could store our painting equipment so that we don't have to drag it up and down the stairs every day?" I asked the desk clerk who was wearing a name tag that read Bonnie Abernathy.

"Yes, we do. It's right behind me. We can lock everything in at night and someone will be here before 6:00 in the morning to open the door for you. Your things will be perfectly safe."

"That's great. Then we'll only need to take our suitcases up the stairs. Do you still have the continental breakfast every morning?" I asked.

"Yes, it's just muffins, rolls, bananas, and apples with coffee, tea and apple juice," Bonnie answered.

"Great! That's all we need," David said.

We climbed up the two flights of steep stairs, panting by the time we got to the third floor. It was not a problem, for in a couple of days we would be used to the climb. Our room, with the number 301 on the door, was a nice room at the back of the hotel. Hopefully, it would be a quiet room. There were twin beds which were small but sufficient. Right next to our door was a back entrance in the hallway with stairway leading outside and down to the back of the hotel. That pleased me in one respect, since I was terribly afraid of fire. It was nice to know an escape route was close by, but there were safety and security concerns I had as well. It would be easy to accidently leave the old twist button on the doorknob unlocked allowing someone from outside to enter without being noticed. I would have to remember to check it each night before I went to bed.

It was a little early to meet Mr. Moghaswammi, but David and I decided to stroll down to the Busy Bee restaurant to sit out in the fresh air for a few minutes to relax while we waited to meet our newfound benefactor. Though I initially found Raj to be insolent, he was interesting, exotically handsome, and from what Captain Tom implied, highly intelligent. Even so, I had my reservations. What would I have in common with a computer expert? It sounded so terribly boring. If I didn't fall asleep listening to him drone on about networks, operating systems, modems, and floppy discs, maybe the private investigatory work he was doing might hold my interest. Yes, I think that would be quite interesting.

"Can you seat us on the patio close to the water and in the shade of one of those lovely blue umbrellas?" I asked.

"Certainly," the hostess replied. "Would you please follow me."

David and I settled for a table near the water with a nice view. I began to look over the menu to be able to order quickly if the conversation with the detective or computer expert, or whatever he was became strained or awkwardly silent.

"I've forgotten what the menu was like here, but I remember the food was good," I said perusing the selections. When I look up to see if David had found anything he would like, over his shoulder I saw Mr. Moghaswammi heading toward our table.

"Hi," I said, giving him an unenthusiastic little wave.

"Smart girl, keeping out of the sun. I guess tanning isn't for you," he said as he seated himself at the table.

What was he implying? Was that another dig, I wondered? I had a little tan but had learned my lessons about spending too much time in the sun long ago.

"The sun loves some people coloring their skin with a golden, glowing bronze, but for me, it turns my skin a bright, lobster red. Some people can handle the sun, I'm certainly not one of them," I said trying to brush off his sarcastic remark.

"Why would anyone want to tan such a lovely, alabaster complexion. That would be criminal," he said. Was he putting me on, or was he trying to be nice? I wasn't sure.

So, tell me more about what you do as a private investigator for Captain Derringer?" I asked.

"I helped him set up a new, state of the art computer system in his office that would allow him to function with his work more efficiently. The system he was working with was pitifully outdated and ineffective. We got rid of the old system, though he gave me a terrible time not wanting to let it go. He finally capitulated," he said shaking his head.

"Boy, I can relate to that," David said. "I'm a complete Luddite. Computers give me a headache."

"I try to keep up," I said with a shrug. "It's hard to share the time of improving my work and learning to be proficient on the computer. Because I enjoy painting so much more, it usually wins out."

"If I were as talented as you, I would probably do the same," he said.

"How did you become familiar with my work?" I asked.

"I saw you painting here the last time you were on the island. You were so engrossed in what you were doing you didn't even notice me or the crowd of people that had gathered around you. The same thing happened when you were working on some other paintings as well. It must be wonderful to have that kind of concentration. In addition to that... I looked up your website."

"That's nice to hear. So, tell me, how did you become a private detective? Have you done police work before?"

"No, I'm not really a private detective, Annabel. Tom just likes to call me that. He thinks I'm like some kid who wants to wear a badge. It's not about the titles or trapping of authority that interest me, I'm more of an amateur sleuth who enjoys putting pieces of puzzles together. I become obsessed with finding answers and solving puzzles and problems of any kind, and in this case, it's crimes. For me, it's more of an interesting hobby. I also find the police mentality to be fascinating," he explained.

"In what respect?" I asked, leaning forward.

"They see things so simply. For them, everything is so black and white. They have their rules and laws and believe in their code so strongly that they are willing to die for them. They are passionate about their work. I see things in black, white, as well, but also in many shades of grey," Raj explained.

"I see everything in brilliant, dazzling technicolor," I said, lifting my hands toward the sky.

"That must be wonderful for you," he said. Was he being sarcastic again, I wondered.

"It is. Being tuned into color is like living continually on some life enhancing drug. I never grow tired of it," I said. David was nodding in agreement.

The waitress finally came by with her pencil and pad ready to take our orders.

Hello, Mr. M," she said furtively flirting with him.

He politely returned her greeting then said, "They have a great Cobb salad here, if you're in the mood for a salad."

David took his advice and ordered the Cobb, but I ordered a chicken Caesar instead. Throughout the hour, Raj peppered me with questions, and I began to feel like I was being interviewed. When I asked him questions, he turned the focus back to me. There were so many things I wanted to know about him but he was giving brusque answers. Was he being evasive or was I just being too inquisitive. It didn't matter, I was curious and kept on with my questioning.

Finally, I began to make headway. "So, where did you learn about computer technology?"

"I went to Stanford. Then to MIT where I got my master's degree. I was in the process of beginning my doctorate when my father and I decided to put my technical advancements into practice rather than writing about them."

"How old were you when you went into Stanford?'

"I was fifteen. I graduated from high school early."

"I'll say you did. How long ago were you working on your doctorate?" I asked.

"I began when I was twenty-one. I've been working with my father since then. I only stay in my house on Catalina part time, usually twice a month, mostly on weekends. My father and I are partners in a tech firm called Envarna. Maybe you've heard of it."

"Yes... I think I have," I said trying not to appear too enthusiastic.

"He handles the marketing and business end, while I concentrate on keeping up with the latest technical advances of our competitors and try to stay several steps ahead of them. Most of the time I'm in San Jose, where I have another house which is my permanent residence.

"Were you born in California?"

"Yes, born and raised in San Jose, but my family likes to travel. We visit family in India as well as those in England. My parents have several homes in the US and in England. They also have one in Switzerland which is beautiful. I think even you would approve," he said with a snicker.

"Do I really seem that critical?" I asked feeling embarrassed and judgmental.

"Yes, you do," he said his eyes widening as he tilted his head. "But I guess it's part of your artistic temperament."

"Ha, talk to me if you want to know about artistic temperament," David interjected. "Annabel's a pussy cat. She rarely loses her temper and has the patience of a saint."

"That's nice to know, and coming from David, someone who knows you so well, it holds a great deal of credibility," Raj responded.

"Well, enough about me and my temperament. Isn't it a long drive from San Jose to Dana Point?" I asked.

I don't drive, I fly between the two cities in my Turbo Arrow stopping at Palomar airport, and from there, on to Catalina. There is an airport here, I'm sure you're aware of that," Raj stated.

If Raj was trying to impress me, it was working. I was somewhat familiar with his company Envarna. It was a company I had investigated on the NASDAQ while doing some stock trading in my tiny 401K. I knew it was a large cap company on the stock exchange. I just didn't want to make a big fuss over it. He just let me know he had two houses, and the houses in Avalon cost a fortune. He also said he owns and flies a Turbo Arrow which I know is a nice plane.

"Yes, I've heard about the airport. Is your house close by?" I asked, not caring if I was being too inquisitive.

"It's on Lower Terrace Road." He leaned in with his face very close to mine and said, "Turn around... it's the white house that overlooks Holly House." He then put his arm around me and pointed me in the direction of his house.

"Yes, I think I see it. It's that large house on the hill. The view from there must be phenomenal. Do you think David and I could paint from your balcony?" I blurted out. Wow, how nervy of me, I thought, but I could get a great painting from that balcony. After all, fortune favors the bold, and he certainly had no qualms about taking liberties with me.

"Of course. I'd be glad to help you out, and if you're nice and don't get paint on my deck, I'll invite you to the Indian dinner I'll be preparing for some of my police friends and artists I've met on the island."

"Oh, that would be wonderful! I love Indian food. I even had a dinner party with a dozen friends where I prepared quite a few Indian dishes with all the condiments.

"That's surprising, most people aren't familiar with It."

"I love it. On what day will you be serving the dinner?" I asked.

"Monday evening, around six or seven," Raj was smiling. I could tell he was happy that I was familiar and approved of his ancestral cuisine.

"Unfortunately, that won't work for me," David said. "Indian food is way too spicy. I'll be up with heartburn all night."

"I can prepare some dishes for you that aren't spicy, David. You both could get a painting done in the morning, have lunch, then call me. I'll pick you up and you can set up your easels and paint all afternoon while I'm preparing dinner."

"That sounds just heavenly. Monday is going to be a special day for me. This is exciting," I said, now squirming in my seat. Raj smiled; he was obviously flattered.

Raj looked at his watch and said, "I need to get going to pick up the ingredients for the dinner and get started with some of the preparations."

We had finished our salads and were ready to get on with the day. Raj insisted on paying for lunch, and though I protested, he handed the waitress his credit card. She obviously knew him and had been especially attentive to him throughout the meal making sure he had everything he wanted, his water glass was full, and his empty dishes were removed as soon as he had finished.

When she gave him back his credit card, her eyes sparkled as she said, "Thank you so much, Mr. M." Apparently, he had given her a big tip.

"Thanks so much for lunch," I said as we walked out of the restaurant.

"My pleasure, I look forward to seeing you on Monday afternoon. If you need anything, let me know. You have my cell and land line numbers."

"Here's my business card. As you can see, it has my number and all my information," I said. David gave him his card too.

He then went on his way. I still had some reservations about Raj, he was so overly confident, and I could tell he was used to getting everything his way. I didn't want to be something else he could purchase with his money and charm. He did seem nice though. Soon after leaving the restaurant, David and I began location scouting when we ran into Alice and Charlotte, the women we met on the Catalina Express.

"Hello there," I said. "Did you just have lunch?"

"No, not yet. We're heading for the Busy Bee. Would you like to join us?"

"Thank you, but we just ate. We're making plans for where we want to paint next. There are so many wonderful locations, it's hard to select, but I think I'll paint in the direction of the Holly House from the Green Pleasure Pier." I pointed in the direction we would be painting.

"That's a wonderful view. I've seen paintings of that location, and it can be a beautiful scene if it's painted by a skillful artist, and that would be you," Alice remarked. She smiled at me and for a split second, she reminded me of someone. I had seen that set jaw in another person's face before, but I kept silent.

"Well, have a nice lunch," I said.

"Thanks," she said as they turned and walked on.

"David, I thought I had seen them somewhere and now I remember where. Sybil showed me a photo of the three of them together. Charlotte is Sybil's mother and Alice is her daughter."

"Holy cow! Now that you mention it, I see the family resemblance, especially in Charlotte. Sybil and Charlotte both have that same sweet face."

"Yes, but I also see Sybil's strength and determination to persevere in Alice's face as well," I said.

"Strange, why do you think they didn't tell us or mention anything about Sybil?" he wondered.

"That's very odd... Hey! Do you know what just occurred to me, Sybil was asked to leave POPOC about two months ago. Hillary knew this event was coming up and Sybil was a better artist than she or Karla. I'll bet she did that to get rid of the competition for this festival," I said.

David gasped and put his hand to his mouth. "I'll bet you're right, and that decision cost Sybil her life. How does Hillary sleep at night?"

"I'm sure she sleeps as soundly as a stone."

Sunday

Chapter 4: The Festival Begins

Waaah... The alarm went off waking us with a start. It was Sunday morning, and David and I were eager for the painting marathon to begin. For the next six days, our plan was to grab a muffin for breakfast, go outside to our location, and paint as fast as we could all morning, hopefully, without compromising the quality of our work.

Speed was an important aspect of plein aire painting because the paintings needed to be finished by the time the sun had reached its zenith. When that occurred, all the shadows and direction of the light changed, and that same scene was vastly altered. Plein aire instructors warned us, "Don't chase the light." That was a good rule and one that I adhered to because it made sense.

There were others such as, "A plein aire painting should be done in one sitting." That rule and some others were nonsense. If my painting needed to be touched up or enhance the next day, so be it. I often wondered who made many of those rules and if the plein aire police would come around and arrest anyone who didn't adhere to them. I decided to only follow the rules that improved my paintings or helped me to become a better artist.

When the sun was high in the sky, it was time to wrap things up. If I was still touching up a completed painting, the plan was for David to stop and purchase our lunches since he wasn't competing in the art show and undergoing the same pressure that I was. We would then wolf down the food and begin our afternoon paintings.

David told me when he agreed to accompany me to this event, that he would only come along with the understanding that he was there to assist me if he could. It was wonderful having my friend there for support. I planned to repay his kindness sometime later, but this morning we would focus on the here and now.

"Okay, here we go!" I said as I jumped out of bed. David went into the bathroom, showered, and dressed, giving me the privacy I needed to get ready. We had worked out a good system alternating our use of the bathroom. I took my showers at night. That system allowed both of us time to change when we were in separate rooms. At the bottom of the two flights of stairs we could count on a continental breakfast waiting for us in the lobby.

"Pretty basic, but it'll do." David said, stuffing a brown sack with muffins, apples, and bananas that we could eat while we walked to the location where I was to get my canvases stamped. "It wouldn't hurt to have some extra food just in case," he said filling an extra bag. Bonnie, the desk clerk opened the room where our equipment was stored, and I grabbed all my canvases which were required to be stamped by the organizers of the festival. It was the practice of all plein aire art events to be certain no one would be cheating by entering any pre-painted art they had brought with them to the show. After placing the blank canvases in a tote bag, we were out the door and sprinting down the street, eating as we went along. We were hoping to be first in line at the stamping station located in front of the Green Pleasure Pier. At the station, I would be given a packet of information compiled for all the artists participating in the show, along with a baseball cap with the PAPOC Art Festival insignia. When we arrived, we could see that there were quite a few artists already waiting in line.

"So much for getting here early," David said as I shook my head in disgust.

As soon as the canvases were stamped, David and I began setting up our French easels in the sand. It was right by the Green Pleasure Pier that I had photographed yesterday when Raj and Tom made fun of my contorted pretzel position. I was glad to be getting an extra day start so I could get extra paintings done for the exhibition and sale next Saturday and Sunday. David and I were quite a comical sight with our oversized sun hats, cargo pants, and vinyl gloves. One elderly gentleman passing by asked me if I was a Proctologist. I didn't get it... David explained. The setting up of our equipment consisted of attaching umbrellas to our easels, putting our canvas boards in place, laying out brushes, and pouring out Gamsol, an odorless paint thinner. David had to squirt his many paint colors out of tubes onto the palette. That was the norm, and most artists had a similar system.

I had devised a completely different method. All my colors were premixed at home ahead of time which took approximately five hours to prepare. The colors were placed into a metal container with three-sides and a bottom that allowed me access to the paint from the open front when uncovered. The cover had four sides and a top which protected the paint inside from drying out or being smeared. The container was eighteen inches long, by three inches wide, and two inches high. I had roughly one hundred premixed colors already available to use without having to repeatedly mix some of the same colors on location. Though I still had to adjust to get the exact colors needed, the system allowed me to be much more efficient than the other artists since I was already halfway there. The many colors in the box were laid out systematically in the same places every time. That way I always knew where the colors were even when the light was poor or it was dark. Setting up my easel and all my equipment usually took a half hour.

The artists in the show were all given name tags that were designed to be worn around our necks allowing the art collectors to know the names of their favorite artists. Since our displays for the exhibition in the Casino would be presented in alphabetical order, favorite artists would be easy for collectors to locate. I unclipped my name tag and attached it to the back of my sun hat knowing that most of the spectators would be watching the artists paint from behind. There were many quality artists, but I had observed that the ones who became prominent were often the self-promoters. Though the quality of one's work was by far the most important aspect of painting, learning to interact with the customers was essential, and for me, most of the time a pleasure.

The onlookers liked to engage with the artists while we painted, but many artists found that conduct to be irritating and sometimes became snippy with the observers or ignored them. One of the most frequently heard and annoying comments was, "My aunt is also a wonderful artist or I'm an artist too. Would you like to see some of my work?" they would say as they pulled out many photographs. Some frequently asked questions were, "What colors did you mix to get that color?" Sometimes there were a dozen colors used to get a specific shade. Trying to explain would be next to impossible. "How long does it take you to do a painting? Can you tell me where I can take plein aire painting lessons?" People simply don't understand that when you're trying to finish a painting before the light changes, you can't give long, involved answers. Most of the time the comments and questions were sensible and easy to answer, and I tried to be patient and polite to the observers. I was once an onlooker myself and appreciated when an artist took a little time to answer my own silly questions. Some of the artists were nice but some were downright rude. Keeping that in mind, I certainly didn't want to be like the rude ones. From a purely practical standpoint, we never know who might want to purchase a painting, so it's wise to always be nice.

Conversely, my friend David hated being interrupted and having his concentration broken. He told me that people don't try to talk to a pianist in the middle of a concerto, but they don't give us the same respect. Though he had a point, I had to remind him that we needed to think of ourselves as art ambassadors and to try being tolerant of the annoying questions we're asked. Artists are often stereotyped as oddballs because we don't always conform to the rules of proper dress or behavior which is often validated by our peculiar, paint-splattered clothing. To be honest, I was proud to be walking around all covered with paint, proud to be an artist. To me, it's almost like wearing a uniform, or a badge. I have no problem if I'm thought of as eccentric. But though we sometimes see ourselves as exceptional, we don't need to behave badly, even when we're pushed to the limit.

For example, while I had once been painting for an hour, a boy who was probably around ten years old was watching me. He moved in way too close to my easel, and with a "know it all" attitude and in front of a lot of people he smugly said, "You need to put some texture here in the water."

He then pointed with his finger almost touching the painting. That kind of behavior, especially coming from a child could've been taken as an afront to my ability, but instead of letting him get to me, I decided not to be nasty or defensive and said,

"Thank you very much for your well-meaning advice, but if you'd been painting as long as I have, you'd know that you never add any texture or details until the very last. They call those last strokes finishing touches," I said as I tried to smile and be sweet. After all, he was a child... smart aleck brat that he was. I heard David who was also there muttering something under his breath. I didn't think it was a good idea to ask him to repeat it in front of the child.

David and I completed our paintings by 1:00 that afternoon and decided to go to Eric's Sandwich Stand for lunch. Eric's was located right at the entrance to the Pleasure Pier, so it was convenient, an important consideration because time was of the essence in the competition. We were in line for a minute when Tony Rossi, who I had met on the boat, came up and stood in line behind us.

"I've been watching you both paint all morning. You know my mother was a wonderful artist too."

"No kidding, did she use oil or watercolor?" I asked.

"She was a very gifted oil painter, maybe even better than David." Tony said.

I cringed hearing that comment. So did David. The last thing an artist wants to hear is that someone is better than he or she is. I looked over at David to see his eyebrows lowered and pinched together reacting to what he had just heard.

"Is she still painting now?" I said trying to move on.

"No, not anymore," Tony responded, looking away.

"Oh, that's too bad," I said. He smiled appreciating my sympathy then looked away. He must have been sorry she was no longer painting.

"Lots of times the talent for music and art goes down through the generations. Did you get any of her artistic gifts, Tony?" I inquired.

"No, I have no desire to paint, but I certainly recognize when someone is good. Some of your work is exceptional, Annabel. I like your work very much as well, David. You have a unique style, very different from the other artists. Both of your paintings are beautiful, but David, I didn't see your name on the list of artists in the show. Why isn't your name there too?" Tony asked.

"The powers that be decided I wasn't good enough," David answered.

"Oh that's ridiculous," Tony scoffed.

"It most certainly is!" I insisted. "Some people capriciously make decisions that adversely affect people's lives."

When we all had ordered, I asked Tony, "Are you only going to have a drink? Don't you need some lunch?"

"No, Annabel, I just stopped my chemotherapy and I'm still having problems with nausea. I've taken some pills and I'm sure I'll be ready to eat by dinner time. I plan to go to the Portofino Restaurant for dinner tonight. I hear the chef there knows how to prepare a terrific steak."

"I don't mean to be intrusive, Tony, but what kind of cancer do you have? I hope it's nothing too serious," I said, hoping I wasn't being too nosy.

"It's Pancreatic cancer and it's terminal. That's one of the reasons I'm here. I just want to focus on enjoying what will be my last days. I want to envelope myself in beauty and there's no better place than Avalon Bay. I'm looking forward to the art exhibition and seeing all the wonderful paintings you artists will produce," he replied. That explained those cryptic comments Tony made when we first met, I thought.

"We're so sorry to hear you're not well, Tony," I said, looking to David for acknowledgement.

"You have such a positive attitude. I respect that," David said.

"Well, you two enjoy your lunches." Tony gave me a pat on the shoulder and was on his way.

"That's so tragic, David. It must be awful to know you're dying, and your days are numbered."

David and I sat on a bench in front of the Pleasure Pier and ate our not very delicious lunches. We had both ordered turkey sandwiches and found the overly processed turkey to have the consistency of a rubber inner tube. The French fries were soggy, and the lemonade was so sweet I had to pour half of it out in the sand and add more water. While we were eating, a seagull tried to steal David's sandwich.

"Hey, get out of here!" David yelled swatting at the bird with his hat.

"Oh no, now he's coming after mine!"

The situation was like an improbable scene from the Alfred Hitchcock thriller, *"The Birds."* No matter how much we yelled or swatted that bird with our hats, he wouldn't go away and was determined to take our sandwiches. David finally got in a good lick which knocked the gull to the sand.

"I don't know why we're fighting so hard for these awful sandwiches, Annabel."

"I'm really hungry," I said, finishing every bite left that the seagull didn't steal.

After that, we had the muffins from the continental breakfast for dessert.

"Tomorrow let's be sure to eat two muffins for breakfast. One wasn't enough to last us till lunchtime," I suggested to David.

"Good idea. Where to now, Annabel?"

Hmm, I'm keeping two things in mind, awards and sales. If I paint in Avalon Bay, I'm likely to meet a lot more art collectors here than If I go off to some remote location. Art collectors like to buy paintings from artists with whom they feel they have a connection. That's why it's good to schmooze with the bystanders, David."

"I know, you've told me and told me," he said frowning. "It pulls me right out of 'the zone' I'm in."

"Let's go out on the Pleasure Pier. I want to paint the boats in the bay in the foreground with the Holly House and other houses on the hill in the background. The light is good and there's a lively blue sky with some billowy clouds right now. The water is a gorgeous shade of turquoise. After dinner I would like to paint a nocturn, so let's keep it simple so I won't be too tired."

"Sounds like a good plan," he said as we walked onto the pier. We don't want to get too tired spending a lot of energy location scouting. This is a good spot for now."

"Nocturns are dramatic, and I want to do something that won't be painted by other artists. Most plein aire artists don't know how to paint night scenes, but I do and those are the paintings that win me awards. I must go above and beyond painting the typical icons of the bay if I want my work to stand out from the crowd."

"That's right, Annabel. To win, an artist must do more than a good painting. It must be well drawn, compositionally perfect, the masses of shapes must be interesting, colors must work well together, there should be excellent brush work, good handling of darks and lights, and the subject matter must be interesting and resonate with the viewer. And you're right, your nocturns are spectacular."

"I must keep all of that in mind to have a chance of winning. I think I'm going to paint the Art Deco murals inside the entrance of the Casino and the front of the Casino tonight. I've been thinking about doing that since we were here last year. I'm sure I can do something that's beautiful and unusual."

We completed our afternoon paintings, and they were good paintings. Even though it would take more than the one I had done to win an award, the painting was saleable and that was important too. Collectors are usually not very adventurous and often like to collect the things that move them emotionally. That's why the icons sell so well, for when people see them, they're reminded of their stay in Catalina. Some of the lesser qualified artists in the show will be satisfied simply to have good sales to cover their expenses. They usually paint typical Catalina icons which are safe, but nothing out of the ordinary or outstanding in their approach. Some of the artists go off to distant locations spending much of their precious time traveling to paint something no one has ever seen before. That's a mistake unless the artist isn't concerned with sales. The best painters know all these things and are the ones going all out for the prizes and the acclaim received by winning. The money is an extra benefit, "the icing on the cake." An artist's whole being and identity is tied to his or her art. Most of the talented artists have been treated as if they were exceptional creatures since they were children. They must perpetually prove that to themselves and others or they might lose that position and have an identity crisis. It's not surprising that some of them carry the desire to prove they're the best way too far.

It had been a productive afternoon, and all went smoothly except for another incident with that nasty seagull.

"What was that?" David exclaimed as he felt something hit his hat. He reached up and touched it. "Yuck, how disgusting," he said looking at the gooey white gunk on his hand.

"David, that darn seagull just pooped on your hat!"

"I hate that bird! Yuck, what a mess." David said taking off his straw sunhat. He bellowed at the seagull as he tried to clean up the hat with a paper towel. We were both laughing so hard it was hard for him to clean off the bird poop. "I'm going to kill that nasty bird," he said through his laughter. After we had settled down, I said, "Let's pack up and go for a Mexican dinner at Diego's Totilliaria. That'll make you feel better. A good fish taco will cure all your woes, my friend."

"Okay, you're right, that sounds good to me."

We then headed up Catalina Avenue which ran parallel on the south side of Sumner Avenue. Mexican meals were full of calories with all the rice, beans, and cheese, and were reasonably inexpensive. We discussed dinner plans for the week, and thanks to Raj buying us lunch and preparing us a dinner tomorrow, we would have extra money. That meant we could splurge and have two nice meals at the Portofino Restaurant during the week. The rest of the evenings we would have to economize by dining at the Busy Bee or Diego's Tortilliaria.

When we reached Diego's, we stood outside looking at the menu posted at the entrance of the restaurant on the sidewalk. After looking it over for a minute, we decided it looked good and the prices were right, so we went inside. As soon as we walked in the door we were met with some raucous salutations from Randy, Mike, and Saul, the three super stars of the art show. There were empty margarita glasses scattered all over their table and it was clear that they had all been drinking... a lot.

"It's 'The Three Amigos' again," I said waving to the guys as we entered.

"Hey, I like that name," Randy said. "Come join us, Annabel. Bring your fa...fren too!" Randy made a clumsy motion to me to come to their table. He pushed Mike sitting in his seat over with his foot and pulled up a chair allowing me to sit next to him. After introducing them to David, I said,

"Where did you paint today, Randy? "

"On Lower Terrace Road, there's a field there overlookin Holly House, lookin toward the Casino. Randy was feeling no pain, and I was amused listening to him. He was slurring his words badly and it took all my resolve not to laugh at him, but I couldn't help smirking."

"Annabel, I don't unerstan why you hang round with that awful Hillary?" Randy said, scrunching up his face.

"Yeah, and that Karla's snooty and rude too," Mike said, trying to push up his nose, but his finger slipped off his nose and poked his eye. "She just thinks she's the bligrrl (undistinguishable) but she's not all that. I've tried to be frenly, and she barely gives me the skolkim (undistinguishable) of the day."

"Once Hillary was paining a scene and I got in fronna her yards away, yards and yards, an she toll me ta move because I was blockin er view, as if she owned the place," Randy said as his elbow slipped off the table.

"Did ja move?" Saul asked, his head popping up, joining in what I would loosely call the conversation.

"Well...(groan) I did... but I was pissed!" he bellowed.

"Getting in front of Hillary is a problem, Randy, but just make sure you don't get behind her. That's when she goes bat shit, ballistic," I warned. "*And*... I don't *ever* hang around with her. That would be an exercise in masochism."

"Hey, you're OKAY, Annabel. Lemme buy you a margarita, oh, and one for your fren David too."

"What about us?" Saul asked.

"Screw you, asshole! Buy your own drink," my plastered friend, Randy, blurted out.

"Well... screw you too," Saul said, giving Randy the finger. It was all done so good naturedly. These guys were close friends.

"Now guys, we have a lady present, watch your language and gestures," David interjected trying to hold back a laugh.

"I beg your pardon, Annabel, and he does too," Randy said, pointing at Saul. Sometimes my frens have no class.

"It's all in fun guys. I'm not at all offended. Not a bit. Everyone's just having a good time, aren't we?" I asked.

"That's right ole buddy, ole pal," Randy said putting his arm around me.

"That's right, ole pal, ole pal," I said putting my arm around him too. Shall we order now?" I said realizing we needed to get our orders in if I was going to have enough time to get a nocturn done later in the evening.

"Okay, but I'm gonna buy you dinner... oh, and your fren too... Wha was your name? Oh, I rember, it's David... You're alright David if you're a fren of Annabel's. You guys are on your own," he said pointing at Saul and Mike.

"Thanks, Randy, that's so nice of you, but no margaritas."

"No margaritas!" he exclaimed in disbelief. "Aww shit!"

"No, Randy. no margaritas. I don't want to wake up with a hangover tomorrow. I don't have your powerful constitution or ability to handle alcohol like you guys. Besides, you could do a great painting, backwards, and standing on your head. All of you could. I've really got to try."

"That's ridiclus. We invited you here to find out where you were gonna paint tomorrow. You're our stiffis competition," Mike blurted out.

"Now you've done it. We were gonna find out without her knowing, you dope!" Randy said throwing a corn chip at Mike.

By then the waitress came by and took our orders. The evening for me was delightful. I was hanging out and becoming friends with the some of the finest artists in California. They were the best and they accepted me even though I was a female. That was something new and a step forward for women. When I first started painting, it was a man's world and though women artists were tolerated, we were not accepted into what was an unofficial men's club. Tonight, I saw a change, I could hold my own with the guy's put downs and I thoroughly enjoyed their raunchy humor. They were all smashed, fun, very funny and I liked them. It was also quite informative. David and I saw the plein aire event as a marathon in which we had to be in top physical condition to endure the extensive walking, scouting locations, and the hours standing on our feet painting. For Randy, Mike, and Saul, painting was a lifestyle. They were so good that they could take the money from the awards they frequently won, enter more events, travel, and have fun drinking and carousing with their buddies. We thanked Randy profusely for the dinner, then said our goodbyes to the guys while they each gave me lots of slobbery kisses and hugs.

"Did you enjoy that?" I asked David as I wiped my wet cheeks.

"Those three guys are animals! We couldn't keep up with that kind of drinking and partying every night."

"That's for sure. I can't believe that they'll be well enough to paint tomorrow. We'll see."

"Are you still up for the night painting, Annabel?"

"I am. Let's head north on Crescent to the Casino. I can't wait to paint the murals at the entrance with some of the Casino structure in the aqua colored shadows of the night. The Art Deco style is such a part of the look of Avalon."

"I noticed that you never mentioned your nocturn plans to the guys," David said.

"Of course I didn't," I answered, with a wily smile.

"Boy, they sure hate Hillary and Karla, especially Mike."

"Wasn't that something, David. They certainly do. I heard about a terrible altercation Mike had with the two of them, but he didn't mention anything about it. I think he was awfully drunk and just wanted to focus on having a good time with his buddies. He seems like a complex fellow. There's an edge to Mike that I picked up on tonight, and there's a look in his eyes that's kind of scary.

"Yes, now that you mention it, I see what you mean. There's something disquieting about the expression of his face," he said.

"Yes, there certainly is, something, hmm... almost sinister."

When we arrived at the Casino, I found a good painting spot and set up the easel in record time. The tiles inlaid into the architectural columns, the light fixtures, and the eighteen feet tall murals were all reminiscent of the Art Deco style popular in the 1920s. Zigzagging patterns surrounded the murals which depicted stylized versions of underwater scenes with schools of bubbly fish, rippling water plants, jellyfish, and seaweed. A pale glow of aqua emanated from the dimly lit murals inside the grand entrance. If my painting could capture that ethereal glow, I would have a successful evening.

"I'm so glad you're here with me David. It's late, and even though we were told the island is perfectly safe in the evenings, it's dark and lonely here and I like having you with me. Thank you for keeping me company."

"It's my pleasure, and even though I'm not officially in the show, this is a way I can practice and share in the experience. Who knows, maybe a miracle will happen, and I might become a Signature Member. I know it's frowned upon for anyone to be painting when they're not juried into the show. And I'm acutely aware you're sticking your neck out by having me to paint with you.

"I did stick my neck out for you, and it was well worth it. That's what we do for our friends," I said with a resolute tone of voice. "So far no one has confronted us. I certainly hope no one says anything to you."

"I've thought about it, and if they do, I'll tell them I'm here as your assistant. I've seen some women with their husbands assisting them. That should silence anyone who has a problem," he said.

"Good thinking, David. That's a great solution and that's just how we're going to handle it."

Chapter 5: The Gruesome Threesome

Hillary, Karla, and Nancy began their Sunday morning getting canvases stamped and painting some typical scenes of the Casino. After lunch, they decided to share the expense of renting a golf cart for the rest of the day hoping to find some interesting afternoon perspectives of the Bay of Avalon. They decided to go up Chimes Tower Road which offered inspiring views of the bay when they were situated close to the bell tower monument. That pleased all three of the women, each one certain she would create the award-winning painting. Hillary and Karla set up their easels close together on the side of the road. They were looking in different directions which was acceptable to Hillary because Karla wouldn't be standing behind her painting the same scene. Nancy found another painting spot farther down the road.

"Did you see what Annabel was painting this morning?" Hillary asked Karla.

"Yes, it was a typical scene, and though it was well done, it was rather commonplace," Karla answered.

"She won't win any awards with that," Hillary responded. "Oh tonight, I want to bring the cart back up here on Chimes Tower Road again. I'm going to paint a shoreline night scene including the Holly House, the Green Pleasure Pier, and the houses on this hill in the foreground. I think all the sparkling lights reflecting in the bay will be dramatic, very exciting!"

"That's a great idea! I'll come with you, and we can paint that scene together," Karla said.

"Yes, me too," Nancy echoed.

"No way! That's my idea. If you want to take the cart on another night, well... okay just don't paint at the same scene I'm going to be painting. Besides, you've never been able to paint a decent nocturn in your life, Nancy. What's the point," Hillary snapped. Nancy was silent, not liking what was said but realizing it was true.

"Hillary, you don't own this island. I can paint anywhere I choose, and even if I paint the same scene, it will look different." Mine will be better, Karla thought to herself.

"In that case, let's not share the expense of the golf cart anymore. We can each rent our own cart from now on," Hillary said knowing full well that Karla would never be that extravagant though she certainly had the money.

Karla was a wealthy woman. Karla was also a skin flint. Karla was beautiful and used to getting her way. But Hillary was going do whatever it took to prevent Karla from painting the same scene.

"Forget the cart, Karla, you need the exercise. You're starting to get cellulite on your legs. Nancy, you run several miles almost every day. You're physically fit and could climb these hills without a problem." Hillary was going to get what she needed, and that was all that mattered to her. Karla was insulted by the cellulite comment and fuming about the cart. The two of them didn't speak for the rest of the afternoon. Nancy, as usual, stayed out of the fray not able to defend herself in an altercation with the more acerbic Hillary, and the much quicker witted Karla. Nancy was seething under her quiet exterior and would eventually get even by undermining Hillary when she wasn't expecting it. I'll just wait until I see the right opportunity to "get her", Nancy thought. By the time the women had completed their paintings, Hillary and Karla were on speaking terms again. It was 5:30 in the late afternoon and the women were hungry. That, of course, took precedent over their residual anger.

"Where do you want to go for dinner?" Karla asked.

"Let's go to the Portofino restaurant. I think it's the best restaurant in town. After we eat, you both can walk back to the hotel. It's not far, and I can drive up Chimes Tower Road by myself," stated Hillary.

The women had made no reservations, but because it was early and they had their artist tags around their necks, the hostess seated them at a nice table having been told to accommodate the artists in the festival. They said "hello" to Alice and Charlotte who were seated at the table next to them. Asher and Miriam Bloomberg were sitting at the bar having drinks. Karla then noticed a man that had been watching them paint earlier that morning.

"Look Hillary, there's that strange old man with the beard and bushy eyebrows who was watching us this morning. I wonder who he is?" Karla asked.

"I have no idea, but someone needs to tell him to comb that scraggly grey hair. I saw him at Sybil's Celebration of Life, but I never saw him before that. He's probably just another artist groupie or collector," Hillary answered unconcerned.

Shortly after their arrival, Tony Rossi came over to their table and asked if he could buy them all a round of drinks. Tony had introduced himself to Hillary while they were on the Catalina Express, and she found him to be nice looking, intelligent, and interesting. Though she hadn't confided in Karla or Nancy, Hillary's marriage had been deteriorating for years, and she was open to having affairs if they suited her purpose. Sensing that Tony seemed generous, she thought he might offer to pay for their dinners, so Hillary invited him to join their party.

"Thank you, I would love to join you," he answered, feeling very popular to be dining with three ladies.

After looking over the menus, Tony informed the women that he was told that the Portofino had the best steaks in town, and just as Hillary had surmised, he said it would be his pleasure to buy them all dinner... and of course, they accepted. Tony ordered some fine wine and Nancy and Karla took advantage of the situation and drank their fill.

"Did you all get some good paintings today, ladies?" Tony asked.

"I did," Hillary replied.

"You all must be very tired, dragging all that heavy equipment around and standing on your feet the whole day."

"I certainly am, Tony, but Hillary's taking the cart up Chimes Tower Road again to paint a nocturn. She probably won't get back to the Glenmore Hotel till midnight," Karla said rolling her eyes.

"I surely wish I had your stamina, Hillary," Tony said offering her another piece of bread.

"I'm tired too, but I want to get something special for the show. That location, I believe, is the best one around and at night, it should be spectacular," Hillary said smiling in anticipation of what she imagined she would paint. As she spoke, she noticed that Charlotte and Alice had been listening.

"Oh yes, that's the best location in Avalon," Alice said, joining in the conversation. I walked up there to get some exercise and thought that the artists in the festival should go there if they wanted a great painting."

"I agree, that's why I'm painting a nocturn there tonight. Please don't mention that location to any of the other artists," Hillary responded.

The waitress finally appeared and took their orders, and when the food arrived, the women ate heartily enjoying their appetizers, juicy steaks, and sumptuous desserts, all at Tony's expense. He didn't seem to mind, for he was having a good time, apparently glad to have their company for the evening. When they had finished their dinners, they thanked him profusely and Nancy and Karla walked back to the Glenmore Hotel. Hillary took the cart and headed up Chimes Tower Road which would bring her to the scenic view.

While she was driving up the road she thought, it's kind of isolated up here at night but it's peaceful and quiet. When she arrived at her destination, she fumbled in the dark and struggled to put on her miner's light to help her set up and be able to see her paints and the painting. It's nice not to have Karla making her "know it all" remarks about art when I'm trying to concentrate. Maybe it's good to be alone because no one will bother me and I can focus strictly on my painting. A warm Santa Ana breeze was gently blowing through the eucalyptus trees that evening. The clouds had blown away and the sky was clear now allowing millions of tiny points of flickering lights to shine above her in the night sky. A pale, crescent moon over the indigo bay reflected its pallid glow on the dark, still waters of the bay. It was an extraordinary night scene where she set up her easel. As she began painting, she thought, this will do it for me. I've got it all to myself. The last thing I needed was for Karla to horn in on my location. I'm going to win that Best of Show with this one and I don't even care about the money. I just want people to finally acknowledge that I'm the best artist of them all. None of these low lifes have anywhere near my talent.

What was that strange noise? "Is someone there?" Hillary asked, with a start. No one answered. She waited a moment and looked around. Oh, I'm just jumpy, she thought. She continued painting for a while but continued hearing the wind rustling in the bushes. It's just the Santa Ana winds, what is it about them that always make me jumpy, she thought. But Hillary was becoming increasingly aware that being alone up there left her vulnerable and prey to things she couldn't imagine. I hope there are no mountain lions on the island. They are nocturnal. I didn't think about that when I started. I'm beginning to wish Karla was with me. Despite her ever-increasing anxiety, she painted on into the night until she sensed the presence of someone standing right close behind her.

"Who's there!" she gasped, turning with a start. "You scared me. What are you doing here?" Hillary demanded.

"I followed you. Do you want to know why?"

Monday

Chapter 6: Where is Hillary

The light that was streaming in through the space between the curtains when Nancy awakened in her hotel room Monday morning. She slowly opened her blurry eyes and sat up in bed. When she looked around she realized she was alone. That's strange, she thought, I wonder where Hillary is. Her bed is made; she must have gotten up early and made it. That's odd, she thought, Hillary usually leaves the bed in a mess knowing that housekeeping will make the bed and clean the room. Isn't that just like her to leave without me so she could catch the best light of morning. Nancy dragged herself out of bed, still feeling some of the effects of the last night's wine indulgence as she headed for the bathroom. After showering, putting on her essential makeup, and getting dressed, she still hadn't heard from Hillary. Maybe she's downstairs eating that awful continental breakfast. I'll call her. Hmm... no answer. I'll go down to breakfast, maybe she's there. Nancy descended the two flights of stairs and entered the breakfast area, but when she looked around, Hillary wasn't there but she saw Karla.

"Have you seen Hillary this morning, Karla?"

"No, I thought you both were sleeping in. Do you think she got an early start painting?"

"Probably, but when I called her, she didn't answer the phone. I'll bet she took the golf cart by herself and didn't want us to know where she is painting, that would be just like her," Nancy said as she shook her head in disgust.

"Let's have breakfast and then you and I can go out on our own. To tell you the truth, Nancy, I'd would prefer not having her around. She's so hard to get along with and the morning will be less irritating without her." Karla snickered. Nancy smiled and nodded in agreement.

"She's so determined to win, she doesn't think or care about anyone else," Nancy said.

"I agree, the only reason I kiss up to her and pretend I like her is because she's in charge of our painting group. If anyone gets on her bad side, she kicks them out of the group," Karla admitted. Nancy said nothing, not wanting to incriminate herself. She didn't trust Karla who she had seen informing on other group members if it was to her benefit to ingratiate herself to Hillary. With Karla, you could never be sure she wasn't trying to get you to say something negative about Hillary so she could tell her on you.

Karla and Nancy worked on their morning paintings till 1:30 and then had a leisurely lunch. While they had been painting and eating, they had been completely engrossed in their own exploits. Since they were annoyed that Hillary had taken the cart and left them without transportation to the best spots, they didn't give her much thought. But now Nancy's focus turned to Hillary for she hadn't tried to contact her companions or had been seen by them since the previous night.

"I'm beginning to wonder about Hillary, Karla. She usually keeps in touch with us."

"Well then, you call her. I'm pissed at her for taking the golf cart. I hope she knows she's paying for the half day yesterday and all day today. That will cover the time she's had the cart to herself." Karla kept on walking and looking for the next location unconcerned about Hillary's whereabouts.

"She's not picking up, Karla. I'm beginning to think something's wrong."

"Why should you care. She never thinks about us," Karla said continuing to look around.

"You're right, Karla. Let's find another good location."

The women finally settled on a scene that was acceptable to both, but by 4:30 that afternoon, they still hadn't heard from Hillary.

"There's the police vehicle, Karla. Watch my stuff, I'm going to talk to him."

"Suit yourself, Nancy. I've got better things to do."

Nancy was gone for about a half hour, when she and the police sergeant, Jim Monaghan, approached Karla who was taking photographs. She stopped and watched as they walked toward her.

"What's going on," she asked the sergeant.

"I called Catalina Golf Carts, and they said one of their golf carts was missing. They checked into it and said it was the one rented by Hillary Applegate yesterday. Do you have any idea where she might be?" Officer Monaghan asked.

"No, from what Nancy told me, she hasn't answered her phone all day. We figured she didn't want us to know where she was painting." Karla answered. A bewildered look crossed her face.

"And why wouldn't she want you to know that?"

"Because this is a competition, and she didn't want us to see what she was painting. She wouldn't want our paintings to overshadow hers," Nancy answered looking at Karla.

"I understand. Do you know where the last place was that she was painting yesterday?" Sergeant Monaghan asked.

"She said she was going to do a night painting up Chimes Tower Road. She took the cart and went there after we all had dinner at the Portofino last night," Karla informed him.

"Okay, I'll go up there and check it out. Don't worry, lots of people lose track of time here. We deal with it all the time. I'm sure everything will be all right. What are your names, phone numbers, and where are you two staying?"

After giving him the information, Sergeant Monaghan thought to himself, this is probably just another typical example of vacation miscommunication. I'm sure the missing woman got engrossed in her painting and forgot to keep in contact with her friends. He then casually took care of some things on his to do list from Captain Derringer.

As the glow of twilight shone in the evening sky, Jim Monaghan took his time enjoying the cool evening air he as he made his way up Chimes Tower Road to the scenic viewing location. As he approached, it appeared that no one was there, but further up the grade he could see a golf cart parked on the side of the road. That's strange, he thought as he climbed out of his vehicle and walked over to the cart. Yes, this is the cart that Catalina Golf Carts described to me, he thought as he walked around the vehicle. Nothing seemed to be out of the ordinary or cause for any concern. Next, he began surveying the side of the road and the downslope when he came across something that caught his eye. There was an artist's easel which had been tipped over on its side. One of the legs on the easel was broken and splintered in the dirt. Paint brushes, art material, and a broken miner's light were strewn over the ground. But then a dreadful spectacle came into Jim Monaghan's view. It was the bluish-white naked legs of a woman which were protruding out from beneath a hillside shrub.

"Holy shit!" Sergeant Monaghan exclaimed. He felt a surge of adrenaline as he groped around in his jacket trying to find his cell phone. When his fumbling fingers pulled it out of his pocket, it fell to the ground. His heart was pounding as he picked it up and didn't even bother to brush it off. His eyes had not left the unbelievable scene before him. His fingers were trembling as he dialed the phone number of the station commander. "Tom, you've got to come up Chimes Tower Road right away! Immediately! Something terrible has happened. Get forensics and Raj up here too. Right away!"

Jim Monaghan was the "Steady Eddie" of the Catalina police force, and this was not the typical conduct of the sergeant. He was known as the calm one who was not prone to drama or exaggeration during any sort of emergency. With that in mind, Tom raced up the hill to meet his right-hand man. When Tom arrived, Jim was waiting in the middle of the road with an anguished expression on his face.

"What is it, Jim?" he said. Jim didn't say a word. He just pointed down the bank to the scene below.

"Oh sheeit!" The two officers stood frozen for a moment realizing the gravity of what they were witnessing. By then Sarah Moreau, the Forensic Scientist had also arrived. Jim grabbed his camera and together they all walked cautiously down the embankment, trying not to disturb the ground of what was now a crime scene. The sergeant took photographs and wrote notes recording the time of the discoveries as they occurred. When they came to the body, the police stood by as Sarah gathered all her forensic evidence. When that was completed, she gingerly turned the victim over as the sergeant recorded the events. Her pants had been ripped off and thrown into the bushes. The blood on her shirt was now a dark brownish red and had coagulated and dried. She had been dead for quite a while. Nancy Hall had informed Officer Monaghan of the time when she realized Hillary was missing. That would help the police to have an idea of the time Hillary was murdered. She had been, stabbed multiple times and her throat had a large slash on it. At first glance, it appeared that she had possibly been raped as well. What was disturbingly macabre was her eyes were closed and had been bleeding. Someone had stabbed them and painted her eyelids black with her oil paint. A gruesome red and black smile was painted on her face. On the back of her sweatshirt the word FORDS was painted in red capital letters. This was not some ordinary murder, it was one that would forever torment the mind of anyone who witnessed its savagery. This was the work of a seriously deranged psychopath.

Chapter 7: Dinner with Karla and Nancy

While the officers were at the crime scene, Karla and Nancy had been sitting on a bench for a while eating ice cream, relaxing, and enjoying the island. Since the police were looking into Hillary's absence, it was no longer their problem. The women's attention had now shifted to their own personal nutritional needs. While they had been engrossed in their conversation they hadn't noticed, but now it was time for dinner, and they were deciding where to go.

"Let's go to dinner at the Portofino. I like the menu there the best. It's right across the street, and I'm starved," Karla said.

"Good idea, me too. Look... there's Tony, maybe we can finagle a dinner out of him again if we play our cards right," Nancy tittered.

"Hi Tony," the two women said putting on big smiles and waving to get his attention. They approached him with affectionate hugs and kisses on his cheeks.

"Hello young ladies. It's so nice to see you again. Would you like to join me again for dinner tonight?" he asked.

"Oh no, Tony, we can't let you buy us dinner again, can we Nancy?"

"No, absolutely not!" she answered.

"Of course you can, you have no idea how you brightened my evening last night!" Tony responded. "I don't think you have the slightest idea of how much I enjoyed being with the three of you. I was hoping I'd see you all again tonight."

"Well okay, Tony, since you put it that way," Karla answered, looking at Nancy with a sly smile. Tony enjoyed having the two women make a fuss over him, but the two women thought he was a dumb sap.

"Where's Hillary tonight," Tony asked, disappointed she wasn't with them.

"I guess she's doing her own thing," Karla said making up an excuse.

Tony, Karla, and Nancy then walked into the Portofino arm in arm. They were immediately seated next to the Bloombergs who had also just arrived with a friend.

"Would the three of you like to join us," Asher asked.

"No thanks, maybe some other time," Karla answered, turning her back on them as she was seated.

Tony, a frequent diner at the Portofino restaurant, was known as a bigger tipper. Because of that and his genial personality, all the employees fussed over him. He loved being given the VIP treatment. After dinner, when his companions had left, Tony had spent the rest of the evening sitting at the bar for hours talking with Henry the bar tender. Tony also left him big tips the past two nights, so he was now a welcome customer to be occupying a barstool. Though he was terminally ill, he seemed to have come to terms with his fate and entertained his companions with great stories of people and places he had been during his interesting life. Tony seemed kind and warm hearted, and his generosity quickly won people over.

"Hi folks, nice to see you back here again," the cocktail waitress said. "I guess you must like us a lot."

"Yes, we certainly do," Karla said, winking at Nancy.

"What will you have to drink tonight?" she asked.

"Hi Suzi, I do like this restaurant, but most of all, I come here to see your sweet smile," Tony said flirting with her. "I'd like to order a nice quality cabernet sauvignon for all of us. It goes well with steak."

"That sound's good," Nancy said, going along with the program.

"Actually, I think I'd like to have something different tonight. I'd like to order a scotch, neat," Karla said.

Several minutes after the drinks were brought to the table, the waitress came by to take their dinner orders.

"There's no rush, we'll have another round of drinks," Tony said, taking charge. After the women had finished their drinks, the waitress again came by to take their orders.

"What will it be tonight," she asked, pen and pad in hand.

"Mmm... I think I'll have the house salad, scalloped potatoes, asparagus and the lobster thermidor," Karla said rubbing her chin as she ordered the most expensive items on the menu.

"That sounds great. I'll have that too." Nancy said. The two women had found themselves a pigeon and were taking him for all he was worth. Though they were pandering to him, they were secretly laughing at him. Tony may have known that he was being taken, but he seemed to be happy to have their company during his final days.

"Uh-huh... that does sound good, but I'm going to have the filet mignon. Would you like another drink, Karla? Nancy, may I pour you another cabernet?" The women gladly obliged. Tony tried to slow his drinking down. He was attempting to stay a little more sober for the evening. At that moment, Charlotte and Alice arrived and were escorted to their table which was right next to Tony and his guests once again.

"Hello, everyone," Charlotte and Alice said, giving Tony hugs. "Looks like we've all decided upon our favorite restaurant and watering hole."

"I think I could safely say we're all in agreement, especially these lovely ladies," Tony said with a big smile.

As he was speaking, Randy and the other two "amigos" showed up and were being seated.

"Oh no, look at what just sauntered in the room," Karla moaned.

"I can tell who it is by the smell," Nancy said putting her napkin to her nose.

Shortly thereafter the dinners arrived, and from that point on, Tony indulged the women to their heart's content. Anything they wanted he provided for them including drinks, multiple appetizers, salads, lobster, more drinks, and crème brulée for dessert. By the time they were finished eating and drinking, Tony, Karla and Nancy appeared to be feeling the effects of the many drinks they had. The two women had become quite loud and boisterous making lewd comments and creating quite a disturbance in the usually sedate Portofino Restaurant.

"Watch what I can do," Karla said as she breathed onto a soup spoon and hung it from her nose. After she accomplished that, she had asked the waitress to bring her a ladle. Showing off, she hung the enormous spoon from her nose as well. Feeling terribly proud of herself she turned around letting all the people sitting in the vicinity see her accomplishment.

"Oh, big deal. I can do that too," Nancy said, grabbing the ladle off Karla's nose. After making several failed attempts, she finally gave up.

"Haaa... Haaa," Karla laughed making an ugly, guttural sound. "You can't do it, Nancy, you can't do it! You do it now, Tony." Karla said handing him the ladle. Tony shook his head not wanting to make a fool of himself.

"No, I don't think so, Karla, I'm not nearly as gifted and talented as you. Let me get you both another drink," and of course, they both accepted.

After finishing their dinners, Tony suggested that he drive the women back to their hotel rooms since they were in no condition to walk there on their own. He also recommended that Karla and Nancy go to the bathroom first before they left.

When they returned, Tony said, "It's time for us ta go, Sweeties," he said slurring his words. Apparently, his attempt to abstain from drinking too much hadn't been successful.

"Here we go ladies," he said staggering to his feet and trying to be a gentleman helping them out of their chairs.

As usual, Tony left an enormous tip. He and the two plastered women stumbled out of the restaurant and into his rented golf cart. While they were driving down Crescent Ave, the women began singing "Goodnight, Ladies" very loudly and terribly off key. Tony cringed as he listened. He had a good ear for music, and in his younger days attempted to imitate famous opera singers.

"Come on Tony, sing along with us," Nancy coaxed.

Tony joined in also singing off key, sardonically making fun of them. The three of them made a spectacle of themselves as Tony swerved the golf cart down Crescent Ave waving at people on the street. When they arrived at the Glenmore Hotel, Tony asked the desk clerk the time.

"It's right up there," Bonnie said pointing to the clock on the wall.

"Oh yeth I see it now. Thang you very mush." He then struggled to help the inebriated women up the hotel's two flights of stairs to their rooms. He got Nancy safely into her room, but Karla had some trouble getting her key card to work so Tony had to help her. On his way out of the lobby, he stopped and talked the desk clerk.

"Wha time is it?" Tony asked again.

"It's three minutes later than when you last asked me," Bonnie said as she looked at the clock.

"They both've ad way too mush ta drink, but I'm sure they'll be okay in the moring affer they sleep it off. We sure had a good time though," Tony said as he stumbling toward the door.

Bonnie looked around at the hotel guest and rolled her eyes.

"Some people just can't hold their liquor," the hotel guest said as the two of them shook their heads, laughing in amusement. "I'm surprised they were able to find their way back to the hotel."

"I'm sure they'll all sleep soundly tonight," Bonnie said.

Chapter 8: Lower Terrace Panorama

David and I awoke before the sun was up. It was Monday morning, the official starting day of the festival. After finishing our continental breakfasts, we were out the door of the hotel and ready to get an early start on our paintings.

"I'm so glad we didn't have margaritas with "The Three Amigos" last night. I don't handle alcohol well, David. It takes very little to get me drunk, and the next day I feel just awful. I was so tempted to join in on all the fun and partying with the guys, but I can't get away with that sort of thing."

"You must stay physically fit if you want to do well in this festival. You're so smart to avoid drinking anything alcoholic, even wine. So... what do you want to paint this morning?" David asked.

"Let's take a walk past the Busy Bee Restaurant and see what we can find there."

While David and I were scurrying down Crescent Avenue, we ran into Alice and Charlotte who were standing taking photographs of the Green Pleasure Pier and the boats in the bay. They were up early capturing the Avalon icons in the glow of the early morning light which was the second-best light of the day. To me, sunset was usually the best. I could tell Charlotte's knee was bothering her as she hobbled along with her cane. Somehow, it didn't seem to deter her from enjoying her stay on the island. She made the rounds with Alice attempting to keep up.

"Good morning" said, as we approached them."

"Hi there! What are you painting today?" Charlotte asked.

"I'm thinking about the Yacht Club. It's an interesting structure and the light on it this morning is terrific. What's on your agenda for the day, ladies?" I asked.

"We're going to stick around here watching the artists as they paint. We're going to decide what we would like to buy ahead of time and create a list so we can make a beeline for those paintings at the exhibition on Saturday. Tonight, I think Alice and I will have dinner again at the Portofino. We seem to be able to find selections there that we both like and the quality of the food seems very fresh and good."

"I might join you there tonight," David said. Annabel is having an Indian dinner with a friend who is supposedly a great cook, but Indian food can be quite spicy, so I haven't decided yet. If I'm free tonight, I might want to have dinner with you," David said inviting himself to sit with them. I was proud of David. He was trying to be more sociable which I knew was difficult for him.

"That would be nice, David. We can all walk to and from the Glenmore Hotel together." Charlotte suggested.

"Alice, you're my hallmate in room 302. I 'll leave a note on your door if I decide to join you. Your room is right across the way from us," David said.

"I'm not there anymore," Alice responded. "Karla takes sleeping pills, and in her sound sleep, she snores like a chainsaw. I moved in with Grandma on the second floor in room 201. We share a small, full-size bed, but at least I can get some sleep. Karla's happy because I'm paying half the cost of the room even though she has it all to herself now."

"That doesn't seem fair, she should at least give you some sort of a rebate," I concluded.

"I suggested that, but she said we made a deal before we came here and if I had any integrity, I would be true to my word and the agreement." David and I just looked at each other knowing that Karla's morals were on a sliding scale which could shift at any moment depending upon what was beneficial to her.

"Well, we've got to set up our easels. Give me your number, and if I decide to go to the Portofino tonight, I'll call and let you know by five o'clock this afternoon. See you later." David said.

We walked south on Crescent Ave and toward the St. Catherine Hotel. When we got to the Art Deco fountain by the Busy Bee, I turned around.

"Look at that, what about a street scene, David. We could paint the Busy Bee Restaurant with its red tile roof, and nautical blue awnings and umbrellas. We could catch the edge of the Art Deco fountain in the foreground," I said holding up my hands, making a square to frame and see the image I wanted to paint.

"I like this scene, it's colorful. Let's set up right here," David said, putting down his backpack.

"Okay, here we go." We set up on a busy area of Crescent Avenue, and shortly after we began painting, we attracted a large crowd of onlookers. True to form, many of them had mothers, sisters, or aunts who were all terrific artists. As usual, I strove to be polite and inquired about their artistic relations. David, as usual, refused to engage in any discussion. I truly didn't understand the degree to why people interrupting him affected him so much when he was trying to paint. To me, it was no more than a minor annoyance that was to be expected. When I had completed most of the street scene, I asked a mother and her two cute little girls in blue sailor dresses to pose for me. The little family group would create an attractive focal point in the foreground of the painting. Mom was happy to oblige. She had carefully dressed her little ones to look adorable, and she was glad to see the children and her efforts appreciated. I had learned that when people have been models in a painting, it almost always guaranteed a sale, especially if their children were included. The weather had been perfect both yesterday and today and the sunshine brought out lots of bright colors, contrasting highlights, and deep shadows.

"This painting turned out nice, but it's not going to win any prizes," I said to David.

"No, but don't worry, it will certainly sell quickly, most likely to that mother," he answered.

"Let's grab a bite for lunch at Eric's Sandwich Stand again. If nothing else, it's convenient."

"How about another rubber turkey sandwich, Annabel?" David motioned, pretending to gag sticking his finger down his throat.

"Sounds delightful," I said as I crossed my eyes. "I hope we don't have another encounter with that seagull. Do you see him anywhere?" David shook his head.

"We haven't heard from Raj, I wonder why?" I asked.

"He's probably busy cooking. He'll call you, Annabel."

While we were sitting having lunch, Raj spotted us as he was driving by in his golf cart. I was glad to see him because since we hadn't heard from him all morning I was beginning to wonder if the offer to let us paint on his balcony and have Indian dinner at his house was still on.

"Hi there," Raj said, waving as he approached us. "I picked up the rest of the ingredients for dinner yesterday and began preparing some of the dishes for tonight. I'm really looking forward to this evening."

"Me too, I can't wait. We're almost done with lunch, so anytime you want to head up the hill, I'm ready to go."

"David, if you would like to join us, I kept the spices to a minimum for three of the dishes, so they won't be too spicy for you. There's plenty food for all." Raj informed us.

"Thank you so much, that's wonderful! And in that case, yes, I would love to join you." David was so happy to be included, and I was happy too. I didn't like David going off on his own when I knew being outgoing was difficult for him.

We piled our equipment into Raj's golf cart and headed up the back roads that took us to his house on Lower Terrace Road. While we were riding in the cart, we continued eyeing the quaint houses with their golf carts parked along the streets. Those back roads were also a part of the charm of the island. When we arrived at our destination, I was impressed. Raj's house was one of the nicest I had seen on the island.

"That must be Mercy O'Reilly and Debra Paisley's cart. Oh look, I see them over there in the field setting up their equipment," Raj said pointing in their direction.

"Yes... I see them too," David said.

"Nice house Raj," I remarked as we pulled into the garage. When we went in, he gave us a quick tour of the house and then took us out onto the balcony to see if it was a scene we would like to paint. "Oh, this is great! This is even better than what I had hoped for. What a view! We can see the whole harbor with the Casino in the background, all the boats in the bay, and in the foreground, the Holly House with the little structures surrounding it. This is perfect."

"Yes, I agree. This is wonderful!" David said, staring out across the water.

I could sense Raj was delighted that we were impressed with his house and the view. He had set down a drop cloth for us to be sure we didn't splatter paint on what I could tell was a freshly painted balcony. It was obvious to me that he took pride in the upkeep of the house. Everything was in perfect order. I wondered why he liked me since my clothing and painting equipment were such a mess. How interesting, I thought.

We set up our easels and went right to work while Raj continued his preparations for dinner in the kitchen. The pungent scent of curry and spices would drift past us from time to time while we were enjoying the scene from Raj's balcony. It was a perfect afternoon for painting, the air was warm and clear, and the Santa Ana breeze was still blowing. We were lucky, the Santa Anas can become so strong that it's nearly impossible to keep the easels from blowing over. If the canvas panel doesn't act like a sail, the shade umbrella will, but today the breeze was gentle. The light on the back of the boats created golden reflections on the sparkling, sapphire water. Both the Casino and the Holly House were beautifully lit by the afternoon sun creating blue-violet shadows on the east side of the structures and objects. This scene of Avalon Bay was an artist's dream, and I could tell this painting was going to be a winner. Occasionally, Raj would come out to see how our work was progressing, making complimentary comments as the images progressed.

"I like your composition, Annabel. You've got a good start. Yours is nice too, David." Raj was sincere in his efforts to learn about some of the most important aspects of art. He had mentioned that he had been reading some art books hoping to learn more about painting. I was impressed that he wanted to make the effort.

Officers Ziggy and Corny eventually arrived and Raj brought them out on the balcony to introduce them to David and me while we were painting. Most of the time that afternoon they kept Raj company as he was cooking, but every now and then, they would come outside to check on David and my progress. The tan, blonde Corny and Ziggy could have come straight out of central casting for the movies. They were both tall, athletic looking, rugged versions of either Robert Redford or Brad Pitt. I had read that the Ziegler family was an important part of the island lore going way back to the early years of Catalina's development. Corny's grandfather purchased land shortly after the turn of the century. Corny's father developed apartments which the family still owned and rented to the residents of Avalon to this day.

"So Corny, how do you and Ziggy manage to tend to your apartments and work for the police department as well?" I asked.

"It's easy," Corny explained. "Ziggy and I turned over the management of the apartments to my wife and daughter. I find dealing with numbers and apartment shit to be tedious and boring. Ziggy and I like to be active."

"I see, that makes perfect sense," I said.

As the afternoon progressed, I realized the two deputies were well meaning fellows, but were both socially awkward, often inserting their feet into their mouths. Whenever they came out to check on David and my paintings, they would pepper us with clueless comments and questions.

"It's just like kindergarten all over again out here with you two, isn't it?" Ziggy said thinking he had said something very clever. He stepped back and forth from one foot to the other as if he could better understand a painting if he observed it from different angles.

Corny was not much better, asking, "Don't you get tired of looking at the same old scene hour after hour?" or "It must be fun to fool around with those pretty paint colors all day long." David was ready to have a fit, but I stepped on his foot reminding him to stay cool and keep silent.

When they went back inside, I said to David, "Remember, they're as ignorant about art as we are about computers." That rang a bell with my irascible friend.

"Okay, I know they were just trying to be friendly and make conversation, gauche as it may have been," David said letting out a big sigh. He realized he should cut the deputies some slack.

Mercy and Debra had come out onto the balcony after completing their paintings, so David and I introduced ourselves to them. They told us dinner would be served a little early, so we quickly cleaned up the palettes and put away our easels. By 5:30 that afternoon we were ready to see what Raj had prepared.

We walked into the dining room where gleaming candles were illuminating the room displaying a table setting with Raj's fine Indian china. The room was decorated with fabric of gold, violet, and magenta which was embellished with tiny, glittering mirrors that reflected the flickering candles. Raj had gone all out creating an exotic atmosphere reminiscent of his family's Indian heritage.

"Oh Raj, this is magnificent! You couldn't have prepared this setting for a more appreciative guest. Thank you, this is very special." All his other guests were also oohing and ahhing.

"You were the one I most wanted to please, knowing how meticulous you can be about almost everything. Now let's see if the dinner matches the setting. I certainly hope so," Raj said, the look on his face revealed the pride he was feeling knowing he had created a magical setting for his guests.

Raj had prepared mulligatawny soup, lamb vindaloo, chicken curry, and cauliflower rice biryani. There was naan bread, mango chutney, yogurt with cucumber, and tamarind condiments. To my delight, Raj had prepared mango lassi.

"Mango lassi is my favorite, Raj. Have you ever had it, David?" I asked.

"No, I haven't."

"Well, you're in for a real treat," I informed him.

The faint sound of Indian music was softly playing in the background adding to the ambience of the setting. David and I were greatly impressed by Raj's skill as an authentic Indian gourmet cook. When all the complimentary comments had been made, we were invited to take a seat at the table. Raj made sure I was seated next to him.

"Where did you learn to prepare these dishes, Raj?" I asked.

"I'm an only child and I used to watch my mother prepare our dinners. She began asking me to help her with the preparations. That's how I got started. When I purchased my own house, I branched out, bought cookbooks, and tried recipes my mother had never prepared for us."

"Were your parents from India?" Mercy O'Reilly asked, batting her eyes at Raj.

"They were but they moved to England when they were young. They met while attending Oxford. My father is Indian, but my maternal grandparents were English. My mother was born in India and spent her formative years there."

"You have a slight English accent. How do you account for that?" Debra Paisley asked.

"Probably because both my parents lived in England for many years. They were the people I first heard speaking English. I think I sound like a typical American."

The entire table laughed. I was obviously not the only one who had noticed a trace of England when he spoke.

"Why is it that people with English accents always sound so intelligent?" Mercy asked, obviously flirting with Raj.

"I really can't explain that. Maybe Indian food raises your IQ," Raj kidded. "I think of myself as American, born and raised in the USA. I like hamburgers and hot dogs as much as the rest of you. "

"Especially if you slather the hamburger with Mango chutney," Ziggy teased.

"Yeah, or how about some biriani sauce and sauerkraut on your hot dog?" Corny suggested.

"Only the Zieglers could come up with combinations like that," Raj said rolling his eyes.

Raj and the Zieglers couldn't have been more different in intellect and temperament. Raj was the brilliant computer genius. He was an innovator creating cutting edge advances to technology. Ziggy and Corny were average, somewhat inarticulate guys. They had been "jocks" in their younger days and now they were men of action as police deputies. But despite their differences, the men clearly liked each other and respected each other's unique abilities.

As the night progressed, Ziggy, Corny and Raj all engaged in competitive banter, playfully insulting each other attempting to make the cleverest remarks. Raj's put downs were witty and esoteric, while Ziggy and Corny resorted to potty talk and slapstick comedy. We all enjoyed both approaches. I now realized that Raj had a terrific sense of humor which I had previously mistaken for sarcasm. I also noticed that while he was entertaining his guests, he was completely at ease and liked being in charge; it seemed to come naturally to him. Only children are often instinctual leaders.

David and I were enjoying ourselves and the company so much, we lost track of the time. Around 7:45 that evening, the phone rang interrupting everyone's enjoyment of the dinner party. Raj excused himself and took the call in the next room, but we could still hear his side of the conversation.

"What! Say that again. You must be kidding! Where? Okay, I'll be there as soon as I can." Raj hung up the phone and came back in the dining room. The look on his face was grim. "I'm so sorry everyone, I've got to meet Tom Derringer immediately. Annabel, I'll take you and David back to the Glenmore."

"Ziggy and I can take them to their hotel, Raj. You go do what you need to do for Tom," Corny offered.

"Is everything okay," I asked. I could tell by the expression on Raj's face something had gone terribly wrong."

"I'm not sure what's going on, but Tom said it was important that I meet him right away. He knew about the dinner here tonight so it must be important."

"Well, it was a delightful evening. Dinner was wonderful. Thank you for everything," we all said as Raj left the house abruptly. The rest of us put away the leftovers and cleaned up for him.

Late that night, I got a call from Raj waking me up. "Annabel, make sure you don't go anywhere without David tomorrow. Always keep him right by your side."

"Why Raj, what's going on?" I asked my voice gravelly from the sudden awakening. This is an odd phone call, I thought.

"I can't talk to you now, but do exactly as I say. I've got to go, bye," with that, he hung up.

"That was so strange." I explained to David what Raj had just said to me.

"Hmm," was all David had to say as he rolled over and went back to sleep.

Tuesday

Chapter 9: Goodbye, Ladies

Tuesday morning Nancy came into the breakfast area looking for Karla, asking Charlotte and Alice if they had seen her. Nancy seemed quite distracted. There was still no word from Hillary, and now Karla was missing.

"You and Karla both had a lot to drink last night, Dear. She's probably sleeping it off," Charlotte said, trying to alleviate Nancy's concerns.

"But I haven't seen Hillary since Monday evening either. Neither of them are answering my phone calls." Nancy was fidgeting nervously with her hands. "Something is not right."

"Why don't you get to work on your painting. I'm sure you'll run into them today sooner or later. Maybe they've taken the cart and are painting somewhere." Alice said, trying to be reassuring.

"Okay, maybe you're right, but they should have called me. She then gathered up her equipment and set out on her own to scout a good location. The morning progressed as usual, Nancy barely thinking of her missing comrades while she was painting. When she completed an almost adequate painting of the Casino, she joined Charlotte and Alice for a leisurely lunch at Portofino. They all decided that as soon as they had finished, something had to be done if no one had seen or heard from either of the women by then. Nancy's desire to do well in the art festival had been enough to keep her focused, but now, she was troubled and becoming increasingly concerned. By the time the women finished their lunch, no one had heard anything of the two women though Nancy had called them several times.

"Okay Nancy, we'll all go to the Glenmore and Alice can open the door to Karla's room with her key card. You do still have the key card, don't you Alice?"

"I do. We'll go check on her. I suspect she's probably just hungover," Alice predicted. They headed down Crescent Avenue and walked to the Glenmore Hotel. Charlotte stayed in the lobby not wanting to climb all the stairs to the third floor.

When Nancy and Alice were at the door of Karla's room, Alice reached into her purse, fumbled around for a moment, then said, "I can't find my key card." She searched through all the compartments in her purse but couldn't locate it. "It's no use, I must have lost it. I'll go down to the desk and get another one."

A few minutes later, the desk clerk returned with Alice and opened the door. "You see, she's just sleeping. Shh... let's let her sleep it off," the clerk said as she quietly closed the door.

"Wait a minute," Karla's former roommate, Alice said. "She's not snoring. Please open the door again."

Alice and Nancy entered the room reluctantly approaching the bed where Karla was lying and buried beneath the covers. Alice hesitated, apprehensive concerning what she was about to behold. Her hands quivered as she pulled back the blanket which revealed some writing on Karla's sweatshirt. She then tentatively rolled over the lifeless body. There were audible gasps in the room as a grimacing, bluish-purple face of Karla emerged from the pillow. Her eye sockets had been painted black, one of her eyes was open, staring into space as if she had witnessed something too horrible to imagine. A freakish smile had been smeared on her face with red oil paint or lipstick, and the gruesome smile had been slashed from ear to ear with a sharp object.

"How horrible!" Nancy exclaimed, burying her face in her hands, turning away as she tried to come to terms with the horror of what she had just witnessed.

"Nancy, call 911. Go get my mother, Bonnie, my mother's a nurse," Alice said to the desk clerk who flew down the stairs and returned with Charlotte. As soon as Charlotte looked at Karla, she instantly knew the gravity of the situation. After going through the motion of taking Karla's pulse she knew it was pointless since rigor mortis had already begun to set in.

"There's nothing we can do. She's gone," Charlotte said after seeing the staring purple face and finding no pulse.

Sergeant Monaghan arrived within a few minutes, followed by Captain Derringer, Raj, and Sarah.

"Did anyone move the body?" Sarah asked.

"I did," Alice responded while the sergeant was taking photographs.

Although the body had been disturbed, Sarah collected all the forensic information she could. Multiple stab wounds in a similar pattern to those of Hillary were found on the body. Four letters written in red on the back of Karla's sweatshirt, spelled out the word "NAZI." Karla's panties had been slashed and thrown onto the floor with her pajama bottoms. Raj began photographing them, the floor, the windows, and the doors observing all he saw while the others collected the evidence. Sarah looked for blood splatter patterns on the walls and ceiling but found none which was telling.

A bottle of sleeping pills near the bed was on the bed stand, but there was no water glass.

"Do any of you know anything about these sleeping pills?" Raj asked Nancy, getting Tom's attention pointing to the sleeping pills.

"She had a lot of trouble sleeping. She used to take one pill every night from what she had told me," Nancy said.

"I know that she took sleeping pills each night because I was her roommate for one night. She told me she needed to get her sleep to be able to get up early the next morning to paint. Last night I saw her consuming a lot of alcohol. She must have overdosed," Alice suggested.

"We'll have forensics look into that." Captain Derringer was pacing around the room and still thinking. He knew more than they did, but he wasn't going to reveal the findings of the previous night to these women. There was an unpleasant task ahead of him. He had to think about what he was going to release to the public and when he would do it.

"And what about Hillary? I haven't seen her in two days or been able to reach her. No one seems to care. Officer Monaghan, were you able to locate her?" Nancy whined. The sergeant obfuscated saying he'd get back to her about that matter, deliberately avoiding her question.

"Who were the last people who saw Karla, and what are their and your names?" Sergeant Monaghan took out his notebook and made sure he had all their names.

"I'm Nancy Hall. You already have my information. Karla and I were having dinner with Tony Rossi at the Portofino restaurant last night."

"I'm Charlotte Fitzsimmons, and this is my granddaughter, Alice Smith. We were at the next table and interacted with the three of them while we were having our dinner last night. All of them were very inebriated when they left together."

"Tony drove Karla and me home, then left," Nancy said.

"I saw them come in around ten o'clock," Bonnie said. "They were all plastered. Tony took them upstairs and immediately returned. He spoke to me briefly slurring his word badly. I could barely understand him."

"Did anyone else see them come in, and who are you, young lady?"

"I'm Bonnie Abernathy, the desk clerk. Another guest who's staying here saw them come in. They made quite a drunken scene in the lobby."

"Anything else unusual that anyone could tell us?" Jim asked.

"Well, Tony is suffering from a terminal form of cancer and is in a lot of pain much of the time," Charlotte said. I had previously told him that being a retired nurse, I made it a practice to keep a lot of medications with me. He told me he was having trouble sleeping. I didn't have sleeping medication, but Alice suggested that she might be able to get a few sleeping pills from Karla."

"Yes, that's right," Alice said. "But Karla didn't want to give me any of her pills to help alleviate his pain. I had moved out of her room because of her snoring, so I pressured her by saying I would have to move back in with her again if she didn't give me a few pills. She finally capitulated and gave me six pills. I immediately gave them to Tony."

"Anything else?" Sergeant Monaghan asked.

"No… no," the four women all said looking at each other not wanting to say anymore.

By then, the coroner had arrived and began examining and photographing the body as he prepared to take it away.

"I'll get her to the forensic pathologist and when he's completed his postmortem exam, I'll certify the causes and manner of death on the death certificate. I'll get it back to you as soon as possible along with the other one." the coroner said. Tom hoped the women hadn't heard that comment.

"Great! Time is of the essence," Captain Derringer responded.

"Okay ladies, Sergeant Monaghan will give me your names, phone numbers, and hotel and home addresses. You can go now, but don't leave the island without letting me know. We're going to have some officers stationed around this hotel for the rest of the week so you all will be safe. Jim, have some chain locks put on the doors to the back entrances." The women all filed out of the room and went downstairs to the room where Charlotte and Alice were staying. Nancy burst into tears. Charlotte held her trying to comfort the distraught woman. Alice attempted to reassure the visibly shaken desk clerk, who called the owner of the Glenmore Hotel. Nothing like this had ever happened on Catalina Island before as far as she knew.

*****

Back upstairs Tom, Jim, and Raj had a serious situation on their hands. There had been a murderer on the island, and now a second artist was dead. The question for them was, when do they make the two deaths public knowing it would scare off the tourists. This was the island's busiest season when most of the income was procured for the restaurants, hotels, stores, and gift shops. This festival was bringing in a tremendous amount of capital for the residents.

"Well sheeit! Doesn't this situation just dill my pickle," Captain Derringer said, his southern accent becoming more pronounced when he was agitated. I think we have a duty to tell the folks. We've gotta put their safety first but I don't look forward to telling everyone about this. As soon as we release it, this is going to be all over the news media. Maybe we can slow it down giving us some more time to find this asshole."

"Well, we better get moving then. Let's go out the back entrance and see what we can find there," Jim said taking the lead down the two flights of stairs behind the hotel.

While they were descending the stairs, Raj said, "Did you notice, there was very little blood on Karla's sweatshirt unlike Hillary who was covered in blood? Dead people don't bleed, so it's quite possible she was dead when she was stabbed."

"Good point, Raj, and yes, I did notice that," Tom said.

Tom, Jim, Raj, and Sarah were careful not to step onto the ground until they had looked it over for footprints or other forms of evidence they might possibly disturb. Jim snapped several photos of the location. There was a tree with a missing branch, and it was obvious that it had recently been broken off.

"It looks as if the killer brushed away the tracks with the branch leaves again. If it were me, I'd throw the branch over that fence over yonder," Tom said pointing.

"I'll check it out," Sarah said treading carefully on the ground. "Yup, here it is."

"We'll take it with us. Now let's scour the area and see what else we can find.

They looked around gathering up anything that seemed out of place on the ground behind the hotel when Jim said, "We better get started deciding what we're going to tell everyone. There's a "Meet and Greet" for all the artists and the organizers of the festival tonight at the Casino. It's a big shindig where they're planning to serve food to all involved. I guess we could tell them about Hillary and Karla there," Jim suggested.

"We'll need to contact Brianna Gleason, the chairwoman of the organizing committee to tell her we need to speak to the people at the event tonight."

"But what on earth are we going to tell everyone?" Raj asked.

"Can you write something for me to say, Raj? You're so much better at those things than I am," Tom pleaded.

Raj shook his head and said, "How can we possibly come up with a way to present this to the artists. This is going to scare the shit out of all of them. Most of them, especially the women, will panic and want to leave the island immediately. I think we've got to talk to Brianna right away and get her involved. Women are so good at wording things in a palatable way. "

"That's right, these are her folks. Good thinking Raj. I'll need to explain what has occurred to her and let her inform the artists. We can be there to answer questions." I'm great when it comes to police business, but when it comes to public speaking, I'm about as worthless as gum on a boot heel," Tom said.

"You're not that bad Tom," Raj snickered. "We'll need to insist that none of the artists should ever paint alone. They must create a buddy system. If they can't find another artist, the large male residents of the island need to be commandeered to accompany them, especially the women. We should begin searching for volunteers right away."

"Great fuckin thinking, Raj. Jim that'll be your job. Begin at some of the gyms and ask for volunteers to accompany the artists. Don't tell them why yet; just make up some lame excuse. Most of these gym rats don't know whether to scratch their watch or wind their ass. So, they'll buy whatever you tell them but try to have some semblance of truth."

Chapter 10: A Day with Annabel and David

On that same Tuesday morning Annabel and David's day began unaware of what had happened the previous night in room 302. As they were coming out of their room, Annabel stopped for a moment, put her hands on her hips and said, "Look at this, David, there are dirty footprints on this rug leading in our back entrance. They must have tracked it in all the way up from the ground behind the hotel. What a dirty mess!"

"I'm sure housekeeping will have it all cleaned up within an hour. Don't be a such a clean freak. That's not like you," David said.

"I guess Raj's tidy ways are rubbing off on me."

We got a late start that morning, so we decided to do a small 8x10" painting of the Yacht Club. There were lots of multicolored naval flags flying on the lines of boat masts. There was an American flag on a tall pole as well. I love the design of our flag and often place a few in my paintings whether they are there or not. People respond to them and so do I.

When David was setting up his easel, he realized there was a problem.

"Annabel, the leg on this easel is stuck. I can't pull it down."

"Give it a good yank."

"No, I don't want to break it and be out of commission for the rest of the week."

French easels have three legs which are lengthened by pulling out an extension at the bottom of each of the legs. That design allows the painter to adjust the legs of the easel to accommodate whatever uneven terrain they are standing upon. One of David's extension legs wouldn't pull out.

"Okay, I have an idea, prop your non-functioning leg up on the green railing that runs along the walkway. How's that?'" I asked as I adjusted the other legs to keep the palette area of the easel flat and parallel to the ground.

"It's okay. I can function the rest of the week if I have a place to prop this easel on."

We were set up and painting along Crescent Avenue's main walkway which meant there was a continual stream of people walking by us wanting to talk and ask questions.

"What's wrong with your easel?" a teenaged girl asked David.

"Guess," David said, agitated by the broken easel situation and even shorter on patience than usual.

"Did you break it? she asked.

"Wow, that's pretty good, you got it on the first guess." After the teenager left, I said,

"Be nice, David." I heard him grumbling something under his breath.

While we were painting, a man walking his huge dog stopped to chat with me for a moment. While we were talking, the dog lifted his leg and peed on my equipment.

"Oh, I'm so, so sorry, Miss," the man said, as he quickly exited the scene of the crime. I heard David hysterically laughing at my predicament.

"I'm sorry, Annabel, but I'm usually the one who deals with those sorts of stupid situations. It's nice to see it happen to someone else for a change," he said half-jokingly.

"Well, I can't complain. I'd rather have dog pee on my stuff than bird poop on my hat," I said swatting his hat.

Shortly after that incident, an old man with a walker came by and was annoyed at us for blocking the sidewalk and voiced his displeasure.

"You hooligans come over here and clog up the town for us homeowners. Get out of my way and stop blocking the street! I'm ninety-three years old and I don't need this!

"Well, yabba dabba doo. Rock on, Fred Flintstone!" David said after the old man had walked off muttering and swearing to himself.

"How did you know his name was Fred Flintstone?" I asked.

"Oh brother, never mind, you're too young to get the joke."

"We weren't blocking the street. Look, there's lots of room," I said pointing to the space on the walkway. Now I was annoyed.

"Forget about it, Annabel. There's an ordinance the says it's legal to set up on the sidewalk if there's room for pedestrians to pass."

When we finished the morning scene of the Yacht Club, the sun was high in the sky and the long shadows we loved to paint had disappeared. That meant it was a perfect time for a lunch break.

"I'm hungry, David, how about having lunch at Diego's today?"

"I could really go for some fish tacos, let's go."

When David was packing up, he gave a tug on his easel leg and it was now working perfectly.

"French easels can be so temperamental," I said.

On our way to Diego's Tortilliaria, we ran into the Bloombergs as they were coming out of one of the little tourist shops along Crescent Avenue.

"Hi there! We're going for lunch now, would you like to join us," I asked. They seemed cheerful and pleasant when we had talked to them before. The more the merrier was my motto. I could tell David would rather that it would have been just the two of us, but this was a good opportunity for him to work on being more outgoing for his own good. I was his friend and felt duty bound to help him to become more extroverted.

"We would love to!" Asher replied. "I truly enjoy talking with people who are interested and knowledgeable about art. Where are you headed?"

"Diego's, do you like Mexican food," I asked.

"Love it," Miriam responded. Asher nodded his head in agreement.

We were seated right away at a booth in the back of the restaurant which was quite full of tourists. Mid-day was almost always busy during the peak of the tourist season, but we arrived just as some people were leaving.

"So, when did you get started painting, Annabel?" Asher asked.

"My mother was a teacher and an amateur artist who was wonderful with color. She realized when I was two that I was drawing at the level of her kindergarten students. She worked with me beginning at an early age, teaching me how to draw and color with my crayons. She also encouraged me to watch her as she did portraits of me and my siblings allowing me to try my hand at it as well. 'You're never too young to start,' she used to say. I was even allowed to use her expensive set of pastels. When I was six, my parents bought me my first set of oil paints, so I got started very early with this medium as well. I won lots of awards throughout my school years, so I think my path as an artist was set from the beginning."

"So, it was from your mother's side of the family where you got your talent?" Miriam asked.

"Oh no, though my father was an electronics engineer, his family was of Swiss ancestry. They were precisionists when it came to art craftmanship. Several members of his family were highly skilled professional lithographers, painters and artisans of various art endeavors. My ability comes from a combination of nature and nurture. And it comes from both sides of the family.

"I have a sister who paints, but our family history is more as collectors than artists. My grandparent's collection included some Monets, Renoirs, van Goghs, Max Liebermans, and Gustav Klimts. From what I heard from my father, it was an amazing collection." Asher explained.

"Wow, those are some of my very favorite artists. I especially love Gustav Klimt. That collection would be worth a fortune today. What happened to it?" I asked.

"It's not a happy story, Annabel. Have you ever heard the name Julius Streicher?" Asher asked.

"I've heard of him, but don't know much about him. I know he was one of Hitler's closest intimates and a rabid antisemite."

"He was responsible for spreading horrible propaganda concerning Jews in several of his publishings. "Der Sturmer" was a sensationalist newspaper where he spread hateful lies about the Jews. He also published children's book where Jews were depicted as children of the devil." Asher explained.

"That's terrible, David have you ever heard of him?" David shook his head, no.

"In 1938, he ordered the Grand Synagogue of Nuremberg to be torn down with the excuse it was ugly architecture. Most importantly, to my family, he was responsible for the death of thirteen of my family members including my grandparents. Streicher ended up with all my grandfather's property including the valuable art collection." Asher's hands were trembling, and I could see he was visibly upset. Though many years had passed, for him, it was as if the atrocity had happened yesterday.

"Have you thought about finding his descendants to see if they have any of the paintings in their possession?" I asked.

Asher and Miriam turned and looked at each other and for a moment were very quiet. Then he looked at me with a penetrating gaze, and with a restrained voice said, "Yes."

"I'm so sorry Asher. I thank God that I will never fully understand how the ramifications of the holocaust affect people's lives for generations."

Our conversation had taken a terribly unsettling turn. Though there were many questions I would have liked to ask, now was not the time. The events that Asher was telling us about were terribly disturbing. I needed to remain upbeat and positive, focusing on creating the best paintings possible. David was shifting uncomfortably in his seat, so I decided to change the subject to lighten the mood of our conversation.

The waitress had just brought the menus, so I asked, "Have you eaten here before?"

"Yes, we have, just once. I had a burrito and Miriam had flautas. We thought they were both delicious."

"Flautas, mmm," David said as he perused the menu. "I usually order fish tacos. You can't go wrong with fish tacos, but I'd like to try something a little different."

"I'm going to stick with fish tacos, and a tall glass of horchata. I love their chips here. Does anyone want guacamole?" I asked.

"Absolutely," the others all said in unison.

Fortunately, the rest of our luncheon remained pleasant and cheerful. Antisemitism for me is deeply personal for I have many wonderful Jewish friends. For now, I wanted to keep a positive attitude which meant I had to avoid upsetting discussions of things that were beyond my control.

"So, what is your personal philosophy of art, Annabel?" Asher asked.

"Wow, that's a serious question," I thought for a moment. "I want to utilize my knowledge, creative talents, and technical skills, to evoke a powerful, emotional and intellectual response to my work. I want to move people by creating images that are so beautiful, that it raises the viewer to a higher spiritual level, the way a powerful symphony does, or a Christmas mass with parishioners singing carols by candlelight. But it's not only that

I'm reaching out to others, I'm finding meaning and beauty in my own life during the process of producing art. After a painting is complete, I sometimes amaze myself at what I was able to create with these two little hands. I'm keenly aware my ability is a gift from God and He could take it away from me at any moment. There's so much I could say about art, Asher, but I hope that answers your question."

"It does." Asher responded.

"It sounds like painting is almost a religious experience for you," Miriam observed.

"No, not quite, art lifts you to a higher level emotionally, but the experience is temporary. Religion is a permanent sense of joy knowing that we're embraced by a loving God, who we will someday join in a place that's even more spectacular than one of God's most glorious sunsets."

"I can tell you've given what you do a lot of serious thought. What about you David?"

"Annabel answered it better than I could. I feel much the same way. But for me, painting is not only my pleasure, it's my frustration too," David said, looking down. We all laughed understanding how difficult the painting process could be. "But excuse me for changing the subject, are the two of you familiar with the word tetrachromacy?" David asked.

"No, I've never heard of it. What's that," Miriam wanted to know.

David looked at me knowing I was more familiar with the subject and motioned for me to explain.

"Some people, mostly women, have four channels for color reception in their eyes, in other words, four cone cells to detect color. Most people have only three, but approximately 12% of women and almost no men are tetrachromats. Many of them enter fields where they can utilize their ability to distinguish subtle color variations, fields such as artists, fashion designers, and interior decorators. I'll bet most of the women here whose work is colorful, are tetrachromats. I'm sure you get the picture," I explained.

"Annabel and her mother are both tetrachromats," David interjected.

"How can you tell if you have that fourth cone?" Miriam wanted to know.

"For one thing, women and girls who have it are often obsessed with color. When I point out certain colors to most people, they often say, 'I don't see that.'" That has been going on since I was a child. Maybe tetrachromacy is the flip side of being color blind, which afflicts mostly men. Maybe they are either missing color cones for perceiving red and green or the ones they have are defective, but that's just a guess. I'm not a scientist." I explained.

"That's a new one on us. We'll look up more information about it on the internet," Asher and Miriam both nodded in agreement.

"Several birds are tetrachromats. I kid Annabel telling her I always knew she was a bird brain."

"David, it's lucky we're friends," I said giving him a light punch in the arm.

"Well, we need to get going if we want to get another painting done before the 'Meet and Greet' at 6:30 in the Casino tonight," David reminded me.

David and I were off to begin another painting. While we were walking to get back to Crescent Ave, we discussed painting something with an unusual perspective. That would best be accomplished by getting up above Avalon Bay either from the south side on Lower, Middle, or Upper Terrace Roads or from the north side of the bay up Chimes Tower Road.

"We've already done Lower Terrace, David, I like the view from Chimes Tower. Up there, the street offers scenes with red tile rooftops, lots of lush eucalyptus trees, and in the background, the point that juts out from the bay and includes the Holly and Wrigley houses. Right behind it is another point in the distance. We can create some great atmospheric perspective with that view." I observed.

"I like the Idea, but how are we going to get up there?" David asked.

"We'll hitch a ride with anyone who is willing to drive us up there. It's a lonely spot, but everyone says it's safe."

We stopped a woman riding alone in her cart, explained we were artists, and asked her to take us up the hill to the bell tower. She was more than happy to comply. We all squeezed into her cart and while we rode up the hill, she said,

"My daughter is a marvelous artist."

"No kidding, what does she like to paint?" I asked. David didn't say a word, as I asked polite and appropriate questions.

When we reached our destination, we noticed a section of the road had been taped off with yellow police tape and some deputies we didn't know were poking around in the brush. Not knowing what that was about, we turned around and went to a lower perspective overlooking the bay. We unloaded our equipment, and thanked our newfound friend,

"Well, we're here, but did you ever think how we were going to get a ride back down again?" David wanted to know.

"That's a good question, it's quite isolated up here, but hopefully sooner or later, someone will be coming down. At worst, we can walk since it's down the hill. I know it's a long walk, but we can do it." David gave me one of his irritated looks.

"Oh, stop it, this is a great location," I said, giving him back a defiant look.

"I wonder what the police tape is about?" David asked curious to know.

"Maybe there was an accident," but as far as I was concerned, it wasn't a priority.

There was a slight trace of humidity still hanging in the afternoon air and a golden glow was beginning to illuminate the mist. The scent of nearby eucalyptus trees washed over the hillside as a gentle breeze enveloped us in its warm, fragrant embrace. We were well above the little bay town and instead of the sounds of traffic, we heard the songs of the variety of island birds, and the sounds of eucalyptus leaves fluttering in the afternoon breeze. I discovered the moon faintly emerging in the September sky and added it to my painting. We painted for a few hours and when we were almost ready to bring things to a close for the afternoon, we saw Tony coming up the hill.

"Hey Tony, I said waving as he approached. Can you give us a ride back into town? We're almost finished."

"Of course I can. Don't rush, I'm in no hurry. I was looking for some artists to watch paint and hoping I might find someone up here. I know that this is a great location, and I thought maybe you'd be painting here."

"Thank you, Tony. That's great! You certainly are an art lover; don't you ever get the urge to paint? I know your mother was a terrific artist," I asked.

"Never! After seeing how my mother's life was completely centered around her art, I never wanted to try. My father and I hardly ever saw her. She was always with her painting friends, at events, or working in her studio."

"She must have been very gifted to have put that much of herself into her work. We're the two of you close?" I asked.

"No, we weren't. We didn't like each other."

"I'm surprised. How sad!" I was startled by his response and didn't know quite what to say. I continued mixing the paint on my palette not wanting to hear more about his dysfunctional family. Why did people always want to tell me about their woes when I was trying so hard to stay positive? David was in his own world and not listening to the conversation.

"My mother neglected and berated me and my father," he continued. "She was driving us on the freeway and went into one of her raging tirades. Dad became so despondent wanting to flee from her diatribe, he jumped out of her speeding car. He was smashed up on the freeway by a large truck and other cars." I heard a catch in his voice as he divulged his story.

With that, I stopped what I was doing and turned around, shocked at his revelation.

"I'm so sorry Tony. That's simply horrible! I guess you probably don't have much to do with her anymore and who could blame you."

"I have nothing to do with her anymore and I never will."

David and I were not quite finished, but it was getting late, and we needed to leave. I could put the finishing touches on my painting tomorrow. I looked at my watch and said,

"Okay, David, time to wrap it up. We've got to get ready for the 'Meet and Greet' at the Casino."

The three of us tried to squeeze into Tony's cart. It was tight with the two big men, but we managed. I tried to keep the conversation on a lighter level, talking about the beauty and charm of the island, how we were tired but determined to keep going, and how much we had enjoyed our stay on the island. David occasionally joined in the conversation which was mostly my monologue. Tony was quiet for most of the ride. When we entered the town, he said,

"Nice to see you both again. I hope you enjoy your 'Meet and Greet' tonight."

"We will, and thank you, Tony. You saved the day. I don't know how we would have gotten down the hill if you hadn't come along when you did."

"It was my pleasure," he said, waving as he drove off.

There we were in the street. It wasn't time yet for the "Meet and Greet" but we didn't have enough time to start another painting. I was still somewhat off balance because of the distressing tale Tony had told us about his family. That man seemed to have way more than his share of misfortune. I needed to pick up my spirits again and said,

"Hey David, I've been wanting to get some ice cream from Big Olaf's. We have some time to kill before the 'Meet and Greet' starts. Do you want some pistachio ice cream?"

"Okay, but let's get one scoop. That way we won't completely spoil our appetites for the hors d' oeuvres they'll be serving. What were you and Tony talking about. He seemed upset about something."

"He was. Let's not go into it now. I want to sit somewhere, relax, chill out, and treat myself to a decadent scoop of a sticky sweet pistachio indulgence."

While we were sitting in front of Big Olaf's, enjoying a rare break from constant focus on our paintings, I spotted Randy walking down the street lugging his backpack and equipment.

"Hey Randy." I said standing up and waving. As soon as he saw me, he crossed the street and ambled over to us. "Why don't you have a couple of scoops of ice cream, my treat. It's delicious."

"No thanks, Annabel. Have you heard the rumor going around about Karla Streicher?"

"No, we haven't heard anything," I said with eyes wide open. "But we've been up Chimes Tower painting all afternoon. We just got back into town."

"It's just a rumor, but I've heard it from a few different people. They're saying Karla Streicher is dead!" Disbelief was all over Randy's rugged face.

"Who told you that?" I exclaimed. "It can't be true." Though I didn't like the woman, I wouldn't want anything to happen to her.

"Like I said, it's a rumor."

"I don't believe it, Randy. You know how rumors get started and spread like wildfire. She's staying in the room right across the hall from David and me, and we just saw her yesterday."

"Well, if it is true, they may call off the festival," Randy said.

"Oh no, that would be terrible. Many of us are depending upon this festival for our livelihood. I'm sure they'll discuss it tonight, but I think it's got to be a rumor."

"I certainly want to continue painting in the festival," Randy said.

"If anyone wants to mourn her death or celebrate her life, they can do that after the festival as far as I'm concerned." Though I said jokingly, I meant what I said.

"I doubt if any of us will be at her funeral," David said without any guile.

"I agree, none of us liked her. I don't want to be a be hypocrite and pretend she meant something to me; she didn't. I'm pooped, and we still have the 'Meet and Greet' tonight. I'm going to head back to the Atwater and rest for a while."

"Okay, we'll see you later," I said as I watched him lumber up the street.

I don't believe it," David said to me after Randy left.

"I know, let's head back to the Glenmore. We need to shower again and change to look presentable for the 'Meet and Greet.' This is one of the only times while I'm here that I won't look like a homeless person."

"You know, now that I think about it, I haven't seen either Karla or Hillary for quite a while," David said rubbing his chin.

Chapter 11: Casino "Meet and Greet"

The last light of evening blazed out in a pinkish flare which enveloped the entire bay for several moments. The water was still, and it mirrored the sky's ever evolving colors of peach, rose, fuchsia, and violet. The boats resting in the bay had transformed from their daytime white to a muted shade of blue violet. Several golden points of light reflected onto the water from the vacationers staying overnight on their boats. It was a perfect night for a nocturn, but unfortunately, it was important for me to attend the "Meet and Greet" to dispel what was hopefully the rumor about Karla. The air was cool as the artists converged along the walkway with its bright, green railings that guided pedestrians to the Casino. Many years ago, men and women dressed in their finest evening attire, had once cruised to Avalon on the "Great White Steamship" wanting to spend an evening in the Avalon ballroom to dance to the swing music of Glenn Miller, Benny Goodman, Harry James, and Artie Shaw during the war years. Tonight, a different generation would fill the historic ballroom. Up the crudely built, concrete ramps we walked, finally arriving in the magnificent open chamber with its fifty-foot-high ceiling with Art Deco motifs. The 1929 structure was the largest circular ballroom without supporting pillars in the world. The historical significance of the Casino did not escape me. I could almost sense the spirits of those who had once occupied the same space seventy years ago.

Though David had not been invited, most of the people on the committee and the artists attending the soiree wouldn't know that, and to those who it would perturb, well... that was too bad.

"Pretty impressive, David. They've gone all out for the artists this year."

"Yes, this is quite a spread. I'm concerned that they will ask me to leave," David said, looking around hoping no one would know he wasn't invited or even care.

"If anyone says anything, stick to the plan and tell them you're my assistant. I think that will cover you. Remember, some of the artists have their spouses with them." I was trying to be reassuring. Sometimes you must take a stand for your friends, and I was prepared to leave if David wasn't allowed to stay, but I certainly hoped he wouldn't be confronted. That would be embarrassing for both of us. "Hey look, there's Raj and the police officers. They look serious. Maybe it's true about Karla. Maybe they're going to announce it. Maybe something really did happen to her."

"She probably drank too much and forgot that she wasn't supposed to take sleeping pills. Maybe it was an overdose," he said. I nodded in agreement.

"Do you think we should go over and speak to the police?" I asked.

"Sure, let's see what we can find out. What have we got to lose?"

We stopped on our way to the podium to say hello to some of our fellow artist friends. We knew and liked several of them, and it was hard to move along through the crowd without engaging in small talk for a minute. Most of the artists were pleasant and friendly and I enjoyed talking with them since we all had so much in common, but as it is with all people, there were a few oddballs in the bunch.

There was something wrong. I sensed it as I approached Raj, Tom, and Jim.

"Hi guys," I said with a friendly smile. Their faces told me they didn't want to talk to me. Though Raj tried to force a smile, all he said was a solemn faced "hello" to me. Then he looked away.

"Wow, talk about the cold shoulder, David. That was not pleasant."

"I don't get it; they've all been so friendly to us. Did we do something wrong? Maybe they know I'm a party crasher." David suggested.

"I doubt if they would care about that. Let's brush it off, forget about it, and get something to eat."

"Good attitude," he said realizing I was upset.

I filled my plate with all the goodies provided by the festival committee hoping to assuage my bruised ego. The room was buzzing. Everyone was talking about Karla. Though most made nice comments about her talent as an artist, no one said anything nice about her as a person. She was fiercely competitive, stingy, selfish, and greedy. Most of us knew it but were trying to be decent now that she was possibly deceased. There was one there who refused to be a hypocrite. Mike, and Saul saw David and me in the crowd and came over to speak to us.

"Hi fellas, I guess you've heard the terrible news about Karla," I said.

Mike leaned toward me, cupped his hand over my ear, and whispered,

"It couldn't have happened to a nicer asshole." I tried to repress a smile, but I couldn't hold it back. "Everyone knew she was a lush, a rich, spoiled, nasty lush." I looked at Mike with a wide-eyed expression and flicked my finger on his wine glass. We both broke out with a big smile and then a laugh. "That's different, I'm a guy." he said.

"Yes, you certainly are, Mike. There's no question about that," I said giving him a hug. How horrible to be remembered like that, I thought.

"What about me, don't I get a hug too?" Saul said, as he pulled me toward him.

"Of course you do." I hugged Saul too. I looked over at Raj and could see he was watching. His face registered no expression, but I noticed he had been keeping an eye on me since I began talking to the two guys. Good, that's what Raj gets when he gives me the cold shoulder. Why should that hurt my feelings? I just met him and I'm not even sure I like him. While I was pouting, David was eating and shmoozing with some of the female artists. Both of us were just drinking water with a twist of lime, so no one bothered us about not having anything alcoholic to drink.

Despite the death of a fellow artist, the mood of the room was jovial. We were happy to be in the historic location with friends, some of whom we hadn't seen for a while. When most of us were finished eating, the chairperson stepped to the podium and said,

"May I have your attention please... Hello everyone, I'm Brianna Gleason, Chairperson of the Organizing Committee of the PAPOC Catalina Art Festival. I'm so glad to see you all here tonight. I know you've come here at great expense to you as artists and we've done our best to make this festival a pleasant experience for one and all. Some of you may have heard of the tragic death of one of your friends and fellow artists and I know it must be a tremendous sense of loss that you're feeling. I'm feeling it too. Unfortunately, I have more disturbing information, Karla Streicher's death wasn't accidental, she was murdered." There were gasps and murmurs throughout the room." I'm so sorry you must hear this, but tragically, this isn't the only distressing news that has come to my attention." The room fell deadly silent; there was not even a whisper. "There has been another death on the island, and that death also was not accidental... Hillary Applegate was murdered as well." Once again, the audible gasps and whispers returned and spread through the gathering of artists. "The officers have asked me not to reveal the circumstances of the murders while they are still under investigation."

I spotted Nancy in the crowd and watched as she put her hands to her face and let out a loud wail as she sank into a nearby chair, making a big dramatic show as if it was the first she had heard about Hillary. It may have been, but I couldn't tell if she was acting.

"I know you have all gone to great expense, but I feel it's my duty to ask you if you want to cancel the festival or still proceed. If you choose to leave, we will all understand. May I have a show of hands from those who want the festival to go on." Almost everyone raised their hands and their voices shouting, "Proceed! Proceed!" demanding that we go forward with the exhibition next Saturday. "All those who choose to go home." Only three of the older women raised their hands. "Well then, it's settled, we will proceed. You ladies, of course, may leave if you choose. Tom Derringer, our police captain would like to say a few words to you." Brianna handed him the microphone and turned the podium over to him.

"Hello y'all, I'm so sorry that these deaths have cast such a dark shadow on what should have been a thoroughly enjoyable occasion. Catalina Island has been a safe respite from all the crime and transgressions of the city, and we are all saddened. The island is known as a place of peace and tranquility and this kind of tragedy is something that we don't experience here. I'll take some questions, but please, remember, I can't give specific information about the murders." An artist raised his hand and asked,

"When did the murders happen?"

"We're waiting for the lab reports. We don't know the exact time of the deaths."

"Do you have any suspects?"

"No, this just recently happened. We discovered Hillary last night, and Karla this afternoon. The investigation is just beginning. Our Private Investigator and now Deputy Raj Moghaswammi would like to say a few words." Raj stepped up to the microphone and said,

"Good evening, everyone. I know you have many questions, and we only want to give you correct information. Because we're just beginning the investigation, we don't have a lot that we can tell you yet without jeopardizing the investigation. What is foremost in our minds right now is your safety. Sergeant Monaghan is passing some handouts for you to take home with guidelines on how to stay safe.

"First of all, you all will need to paint in pairs. I know this is a competition and it's important for you to find a special location that is yours alone, but you've got to change your mind set. Safety must come first.

Second, if you can't find another artist to paint with, we have selected some of the island's strongest and most physically fit men from our local gym to accompany the women. These men will essentially be your bodyguards. If any of the men would like a bodyguard as well, we will provide someone to accompany them.

Third, you will need to keep us informed of the location where you will be painting during the day by registering in front of the Green Pier. Our police force and some men we have deputized for the festival will come around and check on you throughout the day.

Fourth, if you change your mind about where you want to paint, you must come back or call in and reregister." There were groans all around the room. "I know, I understand, this cuts into your freedom, but it's a small price to pay for your safety. Remember, there's a killer loose on this island. Don't get complacent.

Fifth, if you see something suspicious, inform us, no matter how insignificant you think it is, let us be the judge. We will be as flexible as possible wanting to serve you all the best we can. Try to cooperative with us. This is a big job for a small police force, so we need to pull together.

"Can't you hire some extra officers to come in from the mainland?" an artist asked.

"We've made calls to the mainland. They're shorthanded too but some will arrive shortly. We'll probably also have the news media arriving here soon. If they pester you and you don't want your painting time interrupted, just tell the reporters to talk to us. I strongly suggest you do that.

Any suggestions from you will be welcomed so don't hesitate to bring them to us. Anything else?" he asked. There were no more additional questions, so he said, "Okay, the 'Meet and Greet' is officially over. Find someone to walk with you to your hotel. If you can't find anyone, that's what we're here for."

I meandered my way through the crowd toward Raj with David close behind. When I got to the stand where the committee and police were standing, I walked up to Raj when he reached out and put his arm around me. I turned and gave him a full-on hug. The gravity of what had transpired was sinking in. I was scared and it was nice to have Raj and David near me.

"That was excellent, officers. You've been terribly busy, I can tell. Thank you." I said praising the policemen.

"I couldn't tell you anything about what we had learned this morning, Annabel, not until we had more information. That didn't stop me from warning you as soon as possible. Now, I'm going to drive you both back to your hotel."

"Do you think it's safe to stay at the Glenmore tonight? Two of the women who are dead were staying on our floor?" David asked.

"Yes, That's a good question. Where was Karla killed?" I asked.

"Next to you, in room 302," Raj answered.

A cold chill went up my spine. Neither David nor I said a word, we just stared at each other trying to absorb of what Raj had just told us.

"We're going to station some officers around the Glenmore. We're also having chain locks put on all three back entrance doors so your hotel will probably be the safest place on the island. But if you would feel more comfortable, you and Annabel are welcome stay at my place."

"That's an awfully nice offer, Raj. We may take you up on that, but for now, the Glenmore is so convenient and with the police there, I feel safe. Fortunately, I have David with me and he's ex-military and a big guy. Maybe we're all being a bit too jittery."

"I don't think so, Annabel. You didn't see the murder scenes. I'm glad you're scared, that will help to keep you safe. Now, I want to get you back to the hotel safely. Shall we go?"

"Yes, let's, it has been a long day. I know you can't talk about the case, but is there anything that we should know that you can tell us?" I asked hoping to learn something... anything more about the murders.

Raj thought for a moment then said, "No, but I can't stress enough that you two must always stay together, even when one of you needs to take a bathroom break."

"That's a problem. That means that we'll have to leave our paintings and equipment unattended," David said.

"Better to lose those things than your life."

"He makes a good point, David. Okay, we'll do as you say." Being a normal man, I was sure Raj loved to hear me say that. "One more thing Raj, when I woke up this morning there was dirt on the rug tracked in from the door to the back entrance in the hallway."

When the three of us entered the hotel and climbed the stairs to our room, we immediately saw the yellow police tape blocking the entrance to Karla's room. The dirt that had been at the back entrance was gone. Bonnie Abernathy informed David and me that they vacuum the rugs in the morning each day. She said that that entrance was always locked and rarely ever used, so I wondered why there was dirt tracked in from the back entrance.

"Raj, the lock on that door would be so easy to twist open from the inside leaving it open to the outside. If someone had come in at some point during the day or evening, they could have unlocked it. I planned to check it each night, but I forgot. I've never noticed anyone else ever checking it," I said.

"I'm not surprised. People on the island are very relaxed about their safety. "

"So I noticed," David said giving me an "I told you so" look.

"I'll tell Tom about the lock and dirty footprints when I see him. Now you two get in your room, lock the door, and don't come out until morning."

"Okay," we both said in unison, then said goodnight.

"Call if you need me for anything." Raj said as he was leaving.

Although David and I needed to be well rested for another physically taxing day tomorrow, I couldn't relax. I laid there tossing and turning for more than an hour, when David said,

"Can't you sleep?"

"No, my mind is racing. I keep trying to figure out who on earth would want to kill artists and why," I said.

"I know, all we do is create beauty. I wonder who the police may be thinking are suspects, maybe us."

"I doubt that, David. Raj would tell them that we're too obsessed with painting."

"Have you ever tried counting sheep?" he asked.

"I have, but it usually doesn't work."

"That's what I do. Why don't you give it another try. Maybe that will help you, goodnight."

"Goodnight." I rolled over but my mind kept turning over the things I had learned about some of the artists in the festival and the collectors who we had met on the boat. I also wondered about the people who observed and spoke to me while I was painting. Could one of them be stalking me? While I was ruminating, I realized I had some information that couldn't wait. I needed to share it with Raj and Tom the first thing in the morning.

Wednesday

Chapter 12: Revealing Confidences

Morning came, gradually illuminating the curtains of our room. I rubbed my eyes trying to focus on that clock. I pressed the alarm button before it went off not wanting to hear that awful sound. I was glad that it was the light that awakened me as I rolled over hoping to get a few more moments of rest. It was 5:30 in the morning, too early to get up, but not early enough to go back to sleep, so I lay there thinking about the things I should tell the police. I didn't want to incriminate anyone; I had come to like some of the people I would reluctantly need to reveal facts I had learned about them. Helping the police catch the murderer had to be my priority. Maybe I could ask them to keep what I was about to tell them confidential. No, that's cowardly. Those people would probably know who it was that talked about them anyway. I would just have to face their potential anger. Now David was stirring.

"Did you sleep okay?" he asked me as he turned over.

"No, hardly at all. How about you?"

"Like a baby. Nothing ever seems to keep me from a sound sleep." David said feeling pleased with himself.

"It's early, but I'm going to get into the shower." I climbed out of bed and headed for the bathroom. A half an hour later, I was clean, had put on full makeup, and I felt much better. If I was going to confront the police, I wanted to look presentable ... no, I wanted to look attractive. I looked in the mirror and thought, <u>not bad</u>! You should make more of an effort to look pretty while you're here on the island. I think I'll eighty-six my cargo pants for the rest of the week and wear something that fits me better and is more flattering.

"Okay David, the bathroom is all yours."

While David was in the shower, I called Raj. It was still early, and I didn't want to wake him, but I decided I should call him before he made plans for the day.

"Hello, Raj. Hi, sorry to wake you but there are quite a few important things I know about some of the people here on the island. The information could be relevant to the police. Could I come to the police station early this morning? Okay, great. Maybe David and I could still get in a morning painting after we talk, but if not, so be it... Uh-huh... Okay, we'll see you then."

"Raj is going to pick us up and take us to the police station. We need to meet him out in front in twenty minutes. Let's see if we can grab some muffins and things to take with us in those paper bags."

"Are we suspects?' David asked with a worried expression on his face.

"No, I called him and told him I needed to talk to him and the others. I realized that I know a lot about some people who could be possible suspects in the murders. That was the reason for my call. Maybe you've thought of some things that I haven't, so you can help inform them as well." We pulled on our clothes, not worrying about modesty and were ready in record time. As we were walking out the door, the hotel handyman was putting a chain lock on our back entrance.

"That was quick," David said as we headed down the stairs.

We filled our brown paper bags with our makeshift breakfast, and David and I waited outside the hotel for Raj.

"Look at this, David, the Catalina Islander newspaper says, "CATALINA ISLAND MURDERS" on the front page in great big letters. They have pictures of the Glenmore Hotel and the location where they had the police tape on Chimes Tower Road. It looks like that's where Hillary was murdered. Let's see what it says. It's amazing how fast they got this paper out," I said handing it to David. Just then, Raj pulled up right on time.

"Good morning, I'm so glad you called, Annabel. We at the police department were planning to question several of the people who were acquainted with the two deceased women today. Your desire to help us is important for several reasons. Thank you for being forthcoming."

"Of course, we probably want to know who the murderer is even more than you and the police. The sooner he or she is caught, the sooner David, I, and the other artists can relax and enjoy what remains of this event. Oh, look at this." I said handing him the newspaper.

"Yes, we've already seen it," Raj said.

"When we walked into the station, David looked around and said, "I've never been in a police station before."

"Really, I was in one once when I was twelve," I said. "I got hauled in for shoplifting with my dopey friend. We didn't take much of anything valuable; it was more about the thrill of taking something and not getting caught. My idiot friend bragged to some boys about the theft and they told the police. I was at her house when a police car pulled up in front and she said to me,

"I'm not going to take this alone. You were in on it too!"

"Then what happened?" Raj asked, trying to hold back a smile.

"We were arrested and taken to the police station. I called my mother, and when she came to pick me up, she was so humiliated, she cried. That put a definitive end to any potential future criminal activities for me." I looked over at Raj, he was smiling and trying hard not to laugh. He wasn't doing a very good job.

"You're a bad girl, Annabel Adams." Raj said. He was giving me jazz again, but this time I didn't mind. I shrugged my shoulders and said,

"We were so dumb." Just as I was finishing my confession, Tom and Jim came into the room with Corny and Ziggy.

"What was that you were saying, Annabel?" Tom asked.

"Nothing of any relevance, Tom," Raj said, protecting my bruised reputation.

"I heard everything you said from my office, young lady. Kids are so dumb. They could throw themselves on the ground and miss, and we've all been there." Tom said.

"So true," I answered, snickering at his southern witticism.

"I want to introduce you to Cornell Palmer Ziegler Junior, and Cornell Palmer Ziegler the third. We call the father, Corny, and sonny boy, here is Ziggy. These are two of our best deputies and even though they haven't the IQ of a tree stump, we want to include them in the conversation."

"We met Corny and Ziggy at Raj's dinner party last night, Captain. Hi guys, nice to see you again," I said waving to them.

"I understand you and David have some information for us. Please come into my office. Tom said motioning to us. We all walked in and he sat down behind his desk and leaned back into a large chair.

"Yes, we do, and it's quite a bit."

"Well... Don't just stand there like a dummy, let's get started. We're going to take some notes. Do you mind if we record y'all?"

"No, not at a bit. Do whatever you need to do to catch this creep," I said.

"Please, sit down and make yourselves comfortable." Della, Captain Derringer's secretary brought in donuts, coffee, apples, and orange juice for us.

"Now, Annabel, what is it that y'all know and want me to hear about?"

"I'm going to start at the beginning and work forward. What I'm going to tell you may seem irrelevant at first, but it's very relevant, so please bear with me. We had an artist friend named Sybil Fairfax who was another PAPOC member. PAPOC is an acronym which stands for Plein Aire Painters of California. About a month ago, we learned that Sybil committed suicide. From what we observed and were told, she was emotionally fragile and had struggled with depression all her life. Sybil was a tremendously talented artist and whenever her work was exhibited, her significant talent upstaged Hillary, Karla, and Nancy, three other prominent members of our organization. Hillary was used to being the "queen bee" of the San Diego group of artists. When Sybil's work outshone hers, Hillary became cold and snippy to Sybil. I saw that on several occasions. Eventually, Hillary and Karla made up a bogus reason to expel Sybil from the PAPOC group.

Sybil and I were close friends, and she confided in me that she had also been involved and fell in love with a man named Fred. Fred had recently been released from a maximum-security prison and Sybil had not shared any information about him with her family who she knew would not approve. Their love affair was clandestine, but after swearing me to secrecy, she told me about Fred and even showed me an old photo of him taken before he went into prison. To Sybil's distress, Fred had been diagnosed with cancer. That sent Sybil into a tailspin, a death spiral that prompted her to put a gun in her mouth and fire."

"That's all very interesting, Annabel, but how does that relate to this case," Captain Derringer asked. I could tell he was becoming impatient with my story by the way he was drumming his fingers on his desk. I needed to talk faster to hold the man's interest.

"I'm getting there. All that I'm telling you is connected. You'll see."

"When David and I were cruising here on the Catalina Express, we sat on the lower level of the boat and spoke with several people, all of them were from San Diego, and ten of them knew Sybil. I can't tell you how I know, but I believe that the murders could possibly be connected to Sybil. There were thirteen of us sharing that lower-level area. Eight of us were artists. Their names are Randy Creighton, Michael Mitchell, Saul Katten, Hillary Applegate, Karla Streicher, Nancy Hall, and David and me. There were five art collectors. Their names are Charlotte Fitzsimmons, Alice Smith, Tony Rossi, Miriam and Asher Bloomberg. I believe that one or more of these people could be connected to the murders."

"You'll have to give me more than just your hunch to go on, Annabel. We base things here on facts," the captain said.

"Hold on, I'll show you what those facts are, I'm getting there. First, I knew I had seen Charlotte and Alice before but couldn't remember where. It finally dawned on me. Sybil had shown me a photo of her mother and her daughter standing with her. Charlotte and Alice are Sybil's mother and daughter. They knew me right away and said they were familiar with my art. I'm sure Sybil told them about our friendship because we were such good friends. Now, I ask you... why didn't they tell me who they were? There's something fishy about that. I see how you're looking at me, Captain, but I read body language and pickup on things that some other people don't see. I know there is more to this than meets the eye. But let me continue.

Second, David and I had lunch with the Bloombergs. We sat and chatted with them for a while until the conversation took a dark turn. Thirteen of the Bloomberg's family members had been sent to concentration camps by the Nazis where they all were murdered. There was one man instrumental in the family's destruction and his name was Julius

Streicher. (At that moment, the look on Raj's face told me he understood where I was going.) Not only was he responsible for the deaths of most of the family, Julius Streicher confiscated their property, their wealth, and their impressionist art collection, including Monets, van Goghs, Gustav Klimts and Max Liebermans. The art collection alone would now be worth hundreds of millions."

"In what way do you think that is connected with the murders here on the island," Ziggy asked.

"Does the name Karla Streicher ring a bell?" I asked. Raj and Tom looked at each other. Of course it did. "Could Karla be related to the infamous Julius Streicher? Could some members of Karla's family be hiding a monumentally valuable art collection?" I asked.

"Uh-huh... I agree, that is certainly very interesting. Anything else?" Tom asked. I could tell by the way he had shifted his position and was now leaning in that I had gotten his attention.

"Yes, there is. I know I've seen Tony Rossi somewhere before, but I can't remember where or when. He's very ill and is dying of terminal pancreatic cancer. Even so, he spends a lot of money eating and drinking at the Portofino Restaurant where he has taken Hillary, Karla, and Nancy to dinner on a couple of occasions. I was told that he brought Karla, and Nancy back to the hotel the night Karla was killed and all of them were plastered. One more thing. I noticed some dirty footprints on the rug in the hallway the first thing Monday morning. There's a back entrance with stairs behind the Glenmore Hotel and the footprints were coming from the back door into the hallway the morning after Karla was killed. They stopped at a certain point, but the trajectory was leading toward Karla's room.

There's something else that bothers me about Tony. While we were painting up on Chimes Tower Road, we saw the police tape not knowing why it was there. David and I had hitched a golf cart ride to our painting spot and painted there all afternoon. Soon after we got there, we realized we didn't have a way to get back down the hill until Tony showed up. During that encounter, he essentially told me that he hated his mother who neglected and abused him and his father. While his mother was driving on the freeway she was in a rage verbally abusing the father causing him to jump out of the speeding car. Tony saw his father smashed on the freeway by cars and trucks as they ran over him. Though Tony didn't explain, he said he'll never see his mother again. You may want to know why. Is his mother still alive? If not, what happened to her? There was something about that conversation that was unsettling. Didn't you sense that, David?"

"No, but I wasn't paying much attention," David said.

"Oh, one last thing. We had dinner with Randy Creighton, Mike Mitchell, and Saul Katten. They all hated both Hillary and Karla. They were very drunk and freely informed us of their true feelings about the women.

But I must let you know; Hillary and Karla were not well liked by any of the artists I know."

"What about Nancy?" Raj asked.

"She's a follower. Though I don't think she was as nasty as the other two, she has no character and went along with whatever the two more dominant women decided, no matter how reprehensible. That's about it. I think that it would serve you well to talk to all the people I have told you about. I hope we've been helpful to you." I stood up realizing that David and I needed to get going on our paintings.

"Y'all have been helpful. This information gives us more pieces to the puzzle," Captain Derringer said standing up as well.

"Raj, could you take us back to the hotel to get our equipment?" I asked trying to find where I had laid my purse.

"Of course," he said.

*****

Shortly after David and I left, Della came into the captain's office. While we were offering Raj and Tom information about some of the victims, artists, and collectors we knew, some forensic evidence arrived in Tom's email.

"Look at this, Della. Karla Streicher's system was way over the limit with benzodiazepine, a sedative. I wasn't sure her death was an accidental overdose and the killer coming to her room to kill her was a coincidence. We can rule out the accidental overdose theory. The death came from a combination of drugs and alcohol. She was poisoned, but the stabbings came later. We'll see what forensics say about her being raped. Man, someone really hated you lady," Tom said.

"So, if Karla was already dead when she was stabbed, that would explain the absence of bleeding from her stab wounds since dead people don't bleed?" Della said.

"That's right," Tom replied.

"So, the big question is, how, when, and where was she poisoned?" Della asked.

"I counted the number of pills that were in the bottle. There was a sixty-day supply dated the Friday before she arrived here. Ten pills were missing. She could've taken the first four on Friday, Saturday, Sunday, and Monday. That plus the six pills Charlotte gave Tony would add up to the ten missing pills."

"Would six pills be enough to kill her if she had ingested the sleeping pills that night?" Della asked.

"They would and then some. Everyone knows we're not supposed to mix sleeping medication with alcohol. Whoever did this to her knew it too. Something else, Temazepam comes in capsule form. That means the capsules can be opened and the powder can be put into someone's food or drink. It can be done very easily by almost anyone."

"Look what else just came in." Della quickly scanned the new information and handed it to Tom.

"This is interesting," Tom said. "Do you remember there was a black plastic raincoat the workers and our deputies found at the Pebbly Beach Landfill? It came from the cans along Crescent Avenue."

"Yes, I do. I guess the trash usually consists of empty cups, dishes, and food containers. The raincoat was an abnormal find that must have stood out," Della concluded.

"Yes, that's right. Forensics said they found a lot of salt water on it. Whoever the owner was, washed it very carefully but there were still traces of blood on it. It was Hillary's blood."

"Oh Tom! Was it a man's or a woman's raincoat?" she asked.

"It's generic. It could have been worn by either," he said. "We found a button Hillary held in a death grip in her hand. It also had her blood on it which was to be expected, her hands were covered in blood. Unfortunately, there are no fingerprints to be found because the killer must have used gloves."

"We also have the shoeprint from Chimes Tower," Della pointed out.

"Yes, we made a plaster cast of that shoeprint. The killer tried to erase the prints with a branch broken off a bush. Whoever it was, did a good job; we only have a partial footprint and it's not very clear. If the killer is smart, and I suspect he or she is, they would've disposed of those shoes by now.

"Did you find the knife or learn what kind of knife was used?"

"No, there's nothing here about that, but something else was very disturbing, Hillary's eyes had been stabbed before they were painted. They were bleeding so it was done while she was still alive." Tom answered. Della shuttered in abject horror. "Hillary's killer is clearly a sadistic monster. This must be a crime of passion. She wasn't raped, maybe because the perpetrator didn't have the time or he or she was scared off, but Hillary's pants were pulled off. Her eyes were destroyed, and her face was disfigured by painting it with an ugly smile. The word FORDS was painted on her sweatshirt. None of us can figure out what that means, but we do know whoever killed her hated her. When we see that kind of violence, it's usually done by men, but women are now beginning to step up to the plate. Women frequently resort more often to poisoning which could account for the Temazepam ingested by Karla.

"Since her pants were ripped off, it probably is a man," Della surmised.

"Not necessarily," Tom said with a disturbed expression.

"Oh, no." Della moaned, understanding Tom's implication. "Why do you think the killer would want to make Karla dead or comatose before she was stabbed?"

"Maybe they didn't want a lot of noise in the hotel room. The killer could go about the slaughter and possible rape in almost complete silence," Tom suggested.

"I see," Della answered nodding her head.

"What disturbs me is the difference in the modus operandi of the two murders. I hate to say it, but it's possible we could have two killers working together on the island."

Chapter 13: More Revelations

"Thanks for the ride, Raj. You've been wonderful. Will we see you around today or will you be working with Tom?"

"I'll be working with Tom. This is a crucial time in the investigation when the evidence is fresh. We'll need to question the people you pointed out, some other artists, plus a few troublemakers on the island. There's so much to be done. Stay together, and don't forget to register at the Green Pleasure Pier."

"What the heck is this?" I said as two cars transporting a camera crew and some reporters pulled up and parked across the street from the beach. We watched as they approached some artists who were painting by the pier and began filming and interviewing them.

"I've got to get back to the station. Tom will want to hear about this." Raj said as he took off.

"So, how do you want to handle the situation if they approach us? Where do you think we should paint this morning now that the reporters are around?" I asked David.

"Wherever we decide to paint, we should do it on a small 9x12" canvas board since we're getting another late start. To avoid the reporters, how about standing out of the way on the Green Pier and painting the people on the beach with all the colorful umbrellas, palm trees, the Hotel Mac Rae, and hills in the background." "Good plan, those umbrellas and beach toys are colorful," I said.

It was still morning, around10:30 when we set up. We had lost most of the early light, and the light now was flat. The weather was a perfect seventy-five degrees, so at least we were comfortable. From where we were standing, we could paint the water and the shoreline with children playing on the beach in the foreground. The sandy beach dotted with umbrellas in front of the Hotel Mac Rae, would be in the middle ground of the painting. In the background, I would paint layers of hills becoming more gray-blue and ever paler as they moved back toward the sky. One of the joys of plein aire painting is the pleasure of being out of doors with the elements of nature. The sound of the children's laughter as they played on the beach, the seagulls flying overhead emitting their carefree cry, and the fresh air and sunlight that surrounded us as we captured the beauty of the bay. This was the life, the artist's life. Though very few of us would ever become wealthy, it was a wonderful way to live. What happened on the island had shattered the peace and tranquility that artists experience when they are in "the zone." Fortunately for me, once I begin painting, I become so focused that all my worries and fears melt away. While David and I were setting up, Nancy spotted us and headed our way on the Green Pier.

"Do you see what I see," I said with a sigh.

"Oh no, what does she want," David groaned. He thought of Nancy as one of the conspirators who participated in keeping him from becoming a Signature Member of PAPOC. Because of her and the other two, he couldn't participate in this festival.

"I don't know if she, or this stupid fly that has been buzzing around my face, is the bigger pest," he said as she walked up to us.

"Good morning how are you two managing with what's been going on here?" she asked.

"We're doing as well as can be expected," I answered.

"There's a strange looking old man with a beard, mustache and heavy eyebrows that's wandering around the beach. It looks like he's wearing a dirty old gray wig. Have you noticed him?" she asked.

"No, not really. There are so many people here on the island and I'm too busy painting to pay much attention to the bystanders."

"Hillary and Karla noticed him. They said he gave them the creeps."

"I'll keep an eye out for him and if I see him, I'll mention it to the police, Nancy."

Did you see the reporters? It didn't take them long to swarm down on us, did it?" she asked.

"No, it's surprising how quickly they can mobilize."

"I'm not going to talk to any of them, are you, Annabel?"

"I will, but only if they're polite," I said thinking it would be great publicity for me, David, and the festival.

"Are you still planning on staying till the end of the week?" she asked.

"The situation is certainly frightening, but I'm not going anywhere," I answered.

"Aren't you concerned that two people who were staying at the Glenmore and were on our floor have been killed. I couldn't sleep last night thinking I could be next. Every sound I heard was alarming. This festival isn't worth our lives, is it?"

"No, it's not. And we are concerned about the hotel. It does seem like it's the vortex of the violence, but with the police guarding us, I feel better."

"I'd like to find another hotel, but the Glenmore is in a great location which is good, I guess. Annabel, I know this is an imposition, but would you mind if I joined you and David when you're painting? Since Hillary and Karla are dead, you two are my only friends here. I'm on my own now and I'm scared," she said.

"Nancy, this is a competition, and we need to be on our own. David isn't in the show so there's no problem for me painting with him. If you call Captain Derringer at police headquarters, he will provide you with a bodyguard. He said that they have asked physically fit men from the local gym to accompany anyone who asks for protection.

"I know, but the person they would provide would be a stranger. That alone would be unnerving, how would I know he isn't the murderer?" Nancy asked.

"Well, you have a good point. That occurred to me too, so I asked. One of the deputies told me that all the gym members they are asking to accompany us are well known residents of the island," I said.

"Maybe so, but I need my friends. I'm just not good at being on my own."

"Quite frankly, Nancy, you haven't been nice to David and he's my best friend and my priority."

"That was Hillary and Karla, not me!" she said making wild hand gestures.

"Maybe not, but you went along with it and that was terrible. Why don't you ask Tony, or Charlotte and Alice to shadow you. They're not in the competition and you know them. Tell you what, try to see if you can come up with an acceptable arrangement, if not, we'll see what we can work out with you, okay?"

"Okay, I'll try," she said with a sullen face as she turned and walked away.

"I was harsh, wasn't I, David."

"You were direct and thank you for standing up for me and confronting her. I don't want her with us, Annabel. We'll have to watch everything we say. I couldn't believe that she said we were her only friends on the island."

"Wasn't that something? Suddenly, she's become our friend. How convenient now that she wants something. I don't want her hanging around us, but I can't help feeling sorry for her. She's lost her support system and has undergone a terrible trauma with the death of her only friends. I think we must help her if she can't find anyone else to paint with. Maybe she could paint at a reasonable distance."

"Oh Annabel," David said with a sigh. "You're too nice and it's not in your best interest."

"Look here comes Tony. Hi Tony," I called out smiling and waving as he was driving by. He turned around his golf cart and stopped to say hello.

"How are the paintings coming along, my friends?" he asked.

"The paintings are coming along great, but this festival feels like we're walking through a horror movie. Beside learning about the murders of two artists, every time we turn around, some crazy catastrophe happens to either David or me."

"Usually it's just me," David said with a snicker. "But recently Annabel's had her share of calamities too."

"How about you, Tony? What have you been up to this morning?" I asked.

"I drove over to Descanso Beach which is just north of this area. Have you ever been there?"

"No, we've always stayed in Avalon Bay. There are so many beautiful things to paint here we haven't ventured out. Now we're going to be especially careful and stay with the crowds where it's safe," I said.

"I can understand how you feel, but it's safe over there. You should check it out. I'll drive you if you have any free time within the next few days. Descanso Beach is much less developed than Avalon. What you will find there are palapas along the shore, people wading in the water, a charming beach club, and teak lounge chairs for people to relax on. Little white sail boats are often floating in the gorgeous turquoise water and if you look, you can see small yellow-orange fish called Garibaldis swimming in the sea," Tony said.

"Wow, you make it sound wonderful. Is it a short enough distance for us to walk?" David asked.

"I think so, but you have so much equipment. I'll drive you over there if you decide to go and pick you up when you're finished. Here, let me give you my cell number." Tony handed us a piece of paper with his number. "Give me a call if you want to give Descanso a try. It's more like Catalina was fifty years ago. I think you could create some wonderful paintings there."

"Thank you, Tony, we appreciate the offer," I said.

"Well, I'll see you later," he said as he drove off.

As Tony left, I saw the camera crew heading our way. One of the women I had frequently seen on TV in San Diego was leading the entourage.

"Look, David, I think we're about to be interviewed."

"No Annabel, *you're* about to be interviewed. I'm not going to say a word. Here she is."

"May we ask you a few questions?" the reporter asked as her makeup artist combed her hair and powdered her face.

"Yes, but keep it short, we need to get our paintings done before twelve-thirty,"

The reporter began by asking us our names while a male videographer filmed our faces and took a long shot of our paintings. She then asked me where we were from and what we were doing here. I told her about PAPOC and spent a long time promoting and telling her about the plein aire festival as I frequently looked toward the videographer and smiled my best smile.

Then she wanted to know about Hillary and Karla and if we knew them or anything about the murders. I told her we knew them very well and clammed up so I wouldn't hurt the investigation. I had made a promise to Raj that I would stay silent, and I fully intended to honor my commitment. Then she asked where the murders had taken place. I pointed at the hill and the Chimes Tower monument and said the Glenmore Hotel without giving any details. After she had done her who, what, where, why, and when, she thanked me and left.

"Annabel, you're such a ham posing like that for the camera!"

"Was I that obvious?" I asked.

"No, you were smooth. You're so good at this. I truly envy you," David said.

"I was very careful not to disclose anything that wasn't already out there in the newspaper."

While we were talking, two women who saw the interview approached us. There was a catalogue that was circulating around Avalon with artists names and photographs of those who were in the festival. Spectators were beginning to approach the artists in the show to ask us to sign their catalogues. The problem with that was David and I wore vinyl gloves since many of our oil colors are very toxic. Every time we had to sign someone's catalogue, we had to take off our gloves, not wanting to expose the public to the toxicity of the paint on our gloves. It was an annoying ordeal because we needed to paint fast. Signing catalogues had become an increasingly bothersome distraction. David avoided giving his signature by saying he wasn't in the festival, but I tried to be pleasant and cordial.

"Will you please autograph my catalogue?" a lady and her friend asked.

"Sure, can you hand me your pen?"

"Oh, I don't have one." Neither did her friend. "Don't you have one in your purse?"

"I do, but as you can see, I have on vinyl gloves which are covered with paint. I don't want to get paint all over my purse. See if you can find a pen, then I'll sign the catalogue." The women scurried off asking anyone they met if they could borrow a pen. I had reached my limit. I drew the line when it came to me providing the means with which I could be irritated.

"This is one time I'm glad I'm not in the show. How do you put up with that?" David said scrunching up his face.

"I'm about at my limit, but I must remember that I'm a representative of this festival. I must keep that in mind no matter how annoying the onlookers become."

"You can have it! They drive me nuts." David closed his eyes and shook his head in disgust.

"Oh no, look, here they come again," I said through my teeth like a ventriloquist, smiling and waving to them as they approached me.

"We found a pen. Can you sign these now?" she said as she handed me the catalogue. I was going to try a new approach. I would put a paper towel between my glove and the pen, that way I wouldn't have to remove my gloves. All I needed to do was make a rough scrawl for my name and that seemed to satisfy them. Now in addition to the two women, the people who had loaned the ladies their pens and some others that the women had approached got in line with their catalogues for signatures as well. Now there were eight more. I dutifully signed them all. When I looked at David, he was rolling his eyes and shaking his head.

Shortly after the people left, a woman came up to me with her little girl and said, "My daughter is a very gifted artist. She wants to someday be an artist just like you. May we watch you paint?

"Of course! It's nice to meet young people who are interested in art." I was sincere. Guiding and teaching children about art was truly rewarding. Seeing their sweet little faces quietly observing me paint was delightful.

My mind drifted back to a day when I was nine years old and my parents took me to an art gallery in Laguna Beach, CA. I wandered around the gallery observing the wonderful paintings created by the artist and gallery owner on display. One of his paintings especially caught my eye. It was a painting of a deer in a forest with light streaming through the leaves on the trees. I wanted to know how the artist was able to capture the mood of that fleeting moment, so I moved in close to the painting and tried to see how the paint was applied. The artist came up from behind and said very quietly not wanting to interrupt my thoughts,

"You're an artist too, aren't you?"

I whirled around surprised by his voice which had shattered the private world I was experiencing.

"Yes, I am. How could you tell?"

"Because only artists do what you're doing. Other people stand back and observe from a distance. You wanted to know how I made the painting look so real, didn't you?"

"Yes, it almost looked like a photograph until I got up close and saw that it's really not like a photograph at all," I explained.

"Ahh, you really do have an artist's eye," he said.

After that, he took some time with me and gave me advice that I remember to this day. He told me to, "Stay a long time in the preliminary stages of a painting. Don't move forward until your compositional sketch is perfect. Keep wiping off your sketch until it's just right. Your sketch is the foundation of the painting." That was the most important advice I was ever given.

*****

While Annabel and David were painting, Raj had returned to the station only to find another camera crew waiting outside the building. They swarmed over him, peppering him with questions as he tried to enter the station.

"Do you have any idea of who the killer is? When were the women killed? Do the murders have anything to do with the art festival?" The reporters crowded in, pushing him and making it difficult to get in through the door. Raj entered the station rattled and disheveled. His usual neatly combed hair looked as if he had just gotten out of bed after a bad night.

"They were all over you like flies on a hot poop pile." Tom said with a twinkle in his eye.

"Thank you, Tom, I certainly appreciate the comparison," Raj said with a wide, annoyed grin.

Tom and Jim said they had already spoken to the news media and got rid of them by saying they needed to focus on the investigation. Trying to block out the noise of the media, Raj, Tom, and Jim begin discussing the forensic evidence and the information Annabel had contributed. Since they had never delt with a murder on the island, the officers had to recollect what they had been trained to do under these circumstances at the police academy. They set up two white boards on which Tom jotted down what they knew. The first board contained everything they had learned and gathered at the crime scenes about the two deceased artists, all the forensic facts that had come in, and all of what they thought was relevant information that I had given them. Another white board not yet assembled was going to provide a timeline of the events and locations of persons of interest before, during, and after, the two murders. Raj was now placed officially on the payroll as an advisor to the Sheriff Station Commander, Tom's official title.

"Alright, Raj, I want you to get in touch with the eight people Annabel suggested we speak with. Probably the easiest way to find them is to have Annabel point them out to you since none of us know all of them on sight. Why don't you give her a call. That way we can get some of them in here right away."

"Okay, but I can't keep interrupting her while she's painting," Raj responded.

"Raj is totally in awe of Annabel and her talent," Jim said teasing him.

Just then a call came into the station.

"Tom... Corny wants to talk to you. He says it's important," Della said.

"What is it Corny? She did what? Where is she now? That girl doesn't know shit from Shinola," Tom said slamming down the phone. His face was red as a beet. Raj, it appears your girlfriend has just done an interview with the news media. This is on you. You brought her into this case. Go silence her!"

Raj got up and left the station without saying a word, but he was fuming as he drove down Sumner Ave to the Green Pier. She had promised him to keep all the information quiet. Now she was blabbing it to the world, making a fool of him and the police department. He trudged right toward her on the pier.

*****

"Hi Raj," I said, happy to see him.

"Annabel, I need to talk to you," he demanded as he grabbed my arm and pulled me away from my painting. He pointed his finger right in my face, way too close and said, "You promised me that you wouldn't say a word to anyone about this case and now I hear that you just talked to the news media." Raj got right in my face while he was standing there with his hands on his hips and his eyes blazing mad.

"I didn't tell them anything more than what Tom told us at the 'Meet and Greet' and I said nothing other than general information that was already out there in the Catalina Island newspaper. Believe me, I'm not that dumb. Most importantly, you told me not to say anything about the case, and I kept my word to you and didn't disclose anything other than useless information. Give me a little more credit!" At first, I was flabbergasted and tried to defend myself, but then I was furious. "How dare you accuse me of being a leaker. That's insulting!" Raj backed off realizing he had overreacted. He was calming down, but I wasn't.

"What else did you say to them," he asked in a reasonable tone of voice.

"Nothing! I gave them my name and told them all about the festival. It was good publicity and that's what I'm here for and focused on. The only thing I told them about the case was the location of the murders and that's common knowledge. They can get that information from the newspaper." I said, my voice raised.

"That's all?" he asked, his tone now softening.

"That's...ALL!" I said, scowling.

We'll, okay then," he said moving toward me and reaching out. I moved away. "I overreacted and I'm sorry," he said.

"I don't want to talk to you anymore, Raj. Go away, I'm very angry with you!"

"No, don't be. This is just a misunderstanding. Let's forget about it. I know this is a bad time, but I need to ask you both for a favor."

"What?" I responded coldly, folding my arms.

"Tom wants me to locate some of the people you suggested we question. We don't know what most of them look like and the quickest way to find them is for you to point them out. Can you do that?"

"Yes, I can do that. Look, there go Miriam and Asher Bloomberg. Maybe you can catch them before they go to lunch," I said.

"I may need to touch base with you throughout the day to help me locate some of the six other people you thought we should talk to. Time is of the essence," he said trying to squeeze my hand as I pulled it away. "Thanks a lot." He then hurried to catch the Bloombergs.

We watched as he confronted them. At first, they resisted not knowing who the strange man was who wanted to take them to the police station. When he pulled out his recently acquired badge, the pair cooperated. The Bloombergs obediently climbed into the police vehicle that Raj was now driving.

"You were SO mad! I've never seen that side of you," David said smiling at my temper tantrum.

" It was insulting for him to think I would break my word."

"He doesn't know you well. He doesn't know if he can trust you yet."

"But he grabbed my arm way too hard, David, and it hurt. He had no right to do that."

"No, he didn't but cut him some slack. He thought you had betrayed him."

"Well...okay, I guess you're right, but I'm still fuming!"

"I guess the cops think you were on to something," David observed.

It was almost 1:00 and the sun and the shadows had moved to the point when David and I knew it was time to stop. While I was packing up, my painting slipped from my hand and fell face down onto the pier walkway.

"Oh crap," I exclaimed. Luckily my painting fell into a patch of sand that had accumulated on the pier.

"Oh no. It's ruined," David said as I turned the painting over covered with so much sand it obscured the image.

"No, it's okay. All I need to do is let it dry for two days, and then I can brush off the sand. It'll be just fine, but it's always upsetting when it happens."

"I've never heard that before. I would have tried to get the sand off right away hoping it wouldn't stick to the painting. That's a good trick to know."

"I'm just full of helpful hints to salvage ruined works of art. You would be amazed at how often I screw things up," I said chuckling.

"Where to for lunch?" David asked.

"Eric's is right here. Let's give it another try and order a hamburger this time. You've gotta try awfully hard to screw up a hamburger."

"I'm going for rubber turkey again. Oh no, there's that horrible seagull, Annabel. I think that bench we sat at before is his territory. After we get our lunch, let's take it to another bench so that he doesn't try to steal our food again."

Chapter 14: The Inquiry Begins

"I hope they find the killer soon, David, but if he doesn't kill me, this fast food will. How was your rubber turkey sandwich today?"

"Rubbery, how was your hamburger?

"Like cheap shoe leather, but it was cheap!" I said, putting my finger up to help make my point.

"How about tomorrow we go to Portofino's and split a delicious, Mediterranean chicken salad I remember they have for lunch. We can fill up on that nice bread they serve with the meals. We can also make lemonade if we ask for lemons in our water. Sugar is provided on the table." We both smiled a scheming smile at each other. I gave David a thumbs up.

"David, I like the way you think. Let's do that and have lunch there from now on. We can split lots of different items they have on their menu."

"Definitely, even these French fries were soggy, and the lemonade was all ice and way too sweet... blarf," he said.

"So, we need to figure out what we want to paint next. The one good thing I can say about Eric's is that it truly is fast food. We don't have to waste time waiting for the food to be served or the check to come when we should be painting. Let's do a larger painting this afternoon. How about a 12 x16?"

"That's fine with me. Where do you want to go?" he asked.

"Let's go down Crescent Avenue to the other Art Deco fountain by the Landing. The Hotel Metropole is there and maybe we could find something interesting. We've never scouted out that area. If we don't find anything there, the fountain and all the palm trees will be backlit creating interesting lavender shadow patterns on the street."

"Ooo... that sounds wonderful. Rather than scouting, I think I'd like to paint the fountain," he said.

When we arrived, Randy and Saul where already there and had set up their easels in the best spots. But, as David had once said to me, no one owns the island or has a monopoly on where we can paint.

"Oh no, no, no! Go away Annabel," Randy and Mike said holding up their fingers made into a cross as if we were vampires."

I went up to Randy's face, took off my sunglasses, and with crossed eyes I scrunched up my face and said, "Can anyone point me in the direction of the fountain?" Randy and Saul burst out laughing.

"Oh okay... I guess you can join us. But don't be surprised if someone accidently trips and knocks over you and your painting before you're done," Saul said.

"That's okay, I might just have to send that seagull I've trained to shit on other artists paintings... and he has the accuracy of a B2 bomber when he drops his load. Trust me, I know!" Now David was laughing too.

"So, I'll bet you're planning on doing a nocturn tonight, Annabel," Randy said attempting to second guess me.

"Oh... trying to worm it out of me, are you?" I asked kidding on the square.

You're on to me, Kiddo," Randy said.

"Come on Randy, you, Mike, and Saul are the best. I'm just a small-town girl who's only a beginning plein aire painter."

"Annabel, you remind me of the small-town country lawyer who comes to the big city with his aw-shucks attitude. Before the big city slicker lawyers know what hit them, he blows them out of the water, and they lose the case."

"Moi," I said putting my hand on my chest, playing the innocent.

"Yes, Annabel, you."

The whole afternoon went that way. Whenever Randy or Saul could think of something snarky to say to me, they gave me a real hard time. I might have been annoyed if it was just me they were picking on, but they were doing it to each other as well. I figured that it must have been a guy thing. One thing was certain; it kept me on my toes when I should have been focusing on my painting. These guys were famous, seasoned professionals who could turn out masterpieces with very little effort. I had to concentrate and think carefully about what I was doing. Though my lack of focus may have cost me a good painting that afternoon, I was glad that some of the best artists in the country considered me to be a worthy opponent. I was tremendously flattered. Hillary and Karla treated me like a third string artist, but not these guys. On a personal note, I liked them a lot, and it was clear that they respected and liked me too. To be sure, they were giving me jazz, but I was giving it right back to them, and sometimes I got in some real zingers.

It was getting close to dinner time and my painting was about finished. David was unaware of the whole put-down fest, and I don't recall him saying a word the whole afternoon. The guys could tell he wanted to concentrate on his painting and left him alone.

"Let's see what you did," Randy said as he and Saul came over to evaluate my work.

"Woah. That's good," Saul said. Randy just stood looking for a minute and nodded his head. All he said was, "yuh." I could tell he was impressed.

It was good. Although I had been distracted, I stayed with my original plan. I had an image in my head of what I wanted the finished painting to look like, and I was able to stick to that vision. Now that I had been plein aire painting for a few years, something astonishing was developing that wasn't there before. Images in dreams could be seen in minute detail while I was still sleeping. Something else was also occurring. While I was dreaming, with my eyes closed, I could see every rock and blade of grass as the dream scene moved before my eyes. It was as if my mind was a video camera recording everything in view in perfect detail. Because I was so tuned into memorizing my surroundings, I was building up a repertoire of visual information that was being stored in my mind. My dreams were revealing to me what had been warehoused. I believe because of that, I was able to envision the result of a painting before I had even started. I was no longer simply replicating whatever scene was in front of me.

"Let me see what you guys have painted." I walked over and looked at theirs. They were wonderful. "Wow, these are just great. You both are truly masters. Good job!" Something told me that Randy and Saul liked mine better. So did I.

"Where are you headed for dinner," I asked.

"Diego's, as you know, we love their margaritas, would you like to join us again?"

"Thanks a lot, Randy, we'd love to join you, but I promised David that we would split a Mediterranean chicken salad at Portofino's. We've been eating way too much junk food recently."

"Let me guess... Eric's?" he asked.

"Oh, you got it, Randy. Do you know if there's anything better there than the rubber turkey sandwich or the shoe leather hamburgers?" I asked hoping that he could suggest something.

"Well, there's the bean burritos that are pretty good if you don't mind farting all night."

"You may not mind, but Mike and I do," Saul said pinching his nose.

"I get the picture, I get it!" All I could do was roll my eyes as my olfactory senses went into imaginary overdrive. "We need to have a quality meal at least once since we've been here. But thanks for asking, guys. I surely enjoyed painting with you both today. I may be forever emotionally scarred from the battering I got from you, but it was a lot of fun. Now I need to go and lick my wounds." The guys just looked at each other and burst out laughing. I knew what they were thinking and realized I had left myself wide open for a lewd comment. I just shook my head and then gave them both a hug. We said our goodbyes and David and I headed for Portofino's which was just down the street.

*****

After my altercation with Raj, he returned to the station with Asher and Miriam Bloomberg. Before he took them into Tom's office, he took Tom aside and explained that I hadn't divulged anything other than the location of the murders which he reminded him was already common knowledge.

"That's all?" Tom asked.

"That's all. She's a smart girl and she knew better. She didn't break her promise to me," Raj said, happy that his confidence hadn't been betrayed.

He then brought the Bloombergs into Tom Derringer's office, they were nervous not understanding why they were there.

"I'd like to question you first, Asher. I understand that you're wondering why we've asked you to come here so let me explain. As you have probably heard, there have been two murders on the island. We are questioning everyone who knew the victims. You're not suspects, we're just collecting information to help us solve the case. It's customary to separate you both so that we can get two different perspectives on what you may have noticed. Miriam, I would like Sergeant Monaghan to question you." Jim took her into a separate room.

"Asher, is there anything you can tell us that might give us insight into why these women are now dead?"

Asher looked down and thought for a minute. He then said,

"I've noticed that some of the people who came over on the Catalina Express have been socializing with each other. Also, there are several people who were on the boat that are staying at the Glenmore Hotel. Two of the deceased women were staying there and from what I understand had rooms on the same floor. That alone seems like a strange coincidence."

"Uh-huh... yes, it certainly does. We have done some inquiring concerning your background. We learned that many of your family members were killed in the Holocaust." Asher nodded his head. "I say this with all sincerity, I'm so sorry for the great tragedy that befell your family."

"Thank you, Captain," Asher muttered.

"From what we were able to determine, a man named Julius Streicher was principally responsible for what happened. Of course, the loss of life was the greatest part of the tragedy, but we also learned that your family members that died were extremely wealthy. They owned real estate, gold, and a fabulous art collection."

"Yes, that's true," Asher responded, and as he spoke a tear ran down his cheek. Asher immediately realized that they had spoken to me, and I had revealed the story of his family tragedy. He wasn't sure if he should be angry with me or not.

"I'm terribly sorry, I know this is difficult. Are you aware that one of the deceased woman's names was Streicher. That is not her married name. As an artist, she kept her maiden name."

"Yes, my wife and I knew that she was the granddaughter of Julius Streicher. We tracked her down with a great deal of effort. One of the reasons we came here was to meet her and develop a relationship with her. It was our plan to ask her if we could go to her home which is where we understood she had her studio. The problem was, we soon realized Karla was also antisemitic. She rebuffed us when we tried to be friendly. We planned to befriend her to discover as much information as we could about what happened to our family's art collection. We were certain that the gold couldn't be traced, and the money and property had long since been liquidated. Our only hope was to locate the art which may still be in the Streicher family's possession. Miriam and I are both retired now and have decided to try to retrieve what was stolen from our family for the sake of our children and grandchildren.

"I understand. I guess Karla's death robbed you of the chance to go forward with that investigation. You must be terribly disappointed," Tom said.

"Yes, with Karla, but there are other family members and I'm not giving up."

"Can you please make us a list of where you and Miriam have been all day and night Sunday, and day and night Monday. We're doing this with several other people. Please get it to us as soon as possible today, people's lives might depend on it. That's all for now Asher, thank you so much for your cooperation and for being so forthcoming. If you remember anything that will help us, anything at all, please don't hesitate to contact me."

"I certainly will." The two men shook hands and Captain Derringer walked Asher into the reception area where Miriam was already waiting.

While Tom was questioning Asher, Jim had been questioning Miriam. Miriam had also been open about their plans to befriend Karla. The two officers compared notes and found the Bloomberg's responses to be consistent with each other.

"Who's next on our list?" Jim asked.

"The three artists, I have their names here, Randy Creighton, Michael Mitchell, and Saul Katten. I've got a list of all the artists cell phone numbers who are in the festival from Brianna. We'll begin with getting in touch with the three men after dinner so we can begin our timelines ASAP. I'd like to have fish tacos tonight, Della, will you call in the order to Diego's Tortilliaria." Twenty minutes later, Della walked to the restaurant and came back with the officer's Mexican meals. That was not all she returned with since she had been listening to the officer's conversations.

"I heard you say that you wanted to talk to the three artists. While I was waiting for your dinners, I saw the name tags of the artists who were eating there. They were the ones you wanted to speak with. I told them who I was and asked them to come to the station with me," Della explained.

"Where are they now, Della?" Jim asked.

"They're waiting outside."

"Good going Della! Bring them in."

The three artists entered the room lackadaisically joking around with each other about spending the night in jail. Their clothes were covered with paint splotches. It was hard to distinguish where paint smears began, and the food stains ended with these guys.

"Get out your handcuff's officers, I can tell you right now, this guy's guilty... of what, I don't know, but I'm sure he did it," Randy said, pointing at Mike and giving him a push, almost knocking him off balance. That wouldn't have been difficult, the guys had been swigging the margaritas again."

"Have a seat, gentlemen," Captain Derringer said, somewhat tongue in cheek, gesturing with his hand toward the seats where he wanted the artists to sit. "I'm sure you're wondering why we brought you here." Tom stated.

"Not really, we were wondering why you haven't picked Randy up a long time ago." Mike said trying to get back at Randy. They were all giggling and swaying as they unsuccessfully tried to regain their equilibrium.

"Do you guys think you could stop joking around for a minute. We have some serious business we need to attend to and would appreciate your cooperation," Sargeant Monaghan said. Mike put his fingers on his smile and pushed his mouth to a more serious position. But then he and Saul burst out laughing again.

"Come on now, we need to try to cooperate," Randy said. He was the most disciplined of the trio. He knew why they were there and was now trying to concentrate. Though Randy seemed like a goof ball, he was highly intelligent, and I was told, he had an IQ of 149. I heard that Randy's father was a naval officer, an Admiral, and Randy had been accepted as a cadet to the Naval Academy. In his second year he dropped out, finding military life incompatible with his creative nature and desire to paint, play his guitar, and write songs.

"Thank you, Randy," Tom said as he read the name tag all the artists were wearing around their necks. "We're trying to gather information that may help us discover who was responsible for the murders that have been happening on the island."

"I can't believe they both were murdered," Randy said.

"That is what the evidence tells us," Tom said.

"How were they murdered?" he asked.

"I can't reveal any more than I've already told you, Randy. Tell me, how well did you know Hillary?"

"We were acquaintances. I must be honest with you, none of us liked Hillary and I don't know anyone else who did. She was a cold hearted, egotistical bitch who thought only of herself. She liked to think she was far superior in talent and social station to the rest of us. She looked down her nose at everyone, and that snooty voice of hers was like nails on a chalkboard to me."

"What about Karla?"

"She wasn't much better." Saul answered, now trying to focus so he could contribute to the conversation. The two women competed for the uppermost position of who could look down on other artists from the loftiest position. Both were fiercely competitive, but Karla was antisemitic which didn't sit well with me. Whenever I was around, she avoided the three of us, but when she couldn't, she would occasionally make subtle slurs alluding to my Jewish name or looks,"

"Randy and Saul disliked both of those women to be sure ... but I hated Hillary," Mike said. "I know I'm probably incriminating myself, but for some reason Hillary continually made insulting remarks about my paintings. Maybe I'm overly sensitive, but I *am* my work, and I took the things she said to me to heart. Sometimes it took me weeks to get past the anger and hurt I felt from her stinging comments about my paintings. I don't know why she chose me to pick on, but she did, and it was deliberate. She was sadistic. She knew she could get me rattled and she enjoyed it. I think it made her feel powerful."

"What Saul and Mike are telling you is true. I can vouch for what they've told you. I've never met a couple of more spoiled, self-absorbed women in my life. Mike is kind and sensitive, and Hillary saw him as an easy mark. Karla was antisemitic and frequently made nasty remarks about Saul being Jewish. I did my best to defend my friends, but the remarks those women made were so appalling, they caught me off guard and I didn't know what to say."

"From what you're telling me, the net we're setting out will need to be widened. If the women were as bad as you say, there are others who could want them taken out," Sergeant Jim said as he stood up and looked out the window. Tom leaned forward and said,

"I'd like each one of you to give me a timeline of where you were day and night on Monday and Tuesday. If anything comes to mind that you think would be helpful to us, please write it down on your timeline. Can you think of anything else you want to ask the guys, Jim?

"No, I think we covered what we needed."

"Are we suspects, Captain?" Mike said, nervously twisting his wedding ring.

"Mike, everyone on the island is a suspect, but don't get nervous, we will be talking to other artists as well. You were asked to come here because we're gathering information to help us uncover more puzzle pieces needed to solve this case. Ya'll were forthcoming which we appreciate. What you have told us was helpful. Please relax and enjoy the rest of the evening." With that, Tom stood up from his desk and walked the now more sober men to the door.

"Thanks for your cooperation," Jim said to the men as they left the police station.

The three demoralized friends walked silently toward the Atwater Hotel. The experience of being questioned by the police was alarming and took them out of their pleasantly tipsy state. Their awareness that they could possibly be suspects was finally beginning to sink in as the effects of the margaritas were wearing off. Randy was first to realize the gravity of the situation they were in, for people were wrongfully convicted of crimes they hadn't committed every day. Even if they were exonerated and found not guilty, the price of a decent defense lawyer could cost a fortune. This was not good. He and Mike were large guys and now they knew Hillary and Karla were both murdered. Though the police wouldn't give details, from the demeaner of Brianna Gleason and the officers at the "Meet and Greet," it told Randy that Hillary and Karla's murders were brutal, vicious killings. That would mean it would most likely have been done by a large man or a large, physically fit woman. Saul was small, but he and Mike were both over six feet. Though Mike was a little overweight, Randy had kept up with the physical fitness training which had become habitual since his days at Annapolis.

A horrible thought crossed Randy's mind as he realized Mike could have climbed Chimes Tower Road without anyone knowing he had left his room. The desk clerk was always off duty at 8:00. Did Mike hate Hillary that much? Was he capable of murdering her? What about Saul? How deeply did Karla's antisemitic remarks hurt Saul? Could the two of them have worked together? No, they were two great guys, he thought, but suspicion had crept into Randy's mind. Mike eventually broke the silence.

"Do you think they see us as suspects?" Mike asked Randy.

"You heard what he said. Everyone on the island is a suspect."

"This could be very bad, Randy," Saul said, finally realizing how serious the situation was.

"Fortunately, we've spent most of our time together. Try not to worry too much, Saul," Randy said trying to reassure his friend.

"That's right, we can all vouch for each other, can't we." Mike added.

"When we fill out our timelines, we can also make note of all the people who saw us and who could confirm that we are telling the truth. We've got to remember who those people would be. I hate to say this, but our futures could depend on it." Saul said.

"Yes, that's what we must do. We must tell the truth," Randy said. "That way our stories will be consistent. For instance, Annabel and David were with us on Sunday night at Diego's when we were having dinner and drinking margaritas. That was the night Hillary was murdered."

We stayed there drinking margaritas till what time do you think, Mike?" Randy asked.

"Maybe 8:00, I'm not sure, we were all so drunk. The waitress will probably remember. She can also vouch that we were plastered and in no condition to do much of anything other than go back to the hotel to sleep it off," Mike said hoping he was right.

"When lab reports come in, they'll be able to tell when the women died. Until we know that, we're not in the clear. We all have separate rooms which isn't good. We have no alibis after we went into the hotel," Saul added.

"Sunday night we were at Diego's. They know us there and I hope the waitress would be willing to verify our story. Monday night we were at the Portofino Restaurant together where many people saw us. I think we have pretty good alibis except for the time when we were alone in our hotel rooms," Randy said, uncertain they were in the clear.

"I think we'd better be more responsible in our behavior from now on. Let's get to bed early tonight," Saul suggested.

"That's a good idea; I think it would be wise for us to curtail the drinking for the rest of the week. We're going to need to keep our wits about us from now on. Who knows, we may even do better paintings without hangovers." Randy couldn't believe what he had just heard himself say.

Chapter 15: A Portofino's Dining Treat

After completing our fountain painting, David and I pulled our rolling cart with all our equipment into the Portofino Restaurant. I was still a little shell shocked by the barrage of zingers from Randy and Saul as I stood waiting to be seated at the hostess station with David. I was not often at my best on Tuesdays, it was still early in the week, but this Tuesday I was in rare form. I had to be to keep up with Randy. He was really something, smart as could be, quick witted, great sense of humor, and he had this manly way about him that was very appealing. Even though he was considerably older than me, probably in his late thirties, I found him to be quite attractive. There was one thing for sure, he certainly kept me on my toes. At that moment, David interrupted my train of thought, saying,

"There are a lot of people we know here tonight. There's Tony with some people I don't recognize in the middle of the room. The Bloombergs are in a booth with an artist who is wearing a festival tag. Do you know the two artists who are sitting with Charlotte and Alice?"

"Yes, I do, the one on the right with the dark hair is Tyler, and the one with the brown hair and red beard is Ethan. They're members of our San Diego chapter, but they hardly ever paint with us. They must have rode here on the Catalina Express on Sunday. They knew Sybil though. I wonder if Charlotte and Alice met them at Sybil's Celebration of Life.

"Huh... could be. Are they any good?" David asked.

"Oh, yes, they're both very accomplished, almost everyone in this show is good. I'm competing with the best in California. I'm so intimidated, David," I whined.

"Don't be silly, Annabel. I thought your painting of the Art Deco fountain this afternoon was better than Randy's or Saul's."

"I hate to sound arrogant, David, but I thought so too." I was silently gloating to myself. Just then my phone rang. It was Raj.

"Hi Raj!" I answered. I was relieved to hear his voice even though I was still simmering about how he behaved earlier in the day, so I kept a cool tone of voice. "We're at Portofino's. No, we haven't been seated yet. Yes, I suppose we can do that. Okay, we'll see you then." Raj wants to join us for dinner. He said he'd be here in five minutes."

"Okay, but we're not going to split our Mediterranean chicken salad three ways," David said kidding me.

"Not a chance. On second thought, do you think we should buy him dinner since he treated us to lunch at the Busy Bee and made that Indian dinner? I'm beginning to feel uncomfortably obligated."

"Annabel, we 'll run out of money before the festival ends. Come on, be sensible."

"I have a hundred dollars mad money in my shoe. I could use that. You don't have to pitch in. I'll just pay myself." David looked at me shaking his head in dismay.

"No, you need to be more sensible with your money. You're always trying to be so nice and it's not wise. And don't give me any nonsense about not wanting to be obligated, you like him!" David was wise, an important mentor and advisor to me not only in financial matters but personal concerns as well. I listened to him and often took his advice.

"Okay, David, I'll think about what you said."

We were finally seated close to Tony and his new friends, a male and a female. I now noticed that his female friend was wearing the artist's name tag around her neck.

"Hi Tony, who are your new friends?" I asked, wanting to become acquainted with another artist who was in the competition.

"This is Natalie, who's an artist from San Francisco, and this is her husband, Austin. He's acting as her assistant while she's in the show."

"Hi, I'm Annabel Adams, and this is my friend David Ainsworth. How nice to have someone to help with all the paraphernalia we need to deal with. David and I are on our own, but we do help each other." As we were speaking, Raj came to the table and sat down with us. I felt an interesting surge of elation when he arrived. I couldn't exactly understand why, because I still wasn't sure of how I felt about him.

"Hi," I said as Raj took a seat next me. I then introduced him to Tony and the two new acquaintances. "You've been buying us lunch and made that fabulous Indian dinner, so tonight I'm going to buy your dinner," I said giving him a frigid stare.

"Annabel, that's not going to happen. I invited myself to join you for dinner, so dinner is on me for both of you." I started to object. He shushed me. I tried a second time. He shushed me again. "It ain't gonna happen, stop!" he said putting his hands up in protest. "Look, I know you're still angry with me. I behaved very badly, and you didn't deserve it. I should have trusted you and given you the benefit of the doubt, but I don't know you well yet and I felt betrayed. I was terribly angry thinking you had broken your promise to remain silent about the case. I hope we can put this behind us and move forward," he said. He seemed sincere and I decided that I didn't like having friction between us.

"Okay, let's forget about it. Just make sure you believe me when I tell you something." I said squinting my eyes and pointing my finger at him with a smile. I felt much better. I could tell he did too.

Just then the cocktail waitress came to the table to take our orders. Raj ordered a cabernet sauvignon. David and I ordered water. Raj tried to convince us to try a little cabernet, but we insisted that we needed to avoid alcohol while we were painting. A few minutes later our waitress came by. Raj ordered filet mignon, and David and I tried to order a split Mediterranean chicken salad. Raj insisted that we each have a whole portion. We were both famished and realized we wouldn't have to load up on bread or make our own lemonade from the lemons we planned to ask for. When the cocktail waitress brought Raj's cabernet, I decided to splurge and asked for an Arnold Palmer.

"This is so nice of you Raj," David said. "Annabel was planning on using the mad money she keeps in her shoe to buy you dinner."

"David," I whined and then shushed him feeling terribly embarrassed.

"Were you going to do that, Annabel?" Raj asked. I just looked down and didn't answer. "That's awfully sweet of you. You have no idea how much I appreciate that." There was a moment of awkward silence, and then Raj said,

"You may be wondering why I wanted to have dinner with you tonight. I've spoken to Tom, and he agreed to let me ask you some confidential questions. I explained to him what happened with the news media, and he said it would be alright. I would like to be reseated at a booth so we could have more privacy." David and I agreed, and we were moved to a booth in the back corner of the restaurant.

"This is exciting! I feel like we're becoming private detectives too." I couldn't sit still and found myself squirming in my seat.

"The murder of Hillary was gruesome; it was just horrible. She was stabbed many times, her throat was cut, and her eyes were stabbed then closed and painted black with her oil paint. A hideous smile was painted on her face. On her sweatshirt was painted the word, FORDS. Does any of that ring a bell with either of you?"

"Eew...No Raj, it doesn't, but how horrible! You would have no way of knowing this, but I consider myself to be an expert in handwriting analysis though I have no professional training. I'm completely self-educated. I began teaching myself about handwriting analysis when I was only eight years old. I would like to look at the photos I'm sure you have of the word FORDS so I could examine those and any handwriting specimens you have of suspects. I would also like to see all the photos. I'm very intuitive, I may be able to better help you if I had more knowledge of the crime scene. Would you allow me to do that?"

"I'll have to check with Tom. Personally, Annabel, I think having you look at the word FORDS handwriting is a great idea and would appreciate your help, but that's all. I don't want you to see Hillary's face, or Karla's either. The photos are too gruesome. Once you get that image in your head it won't leave, and I don't want you to have nightmares. You're a sensitive girl and I think you should stick solely to the handwriting analysis." I was quiet for a minute when Raj said, "What are you thinking, Annabel?"

"I'm thinking that I'm a lot tougher than you realize so I don't want to be shielded from the photos. I'd like to see what you have. Boy, somebody really hated her. What do you think she did to make someone so mad?"

"I have no idea. I want you both to think about what I've told you and see if anything rings a bell. You must not, and I can't stress this enough, you must not reveal anything I have told you to anyone."

"Well, you've come to the right people. Annabel and I are both good at keeping our mouths shut. We won't say a word to anyone. I can guarantee that for both of us," David said, making a motion like he was locking his mouth and pretending to throw away the key.

"We have received forensic evidence that confirms that Karla was dead before she was stabbed. There was a tremendous amount of a benzodiazepine, in other words, a strong sedative in her system. She was drinking heavily that night, and the combination of alcohol and benzodiazepine was what killed her."

"I was told by Alice Smith that Karla took a sleeping pill each night. Do you think that because she was drunk, she might have forgotten she had already taken her pill and accidently took another?" I asked.

"There were way more than just two pills in her system. It was no accident; it was a huge overdose. Someone put the sedatives in her food or drink, and we're going to find and question people who may have had the opportunity to do that. There may have been more than one person involved in these murders. We don't know yet. Beside the sedatives, Karla was also stabbed many times, and her face was horribly disfigured. The perpetrator wrote the word NAZI on her sweatshirt, and she may have been raped. We're waiting for forensics to come in. Fortunately for Karla, she was already dead when everything happened. She never experienced the horror that Hillary went through, poor soul," Raj said as he put his head down.

"There is something else I know. Alice Smith was rooming with Karla but moved out because Karla snored so badly. I'll bet Alice still had a key to Karla's room when she was murdered. Something else, Alice is a big girl, probably six feet tall. She was in the military service; I think it was the navy. She is very physically fit. Remember, her mother's suicide may have been precipitated by Karla and Hillary's expulsion of Sybil from PAPOC. I don't want to incriminate anyone, but she and her mother have reasons to hate both Hillary and Karla." I was feeling guilty. What if I was incriminating innocent women. "This is just speculation, Raj, Alice seems like a nice person."

"From what I hear, many murderers are charming. They look and act normal, and no one would ever suspect that they could be cold blooded killers."

While we were engrossed in the details of the murders, our waitress brought our dinners to the table. Although I had decided to avoid filling up on bread, our discussion with Raj was so exciting I had lost control of myself and had eaten most of the bread in the basket.

"Let's try to enjoy our dinners now that I totally spoiled everyone's appetite, bon appetit," Raj said with a smirk lifting his wine glass.

"This is awfully generous of you Raj; we've been eating lunch at Eric's trying to save money. What you're doing for us is very appreciated," David said.

My friend David was a cancer survivor who was living on a pension from his military service. He could barely make ends meet each month. I sometimes tried to help him, but he was proud and refused my offers of monetary assistance.

"I have an idea," Raj said. "I told you that my father and I are partners in a large tech company. I would like to help you both with your meals. I can write them off as a company expense. I'll inform the staff here and at the Busy Bee that you are my guests for the rest of the week while you're on the island for the festival," Raj said. I could tell he was eager to help us alleviate our financial concerns.

"Oh Raj, normally I would say no thank you because I don't like to feel obligated to anyone for anything. But with you it's different. I can tell you sincerely want to help us, so I'll accept your generous offer and ask you to join us whenever possible."

"You've got a deal," he said. He flagged down the manager and informed him of the plan. Raj was a good customer and a big tipper and because of that, he was well known in the town and to the Portofino Restaurant staff. His credit was excellent, and they were glad to oblige him.

"Do you think we could we go the Police Station after dinner tonight to look at the photographs of the word FORDS? David and I hate to miss the morning light. Now would be a perfect time for me to examine what you have, and it wouldn't interrupt our painting time."

"Sure, let me pay the check and we'll go."

Chapter 16: Cryptic Notes

When we arrived at the police station, it was 9:00 that evening and Tom, Jim, and Della were still there. They were all finishing the dinners Della had picked up at Diego's when Raj, David, and I walked in on them. Raj explained that I was practically an expert in handwriting analysis and wanted to examine some of the photos of Hillary and Karla.

"I don't think so, Annabel, they're horribly gruesome. You won't sleep tonight if you look at them," Tom said.

"I'll sleep much better if I can help you catch the murderer," I said. Tom raised his eyebrows not believing my answer as he got up to retrieve the photographs. His face told me he was reluctant to expose me to the horrendous nature of the deaths. He was back in a moment and said,

"Now remember, I warned you." He handed me the photos from Hillary's murder. I began to thumb through them.

"What is this odd-looking brown button? I asked.

"That brown color is blood. We found it clutched in Hillary's hand. As she struggled to survive, she must have pulled it of the killer's shirt," Raj explained.

"Ooo...oh, eew." I had no words to describe the repulsion I was experiencing as I looked at the rest of the photographs.

"I'm sorry, Annabel, I tried to warn you," Tom said hoping to justify allowing me to see what had become of Hillary.

"No, don't apologize, this was necessary. There is something that stands out to me. On the surface the writing reads as FORDS, but if you notice the murderer used all capital letters, but if you take a second look, the F, D, and the S, are considerably larger than the O and the R. The way I see it, the person is not writing FORDS, he or she is writing ForDS. I think the person is avenging someone with the initials DS or it could be two people, one with the initial D and another with the initial S. The three men looked at each other for a minute, all of them thinking, how could we have missed that?

"That's interesting, none of us saw that, but now that you've pointed it out, that makes way more sense. Is there anything else?" Tom asked.

"Well yes, Sybil's name begins with an S. Also, I have no idea what this might mean, but Hillary's face was painted to look like the Joker from Tim Burton's movie, Batman. The character, the Joker, was the personification of evil and Batman's nemesis. The Joker was a remorseless serial killer who wreaked havoc on Gotham City sadistically killing his victims and reveling in his savagery. This murderer may see himself as a Batman like character, a dark knight ridding the world of evil doers."

Raj and the police officers were dumbfounded. How could this sweet kid, this young female artist who did nothing but create beautiful paintings all day have such insight into the darkness that lay buried deep in the human soul. All three of them were feeling embarrassed and mortified by their lack of insight.

"Now what about Karla's photos, could you take a look at these?" Jim asked as he handed me photographs of her sweatshirt.

"It's the same handwriting. NAZI is written in all capital letters, the size and spacing is the same, the slant is vertical, the appearance of the lettering is the same as Hillary's. If there was ever any question about more than one killer, maybe someone else put the sedatives in Karla's food or drink, but the writing was done by the same person.

Jim then reluctantly handed me another photo of Karla.

"Oh, this is horrible," I said. Karla's face was painted like the Joker, like Hillary's, but the hideous smile had been slashed from ear to ear. The flaps of skin were parted revealing all her teeth. I was feeling sick. "This is just terrible, Karla was such a beautiful woman. What kind of monster could ravage someone so beautiful. Please give me a moment, I need to go out for some air." I felt like crying. Raj took my arm, and he and David came with me outside where I sat on a bench by the station. I was feeling lightheaded, so I put my head down between my knees.

"Are you alright?" Raj asked putting his hand on my shoulder.

"No," I said with tears running down my face. How could anyone do that to her? I said barely able to speak. I then realized if I didn't pull myself together, the men wouldn't give me access to the case, so I stood up and said, "I'm fine now. I just needed a minute. Let's go inside and continue."

"Annabel don't look at any more photographs," David said.

"He's right, you've done enough," Raj said as we walked back into the station.

"You certainly have given us a different perspective on this case. You've been tremendously helpful. We're asking for each of our persons of interest to supply us with timelines of their whereabouts on the nights of the murders. As they come in, I would like to have you look at the handwriting samples. Can you do that for me, Annabel?" Tom asked.

"Of course I can. But you must remember, I'm in this plein aire festival. Can you try to work around David's and my schedule?"

"Yes, we can do that," Raj said. "I'll make certain we don't interfere with the reason you're here."

"Right after dinner is good, or at lunch if you could bring in some food for us. David and I must keep up our strength. You may think painting all day is easy, but it takes a lot of physical stamina. Just make sure the food's not from Eric's." We all laughed understanding the lack of quality of the food there. "Oh, on Friday I plan to do a nocturn, so I can't come in Friday night."

"If we get any timelines tomorrow, let's plan on having you come in after your morning painting." Jim said. "Raj will keep you up to date. Okay, that's all for now. Thanks, you two." The officers and Raj got up and walked David and I to the door.

"I'll drive you both home," Raj said.

"We're just a little way down the street, we can walk. Besides, I can use the fresh air."

"I understand, but it's nighttime and I'll sleep better knowing you both are safe at the hotel. You can get plenty of fresh air in my golf cart."

*****

After we left the office, Tom asked,

"Do you feel incompetent or is it just me, Jim?"

"How could we have missed those things? I've seen the movie Batman more than once," Jim responded.

I know, me too. Now that I think about it, the difference in the size of the capital letters in FORDS was right there in front of us. How could we have missed it?"

"She's more perceptive than we are. I guess that's why she's an artist and we aren't. I remember reading that men have many more brain cells than women, but not in this case," Jim said.

"If my wife heard you say that she'd say, 'It's a matter of quality versus quantity' and in this case, I couldn't argue with her."

"So tomorrow let's question Charlotte Fitzsimmons, Alice Smith, and Tony Rossi," Jim suggested.

"Let's see if we can do that in the morning so that we can analyze the timelines and fill out our newfound information on the whiteboard before Annabel comes in for lunch. Make sure Della orders lunch for all of us. Okay, let's wrap it up for tonight."

*****

Annabel and David were tired. It had been a long day, and the strains and stresses of the week were getting to them. On top of everything they were dealing with concerning the festival, now Annabel was going to need to find time to help the police find Hillary and Karla's killers.

"I don't think I can make it up those two flights of stairs tonight, David."

"Come on little old girl, you can do it."

"Just give me a push to keep me moving," Annabel said as she stopped before attacking the last flight.

"Hey, what's this?" David asked as he approached their room.

"What's what?" I asked.

"Look," he said pointing to a paper stuck on the door. Right below the number 301 was a note which read, YOUR NEXT! A cold chill ran down my spine.

"David, this is scary!" As I looked around the hallway, I could see that the same message was also taped on room 303, Nancy's door.

"I'm calling Raj. Hi Raj, David and I just got to our rooms and there's a threatening note on our door which reads, YOUR NEXT! Okay, yes, I will.

"What did he say?"

"He said he'll be right there, don't go inside the room, go immediately down to the lobby. David, the police deputies are outside guarding the hotel. It seems like the killer is either staying in this hotel or has access to its interior.

We were waiting in the lobby of the hotel when the police arrived a minute after we called. They immediately began questioning Bonnie Abernathy, the hotel desk clerk who said she had been in and out of the reception area throughout the afternoon and evening. She hadn't noticed anything unusual or anyone other than the guests of the hotel going up and down the stairs. "What's going on? Am I in danger? Should I quit this job?" Bonnie asked in rapid succession.

"No, it's the artists in the festival that we're worried about. You'll be fine. Remember, the deputies are outside and we're just down the street if you get scared. Don't worry," Tom said, but he was worried now wondering how those notes got on the doors and past his deputies.

Raj stayed with Annabel and David in the lobby as Tom and Jim climbed the stairs to the third floor. With the key card they had been given, the police officers carefully opened the door, and with guns drawn, they entered Annabel and David's rented room. It was clear, and the others were told to come upstairs.

"Is anything out of place that either of you are aware of?" Tom asked.

"The window is open. It was closed when we left this morning," I noticed.

"Housekeeping might have opened it," David offered.

"I suggest you throw everything out that you have in the refrigerator," Raj said.

"Good thinking." I said, knowing what had happened to Karla.

"Lock your doors tonight, and don't open them to anyone," Tom said.

"Tom, I should point out the back door to the hotel. It's right here," I said as I pointed out the door to a stairway.

"Yes, we're aware of that door. Let's go next door to where the second note was placed. What's the name of the person staying in this room?" Jim asked.

"It's Nancy, let me talk to her." I knocked on her door.

"Just a minute," she said, from behind the door. When she opened it, she was without any makeup and in her pajamas. Apparently, she had been asleep. It's late," she whined. "What do you want?"

"Nancy, look what's on your door," I said pointing to the note.

She gasped and put her hand to her mouth. She immediately began crying and needing to sit down. The police did their best to comfort and reassure her, but she continued crying.

"I'll tell you what, we'll have two more deputies stationed inside the hotel for the rest of the week and one will be on this floor. Would that make you feel safer?" Jim asked.

"Yes, I think that would help... and thank you." Nancy whimpered.

"Raj, I want to talk to you. You need to ask Tom to question Nancy and get her to make a timeline," I insisted.

"Why? What are you thinking? Raj asked.

"Oh, it's just a hunch," I said using the vernacular that was frequently used in my favorite film noir murder mysteries of the 1940s. Though I hated to admit it, what was happening here on Catalina was more exciting than any film noir movie I had ever seen.

"A call just came into the station from Randy Creighton. He also got a YOUR NEXT! note on his backpack," Jim said.

"I want you and Jim to be at my office at 6:00 a.m. sharp to meet with Randy. We must put a stop to this immediately."

Thursday

Chapter 17: Persons of Interest

Tom, Jim, and Raj's Thursday morning began with them making phone calls to Charlotte, Alice, Nancy, and Tony. Appointments were set up with them scheduled throughout the morning, one hour apart. Annabel had left a message on the answer machine saying she had more information for them and would come into the police station as soon as she finished her morning painting. Randy arrived right on time and brought the timelines that he, Mike, and Saul had prepared to show their whereabouts during the days and nights when Hillary and Karla were murdered. Tom decided to let Jim question Randy noticing the two of them seemed to be in sync. Tom took notes.

"So Randy, tell me where you were when this note was left on your backpack?"

"Mike, Saul, and I left our stuff in a dark area right outside the Busy Bee while we were having dinner. We all decided it would be wise to cut back on our drinking and shouldn't stay out late anymore under the circumstances. We each only had one drink last night. Right after dinner we picked up our stuff and went straight to the Atwater where we all have rooms right next to each other. When I went into my room and took off my backpack, I noticed there was a note that I hadn't seen before which was right between the shoulder straps."

"Your friends didn't get a note, just you?"

"That's right. I called them and asked. They didn't get one, just me."

"Do you have any idea why you were singled out?"

"I do, but this must remain completely confidential." Jim agreed, nodding his head. "I usually win the best of show award at most plein aire events. I think someone wants me out of the show. My backpack is very recognizable. It's large, black, and is covered in colorful paint smears, so whoever left that note knew it was mine. My suspicion is that it was another artist."

"Annabel and Nancy had the same note taped on the doors of their rooms. Are they good enough artists to be considered a threat?"

"Annabel is, she's young and inexperienced, but she's smart and savvy when it comes to understanding how to create award winning paintings. She's a risk taker and will go out on a limb, so her work is often hit and miss, but when she hits, it's out of the ballpark. All it takes is one great painting to win best of show. I consider Annabel to be my biggest threat in this competition. She has no idea that Mike, Saul, and I think of her that way because she doesn't know how good she really is. Yesterday, Saul and I had our easels set up by the north Art Deco fountain when Annabel and her friend David showed up. She was the last person I wanted to see painting the same scene that we were. By the time we had finished, Annabel's painting was clearly the best. After she left, Saul and I talked about it and realized we might as well throw ours in the trash. There was no way either of us could enter ours in the competition... and we did good, solid paintings. Nancy, on the other hand, is no threat to me at all or Annabel for that matter. Her work is bland, and mediocre at best. That's being kind. I've never seen one of her paintings that I believed was at all compelling."

"I see. Everything you've just told me, Randy, is important in helping me to understand the mind set of artists. You all are fiercely competitive and obsessed with proving your work the best. My previous opinion of artists was that they were all a bunch of day dreamy slackers. After getting to know you and Annabel, man was I was wrong!"

"Our goals are different than most of the population. We think of our work as 'something for the ages.' People will speak of us long after we are gone. In a way it's a form of immortality," Randy explained.

"I see," Jim said, though he really didn't. "Can you think of any other reasons why specifically you, Annabel, and Nancy were the ones who received notes."

"No, I can't." Randy stood thinking for a minute, then said, "That's all I can think of right now. I'll let you know if anything else comes to mind. Meanwhile, do you have any specific advice concerning my safety? Even with my military training and physical fitness, I'm frightened."

"You're a big guy, but don't take any unnecessary chances. Stay in well-traveled areas and always stay close to your friends. Never be alone." Randy nodded, planning to follow Jim's advice.

"Did you get all that?" Jim asked Tom who was still scribbling in his notebook.

"I did. I think I'll use the recorder when Charlotte and Alice come in." Tom looked at his watch and said, "They should be here by now."

Charlotte and Alice were next on the list of persons of interest. As they walked into the lobby, Tom was startled by Alice's size. She was very tall, probably over six feet, and appeared to be quite muscular. Tom remembered that Annabel had told the officers that she was former military. They were late which displeased Tom who was irritable from anxiety and lack of sleep.

"Ladies, you were told to be here by 7:00 a.m. It's 7:30, you are late," he said looking at his watch.

"We're sorry officer, but my mother has an arthritic leg and sometimes can't walk very fast. We don't have a rented a golf cart."

"Oh, I see. I apologize ladies, we're under a lot of stress here. We've never had a murder on the island that I'm aware of, and now we have two." Tom didn't want to give them too much information.

"I understand you were in the military, Alice. Can you tell me about your service?" Jim asked.

"I was a Lieutenant in the Navy?"

"I see, where were you stationed?"

"Bosnia-Herzegovina, I was on the Theodore Roosevelt during operation Deliberate Force."

"You must have been very physically fit while you were in the service. It appears that you've kept up a good exercise regimen."

"Yes, I have. What are you getting at, Captain?" Alice asked, now becoming guarded.

"Just curious, tell me, why did you come to Catalina?"

"We came to see the Plein Aire Festival. My mother and I are both art lovers and Catalina is a wonderful place to have a vacation."

"Is that the only reason?"

"What do you mean?" Alice asked, beginning to wonder if they should call a lawyer.

"It's come to my attention Charlotte, that you lost your daughter about a month ago. I believe Sybil was your mother, Alice. From what I understand, Hillary and Karla may have played some part in Sybil's suicide. Is that true?

"It's true, but what has that to do with us and these two deaths," Alice asked.

"That's what we're trying to discover. I understand that you, Alice, shared a room with Karla. Why would you want to share a room with someone who had treated your mother so badly to the point of possibly contributing to her death?"

Alice shot a probing look at her grandmother. Charlotte nodded her head signaling that she should reveal the real reason they were there.

"We were considering a civil lawsuit with Hillary. I was trying to gather as much incriminating information as I could by befriending Karla. She told me the reason Hillary told my mother that she was no longer welcome to be a member of the San Diego chapter of PAPOC was she was a bitch, and nobody wanted her in the club. I knew that wasn't true. Everybody loved my mother and when she said that I wanted to smack her around so badly. I realized I had to get away from her and out of that room before I lost control of myself. I made up an excuse about her snoring as a reason."

"Y'all had access to her sleeping medication, didn't you?"

"I did, why do you ask?"

"I'm a police officer, I ask questions, that's what I do. Please try to cooperate."

"I made a deal with Karla that if she gave me six of her sleeping pills, she could have the room to herself, otherwise I was going to move back in with her. My grandmother is a nurse, and a man she met on the island is terminally ill and has been having trouble sleeping. It's in my Grandma's DNA to alleviate suffering in anyone who needs help. She asked me to get him some of Karla's sleeping pills."

"I see. Alright ladies, that's all. I want you both to make me a timeline of where you were day and night on Sunday and Monday. If you could get them to me before noon, I would greatly appreciate it. As soon as they left, Jim asked Tom,

"What did you think? Do they seem credible to you"

"Very suspicious. It's plausible, but not very believable. I'll be interested to see their timelines. Alice could have killed Karla. She admitted Karla gave her six sleeping pills. Alice had the pills in her possession that very well could have been the ones that poisoned Karla. Another thing, though they didn't have a cart, Alice is strong enough to climb Chimes Tower Road and still have the strength to overtake Hillary who was considerably older and smaller than Alice."

As the officers were talking, Della interrupted, saying,

"Nancy Hall has just arrived. Shall I send her in?" Della asked. Tom nodded.

"What is it you want to see me about," Nancy blurted out as she walked into Tom's office. She was clearly annoyed that she had to come in.

"You were very upset last night, and I didn't want to put pressure on you then. What time did you enter your room last night?"

"I guess it must have been around 7:30. I picked up a to go order of pizza and salad at the Busy Bee last night then came home. Now that I don't have Hillary and Karla to have dinner with, I'm on my own and I don't like it. I'm afraid to be out on my own alone at night, so I thought I'd be safer if I ate dinner in my room. Two people who were staying at my hotel are now dead. Both were friends of mine. I'm scared."

"Did you hear anything while you were in your room last night?"

"No, I was engrossed in a book I was reading about the history of Catalina Island."

"Do you have any idea why someone would want to threaten you?"

"I can't say for sure, but maybe the person wants me to drop out of the art festival."

"Do you think that the person may be another artist and sees you as a threat to winning one of the prizes?"

"What else could it be?" Nancy said shrugging her shoulders.

I would like you to make a timeline of your whereabouts and activities on the island on Sunday and Monday, both day and night. If you can think of anything that would be helpful to us in solving this case, make a note of it at the bottom of the timeline. Please work on this right away and get it back to me before noon today."

"When am I supposed to do my paintings. I don't have time for this bullshit," Nancy said raising her voice and making wild hand gestures.

"Somebody's life is not bullshit, Nancy," Tom insisted, stunned at her callous indifference at helping to find who murdered her friends.

"Oh, alright," she said with a huff as she stomped out of the office.

"Well, that was really something, quite a change from her behavior last night," Tom observed.

"Huh...was that the same person we comforted at the hotel? What a difference a day makes," Jim responded.

While the two officers were waiting for Tony Rossi to arrive, they occupied their time filling in some of their newly discovered information concerning their persons of interest. With the additional pieces of the murder puzzle, an interesting picture was beginning to appear. Della interrupted the officer's concentration once again to inform them that Tony was waiting in the lobby.

"Great, send him in."

"Hello, Officer Tom, Jim," Tony said as he offered the two men his hand.

"Hello, Mr. Rossi, thank you for being so punctual," Tom said as the officers reached out their hands as well.

"Please, call me Tony," he said.

"I understand that you've been battling cancer, Tony. How are you feeling today?" Tom asked, preparing to take notes.

"I'm feeling well today, but it's touch and go. Sometimes I have moments of overwhelming weakness or pain, and I need to immediately go up to my hotel room and lie down. It can hit me at any time, so I try not to get too far from the Portofino Hotel. I have every meal there because it's close to my bedroom." Tony explained.

"Are you on chemotherapy now?"

"No, the cancer is terminal, and I want to spend my last days free of undergoing the rigors of chemotherapy."

"I'm so sorry to hear that, Tony," Jim said.

"Me too!" Tony said with a good-natured laugh.

"I'd like to change the subject now. From what I understand, you were with both Hillary and Karla the nights they were murdered."

"Yes, I was, but what are you saying? Are you telling me Karla was murdered too? Tony said with a look of shock on his face.

"Yes, she was."

"Oh, that's so sad, they were such nice ladies. I can't believe they're gone, but I didn't know that Karla was murdered. From what I heard, Karla mixed sleeping pills and alcohol. I wondered why she would do that when everyone knows you shouldn't. So why do you think she was murdered?" Tony asked.

"That's confidential information and I can't go into that now," Tom explained. "Can you tell us your whereabouts on Sunday night?"

"Hillary, Nancy, and Karla came in for dinner at the Portofino after they had finished painting. I was lonely so I offered to buy them drinks. Then I decided to ask them if I could buy them dinner because I wanted to spend the evening with some nice ladies. Karla certainly was pretty. It was so nice sitting across the table from her."

"I see, what time did they come into the restaurant, order dinner, and then leave?"

"It must have been around 6:00 when I bought them drinks, and around 6:30 when we ordered our meals. Hillary left around 8:00. The other ladies and I finished our drinks, and they left about a half hour or forty-five minutes later."

"Then what did you do?"

"I went upstairs to my room, went to the bathroom, and laid down for a few minutes. I then went downstairs and sat at the bar talking to Henry when he wasn't busy. "

"So you were with him at the bar the rest of the evening?"

"I was. I went up to bed around midnight."

"Okay, I'll have to check it out, but that's a solid alibi for Hillary. Now I need to find out how you spent Monday evening, Tony? Are you feeling up to it?"

"Yes, mornings are usually pretty good, it's the evenings when I can become exhausted. Monday evening Nancy and Karla came into the Portofino Restaurant after painting. When I saw them around 6:30, I waved to them to come to my table where I was having a drink hoping to see the three ladies again. I had such a nice evening with them before, I wanted to buy them dinner and drinks again."

"That can get pretty expensive buying them all dinner and drinks, can't it Tony?" Jim asked.

"I suppose so, but what am I saving it for. I have no relatives and plenty of money to see me out."

"You don't have any family?" Jim asked.

"No, no one. Now getting back to Monday evening, I usually found the ladies to be pleasant company, but though Nancy seemed nice and was a lot of fun on the surface, there was something that seemed devious about her. I wondered why Hillary wasn't with them, so I asked where she was. Neither of them seemed to know. Karla brushed it off making an excuse that Hillary just thinks about Hillary. Nancy remained strangely silent, almost as if she was hiding something. I can't say why, but I don't trust Nancy. That night Karla wanted Scotch instead of the good cabernet sauvignon I ordered. I think she had two or three glasses before dinner. We all ordered our dinner and after that we had dessert. We were all embarrassingly raucous that evening, I'm ashamed to say. Karla and Nancy were even trying to hang big spoons on their noses. They were so funny. We were all having such a good time. I guess we were all quite drunk."

"Was there any time when anyone was capable of putting something in Karla's food or drink?"

"Oh yes, lots of times. We were all running back and forth to the bathroom, sometimes all three of us at once, so our food and drinks were often unattended. When we finished our drinks, I drove the ladies to the Glenmore Hotel where they were staying. They were in no condition to walk, and with the way they were behaving at the restaurant, I thought they should have someone looking out for them. When we got to the hotel, I walked them both up to their rooms, and saw them in. If anything happened to Karla after that, she must have left the room."

"Did you notice anything on Karla's bedstand?"

"No, I didn't go in the room. I just stayed in the hallway while she went in."

"Did anyone else see you take the women up to their rooms?"

"Yes, the desk clerk and a guest saw us come in together and me leave alone."

"Do you remember their names?"

"No, I don't, but I certainly noticed the desk clerk was a nice-looking blond girl. I spoke to her for a minute as I was leaving. Bonnie... yes, Bonnie, I think that's what I heard the other woman call her."

"Do you remember the time?"

"I asked Bonnie what time it was when we went in, and I guess I forgot and asked the time again when I went down. Maybe Bonnie would remember."

"How long do you think you were upstairs helping Nancy and Karla get safely into their rooms?"

"No more than two or three minutes. I helped Nancy first and then helped Karla with her key card. I didn't go into either of their rooms. Nancy could collaborate everything, but like I said, I don't trust her. Karla could have let her in her room after I left. If I were you, I would take a good look at Nancy."

"Okay Tony, we will do that. Of course we'll have to check out your story, but it looks like you have another solid alibi."

The officers stood up getting ready to escort Tony to the door when Tom said, "Oh, one more thing, Tony, how was your relationship with your parents?"

"My parents? What has that to do with anything?" Tony asked with a smile.

"Maybe nothing, but I'd like to know." Tom said, looking at his watch.

"We got along most of the time. We had our ups and downs like most families."

Okay, that's all, except I would like to have you make me out a timeline of your whereabouts on Sunday and Monday, mornings and nights. Can you do that by noon today?" Tony looked at his watch and said,

"I'll certainly try if I'm feeling up to it. I hope I was helpful to you in getting to the bottom of these murders," Tony said, again offering his hand.

Tony walked out the door, realizing Annabel was the one who had told the police about his father's death and his disdain for his mother, but he was reasonably sure that he had covered his bases with his answers.

"What do you think?" Jim asked Tom.

"He's smooth, and cool as a cucumber. He was evasive about his anger toward his artist mother and his father's death leap from the car onto the freeway."

"I suspect there's another side to Tony's nonchalant personality." Jim said.

Chapter 18: Analyzing Handwriting

For David and I, Thursday morning began with us painting on the little Avalon beach just south of the Busy Bee Restaurant. Looking south, there was a nice view of two iconic landmarks, the Holly House, some other houses in between, and the historic St. Catherine Hotel, all of which were side lit by the morning light. The structures created a nice diagonal pattern as they descended downward on the hillside. The background hill in the distance was a pale, grayed down lavender which would create some atmospheric perspective. In the foreground, the water was a bright turquoise green with the beach a pale, warm beige glowing in the sunlight as gentle white waves rolled onto the shore. The composition was perfect as it was without needing any changes. The morning light on the side of the buildings created a dramatic lighting effect and lots of contrast. It was all planned out in my mind; this was going to be a good one. We immediately set up and got started.

"What a beautiful morning," David said as he held his arms and hands up reaching for the sun.

"This is the reason we're artists." As soon as I had said that a couple of boys who were playing on the beach splashed water on me and my canvas. "Hey kids, be careful!"

The older boy was curious to see what I was doing. He came over to me, looked at my set up and said,

"I'm real sorry lady."

"I'll make you a deal, if you and the other boy will be our bodyguards and keep the other children away from us, I'll give you each a dollar when we're done if you do a good job."

"Hmm... I don't think so. That's not enough, we each want five dollars," the boy said.

"Oh, a negotiation! You're a budding entrepreneur and I like you. I'll tell you what I'll do, I'll buy you both a Big Olaf's ice cream when we're finished painting, but only if you do a good job."

"Two scoops?"

"Of course."

"When will you be done?" the older boy asked.

"Smart kid," I said. "We'll be done in a few hours, but you must stand guard. Otherwise, the deal is off."

The two boys looked at each other, nodded their heads smiling, and said,

"Okay we'll do it," the boys said probably thinking they had outsmarted the dumb artist.

"You have the patience of a saint," David said, shaking his head in dismay. "I would have kicked sand on that smart aleck kid."

"Let's wait and see. We didn't plan for the kids that would be playing on the beach. We may be getting off cheap if these painting turn out as good as I think they will."

About two hours later, Randy spotted us and came down onto the beach. I was hoping he wasn't planning on painting the same scene we were, but as he approached us, I could tell by the look on his face something was wrong.

"Hi Randy, what's up?" I said with my usual friendly greeting.

"Good morning. Annabel, I understand you got a note on the door of your room last night."

"Yes, Randy, I did and so did Nancy who is right across the hall from me."

"I guess you haven't heard, I got one too."

"Yes, I did hear that. The police were at our hotel when the station called and informed the officers about your note. I was shocked by the news. "What's going on here? This is crazy."

"I don't know, Annabel, but I'm a big guy with military training and I've got to tell you, I'm scared. You're just a little woman. Make sure you stay where people can see you... and watch your meals very carefully. Are you aware that Karla overdosed with a combination of alcohol and sedatives."

"Yes, I heard that."

"Word has gotten around that it wasn't an accidental overdose. Someone slipped the sedatives in her food or drink."

"Yes, I heard that as well. Information here certainly spreads quickly here."

"I want you to be careful. Whoever is doing the killing is a resourceful, cold-blooded monster. I'd hate to see anything happen to you," Randy said patting me on the head as if I were a child.

"Thank you, Randy. I feel the same way about you." I put down my brushes and gave him a hug.

"I had better get going. I'll see you later," he said. I blew him a kiss as he left.

"This is getting ugly, David." As I was talking to David, I heard the boys I hired shooing other kids away from our paintings. "Nice job boys. Keep up the good work." I called out, giving them a thumbs up.

Shortly after that, their mother arrived and after talking to her boys, she approached me and said,

"I'm so sorry, but we're leaving now. I know you promised the boys ice cream, but I'm afraid they can't fulfill the bargain they made with you to stay till you were finished," their mother informed me.

"That's okay, they did a good job while they were here. I'll pay them anyway."

"That's very nice of you, but I'll take the boys to Big Olaf's. I'd like to have some ice cream myself so I would have taken them anyway. That way we'll all be happy. The boy's mother noticed my painting and paused for a moment. Oh... that's a wonderful painting. Are the children in the painting my boys?" she asked.

"Yes, those certainly are your boys," I said pointing to them.

"Could you reserve this painting for me, I'd like to buy it."

"I will if you come to the exhibition when it opens at 1:00 on Saturday. I'll hold it for you for an hour. After that I'll have to sell it if someone else wants it."

"That's fair, I'll be there as soon as the exhibition opens. Incidentally, my sister is a wonderful artist too.

"No kidding, what does she like to paint?" I asked, once again trying to sound interested.

"She paints flowers. Here, let me show you some of her work," she said as she pulled out some old photographs from her purse."

"Oh yes, these are lovely, she's very accomplished. Tell her to keep up the good work." I thanked her and the boys, and they were on their way.

"Annabel, those paintings were just awful. I don't know how you can do that. You're so polite, but that's not honest," David said, shaking his head and muttering.

"I know, but I don't want to be responsible for discouraging anyone. My paintings were awful when I first attempted plein aire. People can improve and while they're painting, they can enjoy the process as they progress. I must confess, what drives me crazy is when they want to show me photographs of the paintings done by someone I've never met. That's the last thing I want to do when I'm trying to finish a painting before the light changes. Unless the painter is very good, I don't even like to look at amateur work when I'm not busy."

"Amen to that! Since you were talking about Big Olaf's, I got a hankering for two scoops of pistachio. I know you promised Raj you'd spend some time at the police station, but after that, do you want to get some ice cream when we've finished there?" David asked.

"I do. I hope the guys remember to buy us lunch. I know I'll be hungry by then."

"Me too, Annabel, are you almost done?"

"I am, how about you?

"I'm done. I just need to sign it," he said getting out his smallest brush.

We have about an hour; do you want to call Tony and ask him to take us to Descanso Beach?"

"Call him," David said. Tony was there in a minute.

"That was quick, Tony," I said.

"Yes, I was close by watching you both and some artists I'm not familiar with," Tony replied.

"Were their paintings any good?" I asked hoping he would say no, but he didn't.

"Everyone here is good, some better than others, and some much better than others, but I think your work is the best, Annabel."

"Thank you, my friend. How are you feeling? Are you doing alright today?"

"I'm okay, but I'd rather not talk about that. It's better to keep my mind on positive subjects."

"Of course, that makes perfect sense," I said. "There is so much beauty here and it's food for the soul."

"That's a nice way to put it. I whole heartedly agree. I can't think of anyplace that I would rather be right now. It isn't just this beautiful island; it's the people I've met here that have made this such a pleasant retreat for me," Tony said.

"I guess he hasn't met Fred Flintstone," I said out of the side of my mouth. David was holding back a smile, but Tony was oblivious to my comment and continued.

"They've all been so kind and caring to me," Tony said as his eyes welled up with tears. I pretended not to notice because some men don't like to be vulnerable or emotional. "Here we are," he said pulling to a stop.

"This is truly lovely, how peaceful and serene. We've got to paint this sometime, David."

"Yes, but not now. We're running out of time and if you want to paint the things you planned, you won't be able to do this too. We'll have to paint it the next time we come here. Let's just look and enjoy. We can also take photographs and paint this beach in our studios when we get home."

"Okay, David, let's get out and walk around so that we can get some shots from good angles. We climbed out of the cart and enjoyed our time with Tony. As we walked around, photographing, I couldn't help but think about how life is so precious, and it can be taken from us in the blink of an eye. I was sorry for Tony. He was so sensitive and someone who enjoyed life to the fullest. While David and I were photographing, Tony was staring out into the ocean. I wondered what he was thinking. Suddenly David's voice broke my train of thought.

"Time to get going, Annabel. Remember, we've got to get to the police station," he said.

"This has been wonderful. Thanks so much for showing us this place, Tony. I'll never forget this time we spent here with you," I said.

We all got situated in the cart and rode back to the Green Pier where Tony dropped us off.

"Bye, and thanks again," I said. He waved as he drove off.

"Didn't you think Descanso Beach was a good location?" I asked.

"It's a beautiful location, but I don't think it will be as compelling to the buyers as paintings that include some of these iconic structures. That's what people want to take home to remind them of what they saw in Avalon. Most people have never been to Descanso Beach."

"You are so right, David. Thank you for intervening and getting me back here. Good move!"

While we were standing there, I said,

"Hey look, there's that seagull again. Oh no! He just stole part of that man's sandwich." We both watched and laughed as the man swatted at the bird with his hat. While he was swatting, the bird grabbed the rest of his sandwich and flew up to the rooftop of Eric's where he happily feasted on his rubbery meal.

David and I arrived at the police station at 1:15 that afternoon. Della greeted us then asked us to wait a minute. Raj, Tom, and Jim were enjoying their Diego's burritos when Della informed them that we had arrived.

"Let them come in," I heard Tom say.

"Hi, they all said as Della escorted us into Tom's office."

"We got you both some fish tacos with chips, salsa, and guacamole. Is that okay?" Jim asked.

"Oh, it's more than okay, that's perfect, our favorite," I responded looking at David who was nodding his head and rubbing his hand together ready to indulge.

"Did you get good paintings?" Raj asked.

"We sure did. Both of us were very pleased with the outcome."

"You're probably wondering why I called Raj this morning and wanted to see you again," I said.

"Yes, we were. What is it you wanted to talk about?" Jim asked.

"There are two reasons I called. First, as we discussed, it was to look at the handwriting samples of the timelines you've been collecting. But secondly, there was something that disturbed me about Nancy's behavior last night. It seemed to me as if she was putting on a big, phony show. I didn't buy her hysterical fifteen-minute-long crying jag. Did any of you notice, while she was making a lot of noise and fuss crying, there were no tears.

"No, I don't think any of us noticed that. She kept wiping her eyes, so I assumed it was to wipe away her tears," Jim said, but now that I think about it, you're right. There were side glances between the men as I continued.

"She was going through all the motions, scrunching her eyes, wiping her face, burying her head in her hands, making all sorts of crying noises, but there were no tears. Have you ever heard the phrase, 'don't let a good crisis go to waste?' I kept turning that phrase over in my mind last night. I'm not saying I think Nancy is the murderer, but I certainly think she could be capable of trying to get Randy and me to drop out of the competition leaving her the possibility of having a better chance of winning."

"Do you think she's good enough to win, Annabel?"

"No, I certainly don't, but she deludes herself in thinking she's way more talented than she is. She may have put a note on her own door to divert suspicion away from her while her real objective may have been to get rid of Randy and me. This is just a hunch," I said looking around the room to see how the others were reacting. They had put down their food, stopped eating, and were listening.

"That's interesting, Tony also had some suspicions about Nancy, but for other reasons," Raj said. So, if what you're saying is true, the notes may not have any connections to the murders."

I shrugged my shoulders and said,

"I don't know, but alarm bells were going off in my head as I watched her fake blubbering."

"It seemed sincere to us. She appeared to be terribly distraught. Her face was flushed and when I hugged her, and she was sweating" Tom admitted.

"You can work up a sweat putting on a big act like that. Women can pick up on phony crying in other women because we're all guilty of doing it ourselves. I could tell something wasn't legit. Oh, one more thing, the notes say, "YOUR NEXT!" The correct way it should have been written is "YOU'RE NEXT!"

"Yes, Raj saw that too. Well, that certainly gives us another perspective," Tom said. "Now to get to the first reason you're here, throughout the morning, the persons of interest had been dropping off their timelines. They certainly were a diverse group. None of them had the same perspective on what a timeline should look like, and since we weren't specific on their instructions, the possible suspects devised their own systems."

While Tom was talking, I was thinking. All my books on handwriting analysis were back home in San Diego. I wish I had them now, but I was sure I could give enough information from memory to be helpful to the police. When we all had finished lunch, we headed for the back room where the computers and much of the paperwork regarding the case was stored.

"Here you go Annabel," Tom said handing me the timeline with Asher Bloomberg's name covered. "As you can see, we've taped out the person's name. I'm not going to tell you who these timelines belong to, so you're not prejudiced before you start. What can you tell us about this handwriting?"

I took a minute examining the handwriting, I wasn't focusing on *what* was written in the timeline, but the *way* it was written and how it looked on the surface. Though I had made a practice of analyzing friend's handwriting at parties for fun, it had been a while since I had done that. Though I was concerned that I was rusty, I was pleased that I had retained most of the information. To begin with, I would be looking for the signs of a healthy, well-adjusted person so that he or she could be eliminated as possible suspects. Through our scripts we subconsciously express and demonstrate our emotions, character, social development, personal temperament, mood changes and more. Handwriting changes throughout life as people first gain control, mature, and decline with age. Those stages of life will show up in scripts. Most of all, I was interested in detecting certain danger signs that appear in the script formations of people who are prone to violence, dishonesty, emotional instability, sexual appetites, and perversions.

"I want you all to know that I'm focusing solely on handwriting analysis. I'm not going to be paying attention to the timeline. That's your expertise. This handwriting appears to be normal on the surface. The writer has small letter formation which is consistent with someone who has tremendous ability to concentrate and can focus for long periods on details. They're cautious, reserved, and precise. He or she keeps their thoughts and feelings to themselves. In other words, 'plays their cards close to their vest.' The slant is vertical, straight up and down, which means they're analytical, independent, reserved and cautious. The base line is straight, which means they persevere, are composed, orderly, emotionally stable, dependable, reserved, self-controlled and cautious. I see no red flags in this handwriting. I think this person is not dangerous.

"Would you stake your life on that," Jim asked. I smiled, shook my head no, and said,

"Jim, I wouldn't ever stake my life on anything, but it's my opinion that this person is okay. I would guess that this person is probably an accountant, a bank president, or someone who is involved in finance."

"Asher had been an investment banker before he had retired, and this now became a kind of game to the policemen. From that point on, all the men in the room were given the name of the writer I was analyzing. They wanted me to guess who it belonged to as a test to see if I was credible.

"May I have the next one?" Tom was impatient and wanted to keep the meeting moving. "He whispered to Jim, "This is Miriam Bloomberg's. She's an older woman who looks rather frail. That makes her less likely to be a suspect but let's see what Annabel can find." Though Tom didn't like to admit it, he was becoming intrigued.

"The slant inclines to the right, which means the person is extroverted, demonstrative, sympathetic, emotional, and sentimental. The letter shapes are full of garlands, meaning they're receptive, adaptable, easy to get along with, and peace-loving. The capital I is a stick figure, a sign of someone who is independent, culturally aware, mature, and lacks façades. The baseline slants slightly upward suggesting an ambitious, optimistic, and active person. If you look at the overall appearance of the handwriting, it's fluid, well formed, well-spaced, and consistently neat. I don't think this writer would hurt a fly. This is the handwriting of a nice person."

"Do you have any idea who this could be?" Tom asked hoping to stump me.

"Well, I think it's either Miriam or Charlotte. But now that I think about it, it's Miriam. No one said anything, they just looked at each other.

"Will you please hand me the next one." Tom cupped his hand over Raj's ear and whispered, "this is Charlotte's timeline. Since she's a nurse, she probably knows a lot about medications and their effects. She was the one who gave Tony the sleeping pills that Alice got from Karla. Charlotte could have removed the contents, and refilled the capsules with sugar, then given them to Tony who was having trouble sleeping because of his cancer. She seems nice on the surface, but she and Alice both had contact with the Temazepam capsules. Remember, Sybil is her daughter. Revenge is one of the important motivations for murder," Tom was now checking his watch.

"Once again, I'm trying not to read what the timeline says so they don't influence me." I looked at Tom for affirmation. He nodded his head but was still somewhat skeptical.

"The baseline says this writer is dependable and straightforward. The slant tells me they're sympathetic, emotional, and sensitive. The pressure is light, revealing a sensitive, spiritual person. All the words are connected meaning they rely upon logic to build careful conclusions, so they're consistent and reliable. You can depend on this person. The upper zone is normal meaning they're primarily interested in intellectual pursuits and spiritual aspirations. Their conscience guides their actions. The jury is out on this one. On the surface, they seem fine, but a powerful conscience sometimes demands justice. But I can't see any red flags in this handwriting. Is this Charlotte's timeline?"

Tom looked at Jim, both were thinking that Charlotte had every reason to want justice for her daughter. Then Tom said,

"We're not going to tell you, so you don't start to eliminate people."

"Okay, that makes sense. May I have the next one?" I asked. Jim handed me Alice's timeline.

"Uh-oh, I said. Right away I see some things that are very disturbing. There is extreme angularity with heavy pressure indicating a bad temper with violent tendencies. The handwriting tells me the writer is aggressive, decisive, and energetic. Although they are analytical and logical, they are also rigid, inflexible and unyielding in their positions. They would rather argue than compromise. This writer will be disciplined, firm, and steadfast in their convictions. When their mind is made up, they won't be sidetracked from their goals. Look at the end strokes here," I said holding them up for everyone to see. "They are long with a club at the end indicating brutality, tenacity, and enormous energy. This person would make the perfect, military officer. This must be Alice's timeline?"

"Huh," Tom said, looking quite surprised.

"Do you think the writer is capable of murder?" Raj asked, as he leaned forward, closer to me in his seat. They all were leaning in now.

"Yes, I most certainly do, but we must remember, the military are trained to be killers. That doesn't mean she did it. There are thousands, maybe millions of military folks walking around and they don't kill in civilian life. My father was an ex-naval officer, and he adapted well to civilian life. The potential to kill in Alice is there. She certainly could have climbed Chimes Tower Road and had the strength to overpower Hillary, but I would check her timeline to see if she has a good alibi."

"That's very interesting, Annabel. I never put much credence in handwriting analysis, but what you're doing seems credible," Jim said. I may have won over Jim and possibly even Raj, but I could tell Tom was still skeptical.

"Okay, here's the next one," Tom said, as he handed me Nancy's timeline.

"Wow, this one has very interesting handwriting," I said. "To begin with, the baseline is unstable, up and down which means the person is careless, moody, and morally confused. They can be nice one minute then nasty the next, they're unpredictable." There were side glances going on between the two policemen. Jim raised his eyebrows and looked at Tom who pressed his lips together. Obviously, they knew something I didn't after their previously bewildering encounter with Nancy. "The slant is erratic, though they usually have a back hand slant, which means they are cold and selfish, it sometimes shifts to the right which means they can be emotional and sentimental, probably when it pertains to themself. This person is erratic and unstable. Someone with this kind of script lacks good judgement and common sense. Their moods swing between repression and expression. One minute they like you, the next minute they hate you. They're nervous, fickle, capricious, and undisciplined. Uh-oh, here is a downward, thick clubbed ending which is a sign of brutality, sadism, violence and cruelty. There are some dog leg endings which means they're vain, pretentious, dishonest, and cunning. The arcaded endings here means that when they feel threatened, they become secretive, protective, and hide things. The capital I is tall with an inflated upper loop indicating a vain person whose self-esteem can quickly vanish with adversity or when challenged. They love being in the spotlight and being the center of attention. There are erratic changes in the slant, pressure, and sizing. This is a red flag for a person who is willing to lie, defraud, forge, or deceive if it is to their benefit. Egad, this is a terrible reading! Whoever this person is, and I think I know, I would never trust them."

"So, what are you telling us? Do you think this person is capable of murder?" Tom asked.

"I'm not sure about murder. Other than the one thick, clubbed ending, I don't see a lot of violence showing up in this script, but I suspect that this is Nancy's handwriting because it describes her perfectly."

The men said nothing, but I could tell by the look on their faces, it was Nancy's.

"Though I doubt if she could murder anyone, I certainly think she's capable of putting the notes on our doors and Randy's backpack. Do you have those notes, Tom. I'd like to compare them to her handwriting on her timeline."

"Yes, here they are. What do you think?" Tom asked.

"Okay... she used cursive in her timeline. The letters on the notes are all printed in capital letters just like FORDS and NAZI. What is different from those, is the erratic changes in slant, and in pressure. The notes aren't written by the same person as the murderer. Off hand, I would say the YOUR NEXT! notes could possibly be Nancy's printing, but I would need more samples to give you a reliable answer. I would call her in for more questioning after you check the timeline. Oh, look here, she used the wrong form of 'your' in the message she wrote to you on the bottom of her timeline. What does that tell you?"

"I think it tells me you're on to something when it comes to Nancy," Tom said.

"As far as I'm concerned, I think Nancy wrote these notes. I can relax now that I suspect the notes weren't from the killer," I said.

"I wouldn't rule her out just yet," Jim warned.

"Jim, I've been studying handwriting since I was eight years old. I know how accurate it can be. The handwriting analysis, the misspelling, plus the fake crying tells me Nancy is the note writer, but somehow, I can't see her being as vicious as the murderer."

"Well, all you've told us certainly puts a different slant on this case," Raj said.

"I'd like to take a break now and go to Big Olaf's for some ice cream if that's okay with you?" I asked.

"Of course," Raj said. "I'll drive you both over there. What kind of ice cream do you like?"

"David and I both like their pistachio. How about you?"

"I like rocky road. Well, let's get going."

"Good grief, all that concentrating on handwriting is tiring!" I said as we tootled along the street. "It's so nice to be outside again. I was feeling claustrophobic."

"I can imagine. When we come outside with our ice cream, be careful. There's a nasty bird around here that steals food," Raj warned.

David and I looked at each other and smiled.

"Oh, we know that bird well. We've had a few run ins with that stupid fellow," David said as he took off his hat and showed Raj what remained of the white bird poop. "He got a good piece of my sandwich too," David said.

Big Olaf's was a very popular ice cream shop, so we had to stand in line waiting for a while. Because we were with Raj, the counter girl gave us all extra big scoops and Raj made sure she got an extra big tip. We took our ice cream to a bench near the Spanish style, white stucco archway that read "Via Casino." I liked spending time with Raj now. I liked the sound of his deep voice, and though he didn't talk much, when he did, he had interesting and thoughtful things to say. He seemed to be very secure in himself and didn't need to prove how smart he was or dominate the conversation with the police. After all the insanity is over, I hoped we would keep in touch. Maybe we could occasionally meet each other in San Diego or here on the island. I could tell he liked me, and I was going to make sure he knew I liked him too, though it was a little awkward with David there.

"This is so pleasant sitting here with my best friend, and someone who could become more than a friend." I looked at Raj and smiled. He got my not-so-subtle meaning.

"We'll have to do something about that after the festival is over," Raj said. I nodded, yes.

"I guess we better get back to the handwriting analysis," I said when we all had finished our ice cream.

Back at the police department, Tom and Jim were creating their own timeline and consolidating all the information the people of interest had given them on an all-inclusive whiteboard.

"Shall we get started again?" I asked. The officers nodded and handed me another timeline.

"Ooo... this is truly beautiful handwriting. The first thing I see is that it's shaded, thick and thin. This is a person who responds to color, light, and sound. They're in tune with the environment. This shaded type of writing is seen in artists of all kinds.

"You saw the name on this one, Annabel," Tom said.

"No, I didn't. But I know that this person has great control over their fine motor skills. You see this type of writing in musicians too. Whenever I read something someone has written, I analyze their handwriting. You have no idea what I can tell about perfect strangers from their scripts.

Raj whispered to David, "This is Randy's timeline."

"Look here," I said. "You see these long, graceful lead in strokes, this person has a good sense of humor." David was snickering and then broke into laughter, thinking of our funny afternoon encounter painting alongside Randy. "This writer has a love of body movement. They're probably a good dancer or a good athlete. They're also quite an exhibitionist."

"Uh-oh, another one," David said smiling and looking at me. I gave him a disgusted look.

"Here's a rebellious 'k'. You see, the lower-case 'k' is larger than all the other lower-case letters. That means the person has a rebellious streak. Whoever this is, they love to rattle people's cages. Their lower-case 't's' have a thick to thin cross bar that are slanted upward, meaning they are quick-witted and sarcastic. Their writing speed is fast and slightly inclined upward from left to right. That means the person is vivacious, and a rash escapist. This is an authentic person who is a bright, quick thinker. I can tell this is the handwriting of a real character. They're interesting, and what you see is what you get. This is a lover, not a fighter and I see no trace of violence in this handwriting. I think I know whose script this is. Is it Randy's," I asked.

"Yes, it's Randy's, how well do you know him?" Raj wanted to know. He could tell that I liked Randy, and I think he was trying to find out if he was someone with whom I could be interested.

"Raj, we weren't going to tell her who the writer is," Tom reminded.

"David and I had dinner at Diego's Sunday night with Randy, Mike, and Saul, and they were all 'three sheets to the wind.' On Wednesday afternoon, we painted the north Art Deco fountain with Randy and Saul. Those were the only times I spent any significant time with him other than casual meetings, but I would say, I know him well. I don't think there's much more to Randy than what you see. He's easy to know and very likeable." I looked at Raj to see his reaction to what I had just revealed. He was poker faced.

Jim thumbed through the timelines and pulled out the one compiled by Saul Katten, and said,

"This handwriting looks unusual even to me. I'll be interested to see what you learn from this one."

"Good eye, Jim. It certainly has a unique rhythm pattern all its own. Right off hand I would say that this belongs to a very creative person. There are three zones in handwriting, the upper, middle, and lower zones. The zones determine the balance of the person's ego development. The upper zone, or the tall letters like b, h, k, l, and d and t, deal with a person's fantasies, spiritual development, and intellect. The mid zone with letters such as such as a, c e, i, m, deal with the self, social development, and daily life. The lower zone includes letters such as g, j, q, and y, which are the letters with down strokes. The lower zone is where it gets interesting. It deals with the instinctual self, unconscious drives, security needs, sex drives, and material needs. In other words, we're dealing with the "super ego" in the upper zone, the "ego" in the middle zone, and the "id" in the lower zone. Do you see these sudden thrusts from the mid zone to the upper?" They all nodded. "This person has a keen mind and uses it to their advantage. They are on the hunt for creative ways to approach whatever they are attempting to do. This is an innovator, a brilliant mind who actively takes advantage of their impressive mental talents. This person is clever and loves to show off to everyone just how gifted they are, but they always need an audience. This is a trait seen in authors, actors, artists and musicians. I wouldn't be surprised if the person is gifted in at least one if not all those categories. Let me see what else I can find. Oh... the handwriting is vertical. It doesn't slant one way or another. That shows independence, inner strength, and reliance on their own good judgement. They are self-directed in their action. They aren't warm and fuzzy. This is a no-nonsense person who doesn't suffer fools gladly. Like David, they won't be polite to observers who want to tell them all about their aunt's best friend's daughter, who is a great artist. They will blow them off. This is a cerebral person, and I can't imagine that they would be so stupid as to murder anyone. They think they are way too special to do anything that would jeopardize their well-deserved star power," I said folding the timeline and handing it back to Tom.

"There are a lot of highly intelligent people who think they're so brilliant that they can outsmart the police. We hear about them all the time. There are many differing reasons for killing, sometimes it's a crime of passion, sometimes revenge, or sometimes for sex, but there's always someone who thinks he or she is smarter than everyone and can pull off a murder. But what would the motive for killing be? That's the question," Raj stated.

"Yes, that's the question. You've made some good points," I said.

"So, do you know who this timeline belongs to?" Tom asked.

"Is it Saul's?" I asked.

"Yes, it is," Jim said. "Good guess." Tom had given up on trying to keep anyone from revealing who the timelines belonged to.

Jim then handed me Mike Mitchell's timeline and said,

"We're almost done. We still have one more person who hasn't brought us a timeline yet, but we checked out his alibis and they are airtight, so we're not too concerned.

"Let's move forward. This is the second to last sample." Jim said.

"Well, let's see what this script will reveal to me. Right away I see that the slant is not in one direction. It goes back and forth from reclined to inclined. Sometimes it's vertical. This variation in slant tells me that this person is emotionally and socially unstable. The baseline is made up of words that begin up and move downward, like little descending steps. This indicates the writer fights against depression. The lower zone dominates, see these large loopy bottoms of his j, y, and g. That means the writer is driven by instinctual needs. It also means they bottle up their emotions. They are restless and need constant variety to fill an enormous need for money, sex, and pleasure. When their security is threatened, they become neurotic, lose control, and resort to infantile behavior. They are very emotional, very creative, and have lots of energy. These flamboyant endings suggest an immature person who is theatrical and manic sometimes. The stem of the lower-case d is a circle. We call that the magic circle that protects a neurotic person who is off balance in social situations. Mike is self-protective with deeply, hidden anti-social impulses.

"From what you're telling us, this is not a well-adjusted person, and you said Mike." Jim interjected.

"Yes, I can tell it's Mike's and no, he's not well adjusted at all. Many artists would fall into that category. Many of us are a little off kilter. Not me, of course, but my friend David's a real nut job," I said giving him a gentle push. Discussing Mike's handwriting was unpleasant for me, and I needed a little levity at that moment.

"So, what do you think, Annabel? Do you think Mike is a contender for the murders?" Tom asked.

"His handwriting certainly leaves me wondering. He could possibly be a contender. I wouldn't rule him out."

"Okay, we're almost done. I have just one more," Jim said as he handed me the last sample.

"Now this is some interesting handwriting," I said. Jim and Raj were glancing at each other, and I detected hidden smiles. "Look at the baseline, it's ramrod straight. That means this person is solid, dependable, and straightforward. Their slant is ever so slightly to the right. This person is analytical and independent. They trust their own judgement and though they are open minded enough to listen to other ideas, they make their own decisions. What we have here is a decisive person. The pressure is very heavy meaning they are active and have a strong ego and libido. They are aggressive and forceful. The spacing between words tells me the writer is a friendly extrovert who lacks inhibitions. The writing is large meaning that they place great importance on their own thoughts and actions. Look at the angularity of this writing, it's like a saw blade. This is someone who marches forward making forceful, incremental strides toward their objective. The sharp needle points at the top of the writing show a penetrating mind, a fast and intuitive thinker who delves deeply into situations and grasps facts instantly. This a critical thinker with an investigative mind who explores and digs for knowledge always asking questions and seeking answers. This is an intellectually hungry person who will not stop until he has found the answers to the questions. The lower-case "t' is crossed with a wavy flaglike stroke indicating a good sense of humor, graciousness, sociability, and good-natured gaiety. This person is a lot of fun to be around when they aren't focused on serious matters. It's difficult to discern if writing is male or female, but not in this case. This is a man's writing. As a matter of fact, I think that this is the handwriting of someone who would make a terrific police captain."

As soon as I finished my analysis, Jim and Raj were smiling and clapping.

"Are you still skeptical, Tom?" Jim asked. Raj was squirming in his seat pleased with the trick they had played on Tom.

"Okay, okay, you got me. That was surprisingly accurate." Tom said very pleased with himself and what he had just heard. He leaned back on his chair and had to catch himself when his chair almost toppled over.

Jim looked at me, smiled and said,

"Yes, that was a sample of Tom's writing, and you nailed it! As a matter of fact, you got them all correct."

"Well, what can I say," I said as I sat back in my chair gloating and examining my freshly polished nails. After we all had a good laugh, I said,

"Oh, look at the time. David and I need to get going. We would still like to squeeze in one more painting this afternoon before we go to Karaoke Thursdays at Portofino's."

Chapter 19: Karaoke Krazies

"Even though it's afternoon, I'm going to paint a sunset though I doubt if we'll get much of one tonight," I explained to David. "I'll rough in all the structures I see here and use the colors of this old photograph I took last year at dusk to get me started. I'll paint the scene like this photo with a rosy glow above the horizon, the lights of the Green Pier reflecting on the bay, and the white boats that became a gray blue color when the sun went down. The harbor lights reflecting on the water are beautiful and romantic as the night approaches. Sometimes, you must improvise and combine photographs with natural sources to get something better than what is available for you to see. Hillary used to have all these rules concerning what you could and couldn't do when it came to plein aire painting."

"It was ridiculous. I remember you used to call her and Karla the 'Plein Aire Police,' because of all their stupid rules."

"I never understood why they would want to put restrictions on how a person should paint," I said.

"It was all about power and control with them. Ironic, isn't it. It seems so silly when you look where it got them now," David said scowling.

"So true," I said. "You're such a good sport, my friend. You've stayed right by me for protection, painting whatever I chose to paint."

"Annabel, I'm not in this competition so it doesn't matter what I paint. Whatever you choose is fine with me because everything here is beautiful and you have such a good eye for composition. I'm so grateful to you for standing by me even though I shouldn't be here," David said.

"It's a win, win situation for both of us, isn't it, David?"

"Yes, it certainly is."

After David and I had been painting for a couple of hours, Nancy came by to see what we were doing when she told us,

"I'm planning to leave because of the note on my door. This festival is not worth our lives. Why have you decided to stay, Annabel? You must be crazy!" she exclaimed.

"I have David here protecting me and I'm not afraid." I knew what she was trying to do. I paused for a moment looking at her feeling contempt at first, then disgust, and finally, pity. What kind of person feels so inadequate that they need to resort to such despicable tactics. I never liked her before, but now, she was beneath my contempt.

"I'm on my own again. Do you mind if I set up here and hang out with you? I'd like to attempt inventing a sunset like you're doing." she said contradicting what she had just told me about planning to leave.

"No, go ahead." I was no longer concerned; I had never seen a sunset painting that she had done that was any good. She was capable of painting only what was in front of her, and the light of a sunset moved too fast for her to capture. She had no ability to use nature strictly as a reference and paint from her imagination. Most people don't realize, but there is a big difference between a painter and an artist, and I only understood that difference when I made the difficult leap across that vast chasm. Painters stray very little from replicating photographs as they are. They can't make changes that would improve a scene that is right in front of them... they copy. I know, I've been there. The artist can take bits and pieces of photographs, observations from nature, and what their eyes see in front of them and synthesize that and what has been learned from practice and a lot of trial and error. The painter relies upon the external elements for inspiration. The artist lets their imagination be their guide and foundation, and that's when creativity is set free. It took me a long time to figure that out and even longer to be able to do it.

"David, are you almost finished?" I said as I was beginning to pack up.

"I am. I'll pack up too. So, I guess you want to eat again at Portofino's tonight?" he asked.

"Yes, its karaoke night. That should be a lot of fun," I said.

"Oh no... you're not going to get me up on stage bellowing like a banshee. No, no, no!"

"Come on, it will be fun," I said. David put his hands up in stop position and backed away from me.

"Annabel, you know I sing off key. I was in a boy's glee club when I was in middle school and our instructor told me to mouth the words and not sing when we had a performance."

"No kidding, what a terrible teacher!" I said curling my lip.

"He wasn't a terrible teacher. I was a terrible singer, and he didn't want me to ruin the performance for the other kids. You've got to accept when you're bad at something," he said matter-of-factly.

"Nancy, will you be okay here by yourself?" I asked.

"Yes, thank you, Annabel. There are lots of people around, so I feel quite safe. Anyway, I'm almost done."

As David and I were walking to Portofino's, a rolled-up dollar bill came blowing straight toward me on the sidewalk.

"Look at this David, someone must have dropped their dollar." I bent down to pick it up. "This must be a good omen," I said as I opened it preparing to put it in my organizer purse. "Holy cow! I don't believe this... look," I said as I handed it to him.

"Woah! It's a hundred-dollar bill!" The shocked, happy looks on our faces said it all. "What a stroke of good luck. Someone's loss is our gain. I hope this belonged to some jerk," David said.

"Oh, it did. I just know it. There's going to be a hot time in the old time tonight, David. We're going to have Margaritas paid for by this hundred-dollar bill. Thank you, sweet Jesus!"

Save your money, Annabel. We can put Margaritas on Raj's tab."

"No, he's been so good to us. I don't want to take advantage of his generosity. That's the way I want to do this. You and I have been disciplined all week. We can have one night to ease up a little and enjoy ourselves. I'm going to call Raj and see if he can join us. We can treat him too."

"I suppose that would be a nice gesture," David said.

"Hi Raj, can you join us for dinner at Portofino's? Oh, that late. That's too bad. If for some reason you finish early, maybe you could join us for dessert. Okay, I hope we see you later."

"He can't make it?" David asked.

"No, he's busy doing computer stuff for the police. Here we are."

The Portofino Restaurant was packed when we arrived. I recognized some of the locals I met over the last few years while David and I were painting in Avalon. Apparently, karaoke was an activity where locals gathered on Thursday night to let their hair down. I also recognized several artists I had met at the many plein aire events I had attended. While David and I were in line waiting to be seated by the hostess, Mercy O'Reilly and Debra Paisley, the two artists who were at Raj's dinner party, came into the restaurant and were right behind us in line.

"Hi Mercy and Debra. How's the painting going?" I asked.

"Terrific, you've gotta try awfully hard to get a bad painting on Catalina Island. Hasn't the weather been gorgeous?" Mercy asked.

"Yes, it couldn't have been better. So... are you ready to exercise your vocal cords with karaoke tonight ladies?"

"You better believe it! We're both outrageous exhibitionists," Debra said, striking a pose. "How about you?"

"I wouldn't miss it for the world. I'm a singin fool. My friend David, on the other hand, refuses to make himself look ridiculous. You remember my friend David, don't you ladies?"

"Of course, hi David. Since seating is going to be tight tonight, why don't we all sit together. Maybe we can even convince David to sing along with us," David scrunched up his face and shook his head. It was definitively a NO!

The hostess recognized David and I as Raj's special guests and immediately found a table right by the stage and the karaoke machine for all four of us. Portofino's was a high-quality restaurant, but tonight, it was noisy, and it was still early. There was a different class of patrons who were here for karaoke night.

"Wow, you guys have clout. Look where they put us, and they seated us right away," Mercy said.

"Yes, we do. It's like they say, it's not what you know, but who you know," I said shining my nails on my blouse."

"Oh, excuuuuuse me," Debra said, giggling.

As I looked around, all the people that were persons of interest with the police that I knew were here. Tony was at the bar talking to one of the artists in the festival. Randy, Mike, and Saul were a few tables away. Nancy was now with a group of female artists, and the Bloombergs were with Charlotte and Alice. Knowing what I know now after analyzing their script, I will certainly see some of them from different perspectives. That's the problem with handwriting analysis. It opens a window into people's heart and character. I know secrets that they have kept hidden and are deeply buried in their souls.

The cocktail waitress was dressed more provocatively than usual, probably anticipating big tips from people who were to become a little tipsy or flat out drunk as the evening progressed.

"What would you like to drink tonight, Annabel and David?" she asked, getting ready to take our orders.

"We're going to have margaritas, but we would like to have payment for our drinks separate from our dinner. We'll pay cash for the drinks," I said. The cocktail waitress nodded her head.

"Debra and I will have the same, but we would like our own separate checks for dinner and drinks tonight."

When the cocktail waitress left, Mercy said,

"What do you think about these murders? Do you think we're safe?"

"I don't think so, Mercy. I think we should be careful not to be anywhere alone. Are you two sticking together and checking in regularly at the pier?"

"We certainly are. Have you heard any more details about the murders?"

"I probably don't know much more than what the police officers told us at the 'Meet and Greet,'" I said. That wasn't true, but I was determined to keep everything I had learned a secret.

"Mercy and I heard there are two killers on the loose. I wonder if they are working as a team?"

"We haven't heard anything about that," David said. "The police know what they're doing. I'm sure they'll catch him soon."

"So, you think it's a man, David?" Debra asked.

"I don't know. I guess I assumed it was a man because men tend to be more violent than women... but I have no idea. We don't know anything about that. I'll bet the police don't even know that either."

When the waitress arrived to take our orders, David and I decided to try the salmon for a change. Our artist friends split a salad.

"Have you been up Chimes Tower Road where the first murder took place?" Mercy asked.

"Yes, David and I were painting in that area the following afternoon. We saw the police and the yellow police tape but had no idea what had happened."

"Ooo," Mercy said shuttering. "That gives me the creeps. I wouldn't go up there now if you paid me."

"But that's where all the best locations are. Don't think about what happened. Block it out of your mind and just paint." As I was talking, I realized I was lucky, I could focus on painting no matter what was happening. I was so glad I could tune out my emotions and get whatever job I was doing, done.

"I'll never go back up the hill ever again. I don't even like to look at the Chimes Tower monument anymore," Debra said. All I can think of is Hillary lying dead up there, and I didn't even like her."

We all looked at each other and smiled shaking our heads. None of us had to say a word. We all disliked Hillary, but even though we were smiling, no one should have to die such a horrible death.

We were all ravenous. As usual, it took a lot of energy to create paintings. To our delight, our dinners arrived quickly, and we all dug in. While we were eating, David and I ordered another round of margaritas. The people in the room were becoming increasingly boisterous as their voices had to be raised to be heard over the noise. Dishes were clattering, glasses were clanking, and the speakers and equipment were banging, as they set up the karaoke machine. Thursday night at Portofino's was alive and happening.

"May I have your attention," the restaurant manager said as he took the microphone. Ouww, it whined as he tried to adjust it. "Who will be the first to start off the karaoke tonight," he asked. Right away a few of the local girls got up on the stage as the manager handed them the microphone. By the way they were handling themselves and the applause they were receiving, I could tell that they had done this before. The music began and there was more applause as the beginning strains of "Don't Stop Believing" by Foreigner began. The three girls began singing and motioned to the audience to join in. They were just terrible, off key, forgetting the lyrics, and clearly under the influence, but it didn't seem to matter. The audience loved them. They followed up with, "These Boots Are Made for Walkin," originally sung by Nancy Sinatra, then "Be My Baby" by the Ronettes. The crowd went wild, clapping and banging their feet on the ground.

Next, a guy and two girls got up on stage and sang, "Sweet Dreams Are Made of This" by the Eurythmics, "Stand by Me" by Ben E King, then the guy took the microphone and sang "My Way" by Frank Sinatra. A lot of the audience joined in. There was more applause and stomping.

"Okay girls, It's time for the 'Artofficials.' That's the name I've given our singing group," Get it?" I asked.

"Hey, I like that, it's cute," Mercy said, as she, Debra, and I all stood up together.

We headed for the stage just as Raj was coming in the door. As soon as he spotted David, he joined him at the table sitting down as we walked onto the stage.

"Hi everyone," I said. "We've just named ourselves the 'Artofficials' because we're artists painting in the Plein Aire Festival. This is Debra (she made a bow), Mercy (she did a curtsy), and I'm Annabel. Are you all having a good time." I said, putting my hand behind my ear as if I needed to hear better.

"Yes!!" they all yelled back at me.

I leaned over to the manager who was working the karaoke machine and pointed to "I Wanna Dance with Somebody" by Whitney Houston. The music began and Debra and Mercy chickened out and didn't sing. Nobody cared if we were good, they just wanted to be entertained so I said,

"Wait a minute, hold it, hold it," I said putting up my hands. "Could you please start it again?" This time I sang it by myself. I don't know if I was good or the people appreciated my bravery. Maybe they were just drunk, but the applause and stomping were louder and noisier than ever. Some other people were on their feet standing and clapping. After the reaction to the first song, Mercy and Debra got braver being on stage, found their voices, and sang out. They were surprisingly quite good as we sang "Girls Just Wanna Have Fun" by Cyndi Lauper, followed by the old 50s song "He's a Rebel" by the Crystals. Three songs were enough, so I blew everyone kisses and we all took bows then went back to our seats to find Raj now sitting there with David. He got up and pulled out my chair. He was smiling and enjoying the revelry of the evening.

"You're a good singer, Annabel, and quite the entertainer. Good job!" Raj said as he pushed in my seat.

"I'm a real ham when given the chance, Raj. I'm so glad you were able to make it," I said trying hard not to slur my words. "Would you like a maragita."

"A what," Raj said trying not to laugh.

"A Mara... marageet, oh, you know what I mean."

"Yes, I do. No thanks, I just wanted to stop by to see you and David tonight."

"We're so glad you did," David said. "You'll never guess what happened to us on the way here. A hundred-dollar bill rolled down the street and stopped at our feet. Annabel insisted that if we were drinking a lot, we shouldn't have you pay for it. She didn't want to take advantage of your generosity," David told him.

"You didn't have to do that, Annabel. I was happy to help you enjoy your time here." Raj was clearly touched by my concern for him and gave me a hug.

"That was nice, Raj." I leaned over and gave him a kiss on the cheek. The "maragita" was making me bolder than usual.

It was late, and David and I needed to be up early tomorrow morning. We said goodbye to Mercy and Debra, and Raj gave us a ride home. I'm certain that he knew what karaoke Thursdays at the Portofino were like and planned to arrive to get us to our room safely.

"Goodnight Raj and thank you for all the nice things you've done for us this week."

"It's been my pleasure, Sweetie, goodnight."

We climbed the two flights of stairs and plopped into bed not bothering to do our usual bedtime routines. We were both too tired, and too blitzed. I normally stayed awake at night for an hour or so planning for the next day. Not tonight, I fell into a deep slumber. Several hours later I was awakened by David being sick in the bathroom. I got up to see.

"Are you alright, David?"

"I think I got some food poisoning. I feel terrible."

"All the drinks we had I'm sure didn't help either,"

"Probably not."

"Are you coming back to bed now?"

"Yes, I think I'll be okay now." He pulled himself up from the commode and stumbled back into bed.

"Alright, I hope you can get some sleep and feel better in the morning. Tomorrow's our last day of painting."

Friday

Chapter 20: Hangover

The morning light came way too soon. I shut off the alarm as quickly as possible hoping not to awaken David. Fortunately, he was sound asleep and didn't even hear it go off. I wasn't feeling so well myself. I had a headache, my stomach was upset, and my tongue was stuck to the roof of my mouth. I must have had three margaritas and I'm usually a one drink girl, and that was not often. I tiptoed into the bathroom and shut the door without making a sound. After taking my shower, I looked at myself in the mirror and was taken aback thinking, Whoa... you're gonna need a whole lotta makeup today girl. Since I was feeling so lousy, I decided that today would be a good day to get my framing done. All the frames and framing tools were in the closet downstairs and working there wouldn't disturb David. Though Friday was the last full day for painting, I just wasn't up to it. If I was feeling better later, I could get in another afternoon painting and a nocturn, but those would be my last paintings. On Saturday, I would have to get all my framed paintings to the Casino by 9:00 in the morning and select two of my best for judging. Last night was fun, but I won't ever drink that much during a plein aire festival again.

I quietly closed the door and walked down the stairs, each step pounding in my hungover head. It was another sunny day but way too bright for my bloodshot eyes to handle, so I put on some sunglasses though I was still inside. They didn't help much. I looked over the table serving the continental breakfast, but the only thing that looked good to me was the orange juice. Never-the-less, I filled up a paper bag with enough food for David and me if we regained our appetite at some point later in the day. The orange juice tasted good, so I poured another.

After saying good morning to Bonnie, I asked her to open the door to the storage area which contained my equipment. I found a secluded space in the lobby because I would occasionally be using a hammer on the frames, and I didn't want to disturb the other guests. I then began the tedious task of framing. Working was good for me because I didn't notice how lousy I felt quite as much when I was working. I had heard that if you keep hydrated, it helps you to deal with a hangover, so I kept alternating drinks of water and orange juice. By10:30 I thought I should check on David, so I went upstairs to see how he was doing.

"Hi, are you feeling any better?"

"No, it must be food poisoning. It must have been the fish I ate last night."

"I had the salmon too, and I didn't get sick, David."

"Maybe it was a different piece of fish." he said.

"Could be, or maybe you're just hungover, maybe both. Make sure you take some Tylenol and drink a lot of water. Do you think you'll be up to doing a painting this afternoon?"

"Not a chance."

"Okay, I'll continue doing my framing and I'll do some of yours too. If I sell most of mine, I'll ask Brianna Gleason if you can put your paintings in my space. If you're not up to choosing the paintings you want in the show, I'll choose what I think are your best."

"Thank you, Annabel. How are you feeling this morning."

"Not great, but I'll survive. I took some Tylenol, and I think it helped a little. I'm going to do an afternoon painting and if I can find someone to paint with me, I'd like to go up Chimes Tower for a nocturn."

"Only go if you're with a big guy, preferably someone you know."

"I will," I said hoping I could find someone.

"Promise?" he asked.

"Oh yes, I promise. Maybe Raj or Randy will go up there with me. I hope one of them will be available."

I went back downstairs and continued framing my paintings. My fingers were getting sore from being stuck by the wires for hanging when I twisted them onto the back of the frame. I didn't feel well enough to frame all of David's paintings, but I managed to frame the ones I thought were his best. We would have a little time tomorrow morning to frame them all if we both worked. Instead of climbing the stairs again, I called David on the cell phone.

"Is there anything I can pick you up at the store? "

"No, I have Tylenol with me, and I took two. I'm drinking a lot of water which is all I can do now. Go on out and do your afternoon painting. Just stay in the busy areas."

"Okay, I'll do that. Feel better," I said.

So, what am I going to do now? I thought. It was a little past noon when I walked out of the hotel and down the street toward the Green Pier. The pier was directly across Crescent Ave continuing in the same direction as Sumner Avenue out over the water. Paintings with water in them sell the best and I think they're the most successful for me, but when I turned and looked at the Glenmore Hotel, I had another idea. It was a beautiful structure with an interesting tower that jutted up above some unusually shaped trees. This is it! I'll do another street scene. I thought. The Glenmore was an iconic building and an important part of the history of Avalon. I also liked being close to the hotel if I needed anything. I explained about David's and my hangovers to Bonnie and asked her to let me store our continental breakfasts in the hotel employee's refrigerator... She agreed. There was also a water cooler and a bathroom in the lobby, and I was planning to use both... a lot.

The sky was a deep, cobalt blue, and the bright yellow hotel "popped" by contrast. The scene was brimming with color. There was a bright blue awning over the hotel entryway, a red pizzeria with a red and white striped awning next door, and a white bench with bright green slats which were the same color as the Green Pier. There were cars and golf carts parked on the street and people were walking along, coming and going. It all added up to the makings of a cheerful painting. When I first began, only a few people stopped to watch, but as the painting progressed, a crowd began to gather. There were lots of questions flying my way, and since I knew that I wouldn't be irritating David, I decided to interact with the people who were watching.

"How long does it take you to mix all those colors?"

"About five hours. Everything you see is premixed except for the colors along the back of my 18" long metal paint box."

"Where can you buy a metal box like that? I've never seen any like that in the stores."

"You can't buy them anywhere. I had it specially made by an airplane fabricator and he's long gone now. If you want something similar, you can make one yourself from cardboard. That's what I did for the prototype. The airplane fabricator copied my original cardboard box in metal."

"Have you thought about copyrighting the box and selling it?"

"No, it would be a lot of effort, and I don't think there are enough plain aire painters that would make it worth my while."

"Don't all those colors dry out?"

"I usually store all this paint in the freezer after I'm done for the day. It lasts about a month. Then I scrape what's left over and smoosh it together making all these wonderful gray tones," I said pointing them out to the spectators.

"How long have you been painting, Annabel?"

"I got my first set of oil paints when I was six. You're never too young to begin, but I suggest young people should start with watercolors. These are toxic. That's why I wear gloves."

"When did you decide to become an artist?"

"When I was five. My kindergarten teacher looked at my painting done in poster paint and said, 'Oh, we have an artist in the class.' The next day I was studying the formation of bushes and trees along the road on my walk to school, and I thought to myself, 'You're going to be an artist when you grow up' and I was serious."

"Is there anyone in your family who is an artist?"

"Yes, my mother is an amateur artist. She's very good, though untrained. My father's side of the family has had several professional artists going back generations."

Tony had now joined the onlookers wanting to see what I was painting. I spotted him in the crowd and waved. He tipped his hat.

"Now this is my favorite finishing touch. I'm going to paint some American flags even though they're not actually here. I paint them because they'll look nice with the red and white striped awning, they'll add more bright color, and most of all, I love our flag." Unexpectedly, some people who were observing applauded. A few minutes later, I said,

"Thank you everyone for your company, your questions, and your interest. I'm done now and am going to pack up. I hope to see you all at the Casino tomorrow. Enjoy the rest of your day." Once again, the people applauded. I took a bow, and said, "Thank you." That was so nice, I thought. I enjoyed interacting with those folks. Painting can be such a lonely activity, but today I truly did enjoy the company and being appreciated.

Several people came over to me as I was cleaning up and said they wanted the painting. I told them the first one who comes to me will have the painting, so make sure you get to the Casino early. One lady thanked me and said,

"Most of the time the artists here don't want to be disturbed. It was nice of you to explain things to us."

"It was my pleasure," I said with a smile.

After everyone had left, Tony came over and said,

"That was a good painting. You certainly were patient with all the questions. Most of the artists I observed give a one-word answer and clam up. They clearly don't want to be bothered. Some are snippy and rude, but you treat the people so courteously."

"Thank you, Tony, I appreciate their interest. I'm trying to communicate something and it's good to get a response. I saw you last night at Portofino's. Wasn't karaoke night fun?"

"It was, you were certainly having a good time."

"Yes, I was, but I'm paying for it today."

"I enjoyed your performance last night. You're also a good singer!"

"I was sloshed, so I have no idea if I made a total fool of myself. I was having such a good time, I didn't care."

"I could tell... that you were having fun, I mean."

"Where's your friend David?"

"Food poisoning or a hangover... maybe both. I'm on my own for the rest of the day."

"In that case, would you like to meet me at Portofino's for dinner tonight?"

"I would, but I may have to leave early. If I can find Randy Creighton, I'd like to go up to Chimes Tower Road to do a beautiful nocturn. That would be my last painting."

"Aren't you afraid to go up there after what happened?"

"I won't be if I have a big guy with me."

"I'll take you up there after we eat, if you like. That way you won't have to climb the hill with Randy. I don't think he has a cart, but I do."

"That would be even better. I certainly would appreciate it, Tony, but are you sure you won't get bored sitting in the cart for a few hours?"

"Are you kidding, with you? You're very entertaining, besides, you need someone to protect you with all that's been going on these past few days."

"Yes, that's true. Thank you so much, Tony. I made David a promise that I would only go up there if I could find a big man to go with and now I have you. Let's do it! I'm going to pack up and go into the Glenmore for a while. Shall I meet you for dinner at Portofino's at 6:30?"

"Why don't I pick you up in the golf cart at 6:20?" he said.

"Okay then, I'll be out in front at 6:20."

I packed up and went into the hotel to retrieve my muffins, apples, and orange juice from the refrigerator. Fortunately, I was finally beginning to feel better and with just a snack now and a light dinner later, I think I could handle painting one more nocturn. I was lucky to have run across Tony and nice of him to offer to stay with me while I painted. Waiting for a few hours for me to finish painting I think would be boring, but Tony seems to be so lonely and wants company. It was a win, win situation for both of us.

I checked on David again, and though he was feeling a little better, he would be in bed for the rest of the day. I went back downstairs and continued to frame his paintings. When it was almost time to meet Tony in front of the hotel, I gathered up my equipment and went outside.

"Hi Tony, you're very punctual. You're right on time."

"Yes, punctuality has become a habit with me."

"Oh really, why is that?"

"Just the lifestyle I've led for many years."

"I see," I said. Well, it's a good habit to get into. I like punctuality and try to avoid keeping people waiting," I said as I lifted my equipment into the back of the cart. We headed down Crescent Avenue and looked for a parking spot close to the Portofino.

"Oh shit! I hate the way people park around here. They can be so inconsiderate. Look at this lousy parking job! People have no concern for how the way they park effects other people."

"No, they don't!" I said not wanting to challenge his statement. That was an overreaction to something rather insignificant. I guess he must have his reasons, I thought, so I let it go. "Have you had a nice day, Tony?" I was hoping to change the subject and divert his attention from the parking situation.

"I certainly did. It was a beautiful day, and I walked around looking at the wonderful art all you gifted artists create. Artists are a breed unto themselves. They become so engrossed in their own work that they are oblivious to what is going on around them. Most of them don't speak to anyone while they're working. You're different Annabel. You're such a nice girl. I was so impressed with the way you liked interacting with the spectators."

"I do, but my friend David gets distracted when I or anyone else chit chats. Because of that, I usually keep my interactions while I'm with him to a minimum."

"He's a typical artist, introverted and selfish. You shouldn't let him influence how you want to spend your day painting."

"Tony, I'm so glad to have a nice friend to paint with on a regular basis that I gladly make concessions for him... And you're wrong about him, he helps me with lifting heavy equipment, he usually goes along with wherever I choose to paint, and he's so kind and considerate to me and others in many ways."

"I'm glad to hear that, Annabel. I'd hate to see anyone push you around."

"No, that will never happen. You see this muscle," I said bending my arm making a fist. No one would dare challenge me with this show of awesome physical strength." Tony and I laughed knowing my puny muscle wouldn't impress anyone. "But you're right about my liking to interact with people. That's part of the fun of painting. I hate to admit it, but I do like all the attention."

"I can see that. When you were doing the karaoke last night, you took over. You like to be in control, don't you."

"Doesn't everyone? I asked.

"No, some people like to be taken care of and give up their control to a more dominate person. I'm sure you know people like that."

"Yes, you're so right, understanding people is a lifelong challenge that can never be solved. Churchill once said, 'The human mind is a riddle, wrapped in a mystery, inside an enigma.'"

"You have no idea, my dear."

Though it was Friday evening, the Portofino Restaurant wasn't crowded probably because many of the customers were slightly hungover. I looked around as we waited for the hostess and didn't see any of the people and artists with whom I was acquainted. Most of the artists were probably in their hotel rooms framing what I'm sure they all believed were masterpieces. The hostess who recognized us immediately greeted us by name. She escorted us to Tony's favorite table which was at the front of the restaurant by the window.

"I like this table because you can watch the boats."

"Me too. What is it about boats that is so compelling?" I asked.

"I think boats are a form of escape. The ocean is so vast, and a person could disappear out there and never be found. We're all trying to escape from something, don't you think?"

"Yes, I do, Tony. Painting is a form of escape, so is singing, or playing an instrument. Our imaginations allow us to temporarily leave our bodies and experience a form of freedom we don't experience when we're living in the real world."

"What are you trying to escape from, Annabel?"

"I think I'm trying to escape from life becoming too routine and humdrum. I want to live a life full of excitement and adventure. That means sometimes I must take risks, because when I push my boundaries, that's when I learn and grow."

"But taking risks can be dangerous, especially for a pretty young girl like you."

"I guess so, Tony, but I trust that God will protect me. One way or another I know I'll be fine."

For a moment he stared at me nodding his head, saying nothing.

"What are you thinking, Tony," I asked.

He shuttered, as if he was shaking himself out of a trance.

"Oh nothing, I'm hungry, I'm going to flag down the waitress."

When she came by to take our orders, Tony ordered his usual steak, a twice baked potato, and some vegetables. I had never known anyone who liked steak so much in my life. I was feeling much better and ordered the Cobb salad.

"Tony, you certainly do like steak. Do you also eat fish or chicken?

"Not this week, no, not this week."

"Why not?" I asked.

"I guess I'm feeling like a Neanderthal this week."

I didn't know Tony well, but tonight he seemed distant and cryptic again. Possibly he was trying to come to terms with his own mortality. I wondered about the prognosis for pancreatic cancer. I knew it was almost always fatal, but I wondered how much time he would have left. I decided to do something nice for him tonight.

"You've been so nice offering to buy me dinner and staying with me while I paint. May I at least buy you dinner tonight, my friend."

"Oh no, not a chance! I would never let a woman pay for my dinner."

"Well, okay then." I was surprised at his response. Many men like to have a break from always being the one who pays.

For reasons unknown, our dinner was held up and took a while before it came. I was hoping to finish quickly to get an early start on my painting, but it was not to be. I didn't think it would be polite to gobble down dinner since Tony was treating me. When we finished Tony asked,

"Would you like some dessert?"

"No, it's almost 7:45, I'd like to get set up while there's still a little light."

"Oh, you must try their bread pudding, Annabel, it's wonderful."

"I certainly love bread pudding, but I'm still a little hung over and I don't think I can eat another bite."

"Okay, I'll need to use the bathroom before we go."

Good Idea," I said as we both headed for the restrooms. Tony was in there for about fifteen minutes. I wished he would hurry because the delay would cause me to have to set up in the dark. I had my miner's light, but there was a steep slope next to my chosen location. I would need to be extra careful not to get too close to the edge. Tumbling down that slope would be catastrophic. Tony didn't seem to be in a rush even though I thought I had made it clear to him that I needed light for the set up. Maybe he wasn't feeling well. The ride from the Portofino up the hill in the old golf cart took us less than ten minutes. As soon as we got to the location, Tony turned the cart around, pulled over, and turned off the cart lights.

"Tony, could you please keep the lights on until I've set up my easel?"

"Oh, yes of course, force of habit."

With my miner's light to guide me, I found a flat spot in the dirt just off the side of the road. It was about 8:15 that evening when we arrived. I cautiously looked over the edge of embankment, and though the sight didn't unnerve me during the daytime, it did in the dark. I couldn't see much of anything that lay below, and I was going to need to be extremely careful not to get too close to the edge. I worked at getting set up as quickly as possible. The air was cooling down now that it was dark and I hoped it wouldn't get chilly. If it did, I had a sweater.

It was a beautiful night. The air was a clear ultramarine blue, there were millions of twinkling stars in the sky, and the moon was a perfect sliver of a silver crescent. Beyond the murky darkness of the downslope, it was all there, the glittering little town nestled beneath the stars. The lights of the Casino, the Green Pleasure Pier, and the Holly House reflections glimmered on the water bringing the whole scene to life. There were gentle silver waves breaking on the shore, and many little boats all in rows settling down for the night in the harbor. This was my perfect vision of Avalon. If I could capture the essence of this image, I could hit the jackpot. Tonight, I could be creating my award-winning painting. I got right to work.

"Look, Tony, isn't this the most beautiful scene you've ever seen?"

"Yes, it certainly is."

Chapter 21: Timeline Eliminations

At police headquarters Jim finally got the warrant he was waiting for to go into Nancy's room. When he got to her room, he looked around and in the desk drawer he found a note pad with the same kind of paper on which the threatening notes were written. On the pad was a deep impression left by a pen. By holding it up to the light he could see, "YOUR NEXT!" Annabel and Raj noticed Nancy's timeline message said, "*Your* all working so hard to try to find the person who is threatening me. Thank you from the bottom of my heart." That was the same grammatically incorrect form of *your* used on the threatening notes. With all the new evidence, they decided it was time to call her into the station for questioning. When she arrived, they tried to keep it informal hoping she wouldn't panic and lawyer up.

"Nancy, we're trying to understand the reason someone would write the threatening notes to y'all. So you told us you thought it could be another artist who thinks you're in contention for the best of show award?"

"I didn't want to say that because I thought it would sound arrogant, but yes, I'm sure that's the reason."

"Do you think Annabel and Randy are also contenders?"

"They could be. They're both reasonably good."

"What about Karla and Hillary? Do you think they were possibly killed by someone who wanted to win some of the prizes?"

"Why are you asking me all these questions! How should I know?" she said with a sharp tone.

"We're just trying to find a motive for why someone would want to hurt the artists."

"How should I know, I'm not the police! That's your job," she said becoming increasingly agitated. "Now if you don't mind, I need to get back to work." She was beginning to get up to leave, when Captain Tom said,

"Just a few more questions, Nancy. Please bear with us." Tom was trying to de-escalate the situation. "Do you think it's a crime to write threatening notes to people?"

"I don't know. You're asking me all these stupid questions," she said raising her voice.

"Let me show you something." Tom opened his desk drawer and took out the note pad and said, "This is the note pad we found in your room." Her eyes widened as she began to realize, she was in trouble.

"So... what difference does that make? Lots of people have that brand of note pad. I got it in the Vons market here on the island."

"Yes, lots of people have this make of note pad, but the one in your room at the hotel has an impression on it that reads, "YOUR NEXT!" Jim said.

"Well, then someone must have planted it in my room."

"Nancy... give it up. We're not going to press charges because we've got bigger fish to fry, but we know you planted those notes on the best artists hoping that they would leave the island fearing for their lives. You were trying to eliminate what you saw as your competition. You put a note on your door as a ruse hoping that your being threatened as well would give you an alibi. Sorry Nancy, it didn't work." With that she burst into tears and started hysterically crying again. "We've been down this road once before, haven't we, Nancy? The problem was, strange as it seems, when you cry there are no tears. We're not buying your act this time." Jim stated.

"What are you going to do with me? Are you going to tell the other artists what I did?"

"Maybe you should have thought of that before. That was a nasty thing to do, and it distracted us from the real situation endangering lives." Jim said.

"Please don't tell anyone. Randy and Annabel didn't leave the island. No harm was done."

"No harm done except for terrorizing two decent artists, and we were sent on a wild goose chase." Tom said.

"We'll decide later how we're going to handle this. Meanwhile, you can wonder and worry about what and how we're going to divulge this. You can go now, Nancy, but don't leave the island." Jim said.

Humiliated, Nancy left the station.

"That woman is a double wide livin, pork rind eatin, howlin hound dawg," Tom declared, pressing his fist against his mouth and puffing out his cheeks. "What a piece of work. Do you remember the Tonya Harding/Nancy Kerrigan rivalry? Women will engage in the most despicable acts simply to win a competition."

"Better be careful, Tom, the" Male Chauvinist Police" will get you if you say things like that," Jim warned. Tom shook his head in disgust.

"We didn't even mention how she used 'your' improperly." Raj said.

"We didn't need to. She caved in as soon as she realized we were on to her. We caught her admission on the camera Raj set up for us. Now that the note writing crime is solved, let's look at the timelines for the murders," Jim said.

"We'll begin with Sunday night, the night of Hillary's murder. Tony, Nancy, Karla, and Hillary were having dinner at the Portofino Restaurant. Nancy, Karla, and Tony were drinking a lot of wine, Hillary wasn't. Hillary left to go up Chimes Tower Road around 8:00 that evening which would be around twilight. Tony stayed with the two remaining ladies till they left around 9:00 p.m. to walk to the hotel. The desk clerk said when she saw Karla and Nancy come into the hotel around 9:15 pm. They went right upstairs to their rooms."

"Bonnie, the desk clerk, said Nancy and Karla stayed in their rooms Sunday night. Nancy asked Bonnie to come to her room because she was having trouble with the TV around 9:45. Hillary's watch was broken at 9:45 p.m. There wouldn't be time for her to have anything to do with Hillary's murder. After the women left, Tony stayed and finished his drink till around 9:30. He then went upstairs for about 10 minutes to use the bathroom. He came down to the bar and had drinks and talked to Henry till midnight, only leaving to use the bathroom which he did a few more times. Several people verified his story. Nancy and Tony have alibis and of course, Karla was killed the next evening so I think we can eliminate her." Jim surmised.

"But Tony had a cart, so it's plausible that he could have gone upstairs and down and out the back Portofino entrance. It took me seven minutes to drive up Chimes Tower. Let's say it took ten minutes to kill Hillary and then seven minutes to drive back down to Portofino Hotel. He could then go up the backstairs and down to the lobby without being seen, then straight down to sit at the bar talking to Henry. He could have left, killed Hillary, and got back in about twenty-five minutes," Raj suggested.

"But what about the raincoat, gloves, and knife?" Jim asked. "When would he have gotten rid of those?"

"It could have been later that night. He could have gone out the backway, washed the raincoat and gloves and threw them in the trash. There's good access to the beach across the street by the Portofino where Tony is staying." Raj deduced.

"What did he do with the murder weapon?" Jim wanted to know.

"Remember the serrated marks we saw on Hillary's throat? He could have used a steak knife, washed it off, and left it on a table for the bus boy to pick up," was Raj's answer.

"That's a disgusting theory, Raj, but hold that thought till later," Tom said.

"Charlotte and Alice were also at the Portofino the night of the murder. Charlotte and Alice left a little after Nancy and Karla did, around 9:00 pm. They said they stopped to look at the water on the bench near the pier because it was a beautiful night and Charlotte's leg was hurting. They saw the Bloombergs while they were seated and got to their rooms a little before 10:00 pm, which was verified. And they don't have a golf cart," Jim said.

"David and Annabel were at Diego's the night of Hillary's murder. They ran into Randy, Mike, and Saul who David and Annabel say were plastered. The threesome asked Annabel and David to join them, which they did.

Annabel said the three men could barely talk let alone walk. None of them have a golf cart. Annabel and David left Diego's about 7:15, which was verified by the waitress. They then went to the Casino where Annabel said she painted a nocturn of the art deco murals in the Casino entrance. David sat and watched because he was too tired to do another painting. Annabel looked at the clock in the lobby when they came into the Glenmore and said it was exactly 10:35 pm, which was verified by the desk clerk. Annabel says her painting is proof of her whereabouts that night. They also remembered talking to Tyler, a fellow artist who has collaborated their story. They don't have a cart either," Raj said.

"The Bloombergs were at the bar of the Portofino for a while and had a late dinner. That was the night of Miriam's birthday, and they were celebrating. After dinner they decided to have a romantic walk by the water. They left around 9:30 that evening and walked along the Crescent Ave walkway. They said hello to Charlotte and Alice during their walk and went back to the Hotel Mac Rae a little after 10:00. Their story checks out and they didn't have a golf cart," Jim said.

Jim got up and slowly walked around the room then said,

"So that's our timeline evidence for Hillary's murders. Now for the Monday night timelines for Karla's murder."

"Aren't we going to reach some conclusions about Hillary first?" Raj asked.

"No, we need to do both to get the big picture. Y'all need to hear me out, I know this is complicated," Tom said.

"Raj again joined in the conversation and said,

"Annabel and David were with me all afternoon painting on my balcony on Monday. I then served them an Indian dinner after they were finished painting. They were with me all evening when you called me at 7:45 to join you up Chime's Tower Road. It took Ziggy and Corny around twenty minutes as they helped put the food away. They then drove Annabel and David to the Glenmore. Bonnie, the desk clerk verified the time and said they were in their rooms that night because she delivered for some extra washcloths to Annabel later that evening. She was in her pajamas and David was watching TV in his bed. That's an alibi for Karla's murder, wouldn't you agree?"

"Raj, cardinal rule, don't let your emotions color your judgement. We know you like Annabel, and I agree with you, but let's continue to keep her in the mix of persons of interest," Jim said. Raj just rolled his eyes.

"Let's move forward," Tom said. "Randy, Mike, and Saul were at the Busy Bee Monday night. They arrived and were seated around 6:00, had dinner, and stayed there having drinks till 11:30 that evening. When they left, they went to their rooms at the Atwater Hotel. Everything checks out.

"Now, there were two places that someone could have tampered with Karla's food or beverage, and that's the Portofino restaurant, or the

Glenmore Hotel. Nancy, Tony, Charlotte, Alice, the Bloombergs, and the three artists, were all at the restaurant. Nancy, Charlotte, Alice, Annabel and David were at the Glenmore. Tony was only there for a couple of minutes," Tom concluded.

"Yes Tom, but Tony was in their proximity for most their dinner and he had the greatest opportunity to tamper with Karla's food or drinks." Raj said.

"Yes, that's true and we must keep that in mind, but Nancy, Charlotte, Alice, Annabel, and David were at the hotel, and Alice had a key card to Karla's room. Someone could have entered her room, had drinks with her which they put the Temazepam in, then removed the glasses later. These are possibilities," Jim said.

"But Karla was very drunk and probably not in any condition to have any more drinks with anyone Monday evening. If she wasn't drinking anymore, there would be no opportunity to spike her drink," Raj theorized.

"That's good Raj. In that case, we must consider that , Karla gave Alice some of her Temazepam sleeping pills which comes in capsule form making it easy to put into someone's drink or food. Alice pressured Karla to give her the six pills because Tony was supposedly in pain and having trouble sleeping. Charlotte took the pills and gave them to Tony. That makes three people who had direct access to the pills," Tom concluded.

"Since Tony was the last person in the chain of events receiving the pills, wouldn't you say that's an important factor?" Raj asked.

"It could be," Tom said. But someone else could have removed the Temazepam and refilled the capsules with sugar by the time Tony got them. It's done all the time." Tom explained. He then put his chin down in his hand and sat quietly as he contemplated the situation. Jim then spoke up and said,

"Okay let me proceed, Alice had been rooming with Karla and still had the key card to Karla's room. She could have used it herself or given it to her grandmother, Charlotte. Here's something else to consider, The Bloombergs have a serious reason to hate Karla Streicher since she is the descendent of the Nazi, Julius Streicher. I still think it's possible that more than one person was involved. Since Karla was no longer a useful connection to the Bloomberg's art collection, they may have wanted revenge and could have been somehow involved. Alice, Charlotte, Nancy, Tony, and the Bloombergs were in locations where they could have had access to poison Karla's food or drink. Annabel, David, Randy, Mike, and Saul did not have access," Jim deduced. "We still should consider the possibility that there was collusion."

"We're going round and round here," Raj said. "Now we know that Karla was stabbed and slashed after she was dead. Annabel said she noticed dirt tracks on the rug leading in from the back stairs entrance to the hotel the morning after Karla was killed. The dirt tracks were heading in the direction of Karla's room. The dirt tracks weren't there when she and David went into their room at about 8:10 Monday evening when Corny and Ziggy took them to the hotel after my dinner party ended. Someone could have unlocked the door at some point that day or night and come into Karla's room much later to rape and disfigure her body after she was dead. They could have relocked the door and let themselves out the back entrance again."

"That's good, Raj, but how would they have gotten in her room unless they had a card?" Tom asked.

"Alice had a key card which she said had disappeared when she tried to open Karla's room. She could have thrown it away to get rid of evidence, or someone could have removed Karla's card from her purse that night at some point," Jim suggested.

"From what Annabel told me, the key cards were notoriously temperamental and difficult to use. Tony told us Karla had trouble getting in her room with her card. He could have helped her get in her room, helped her with the key card then put the card in his pocket. Nancy was already in her room, so she wasn't a witness. Tony was alone with Karla, and she was very drunk and may not have noticed he didn't return the card to her purse. It would only take a second for Tony to unlock the back entrance door. He could have come back in later when she was dead and then taken his time to do all those horrible things to her body." Raj deduced.

"Now Raj, we're trying to keep to our process of elimination. Let's stay focused on the timelines," Tom said.

"Before we go forward, Tom, I want you to know, I'm taking a closer look at Tony. Although you said he had an airtight alibi, all it would take was for a few people to get their time frames slightly off by five or ten minutes. He was with both Hillary and Karla on the nights they were killed. He has a golf cart and could get up Chimes Tower and back in less than a half hour. None of the other persons of interest had a golf cart. Yes, I understand Alice, Nancy, and Randy, Mike and Saul are physically fit, but they couldn't get up the hill and back and kill Hillary in less than an hour. I know Tony says he's ill and needs to stay close to the Portofino, but although you've ruled him out, I'm doing a background check on him. The report should be coming in momentarily."

"Okay Raj, it's good to double check. All the background checks we're doing should be coming in soon and we'll go over them. Now let's get back to the timelines," Jim replied.

Della had been listening to the conversation and decided to check to see if anything had come in concerning the background checks. Yes, there was something. It was Tony's.

"OH SHIT!" she said as she burst into the room and handed it to Raj with the results. Raj immediately handed Tony's long rap sheet to Tom. Tom then stood up as he read the shocking revelations.

"Tony had been released from prison four months ago. He was convicted of murdering his mother and given a life sentence but was paroled after serving twenty-five years for being a model prisoner. There was evidence that he had killed and raped three other women, but there was not enough evidence to convict him. Shit!"

"I've got to call Annabel," Raj said pulling his cell phone out of his pocket. The phone rang and rang and then went to voice mail. "Annabel, you must call me immediately, and wherever you are, leave and go straight to the hotel. Keep away from Tony!"

"Do you have her friend, David's, cell number?" Tom asked, an urgency in his voice.

"Yes, I do and I'm on it. Hello David, is Annabel there? She's not, where is she? Oh, no! I've got to go now," Raj said hanging up. "She's up Chime's Tower Road with Tony."

Chapter 22: The Dark Avenger

As soon as Tony and I arrived at the destination overlooking Avalon Bay, I set up my easel and began painting. I tried to keep Tony entertained as the evening progressed. He didn't seem to want to talk much about himself so I told him all about my family, friends, school, and anything I could think of to keep him preoccupied. Thank goodness I could both talk and paint at the same time. Though he didn't have much to say, Tony was in and out of the cart several times that evening standing behind me to see how the painting was advancing.

During one of those times, I noticed that one of the unusual buttons on his shirt was missing. I suddenly felt a rush of adrenaline as I realized, those were the mates of the bloody button that the police found at Hillary's crime scene. A cold chill ran down my spine and my hands began to tremble as what was occurring was now crystalizing in my mind. I was up alone on Chimes Tower Road, close to where Hillary had been killed with her killer. The images of what he had done to her flashed across my racing mind. How could I have been so blind, he was often in the crowd of people who were watching me paint. It wasn't that he was admiring my paintings, Tony had been stalking me and now he was about to make me his third victim. Somehow, I had to draw him out of the cart, so I could climb in and race down the road escaping this deranged lunatic.

"Tony, could you please hand me my sweater, it's gotten chilly." He didn't answer. Instead, I heard his footsteps behind me. I turned to face him. That's when and my miner's light caught the glint of a knife in his hands.

"Tony, where's my sweater?" I asked.

"You won't need your sweater now, Annabel."

"Why not, I'm cold," I said, now fully aware of what was taking place. My heart was pounding as I began to understand that Tony had been setting me up to be his next target.

"All you artists are alike. You're selfish, arrogant, bitches. You just use men and throw us away like garbage."

The light of my miner's cap was shining on Tony's face, and for an instant an image flashed before my eyes. It was the image of the man Sybil had shown me in the old photograph of the man she loved. It was the man she had been writing to while he was in prison and was seeing after he was released. Though the photo was of a man twenty-five years younger, I realized that was where I had seen Tony's face before. He had signed Sybil's photograph, Fred, and that was the name she had been calling him.

"Put out that light!" Tony demanded. I immediately obeyed.

"You're Fred, aren't you?" I asked. Every fiber in my body was on high alert. Keep talking, keep talking.

"Fred is my first name; Anthony is my middle name. I decided to get a fresh start when I got out of prison, so I now go by my middle name."

"I see, Sybil showed me your picture when she was writing to you. She told me how much she loved a guy named Fred."

"Did Sybil say that?" Tony said his tone softening.

"She did. She told me that many, many times." Oh please, God, let someone drive up this hill.

"I loved Sybil, she was the only woman I ever loved. I miss her every day."

"Did you kill Hillary and Karla because they were so horrible to Sybil?" I asked. Keep on talking, keep on talking.

"That's right. I did it and I'd do it again. I hated them."

"I understand, I hated them for what they did to Sybil too."

"It won't work, Annabel, you're reading from my old playbook. Don't try to con an old con."

"I'm not, Tony, I've known it was you all along and I didn't tell. Sybil saw something wonderful in you, and I wanted you to have a chance at a new life." As I was talking, I had been looking for an escape route, but I was blocked in by the cart, by Tony in front of me, and a range of tall bushes on each side of me. My only means of escape was not a good one. It was behind me, down the steep slope.

It's too late, Annabel, I was quite sure you knew I killed Sybil or were close to figuring it out. I like you, Annabel, you're a real nice kid, but you're too much of a liability. I can't take the chance of letting you go."

"No, I didn't know that, Tony. Why would you want to kill Sybil?" Keep him talking. Keep stalling for time.

"Because I had lied to her and told her I was innocent and framed for the murder of my mother. I told Sybil my mother had fallen down a flight of stairs. I told her the prosecutor was corrupt, tampered with the evidence, and lied to the jury. She believed me while I was in prison, but when I got out, she began seeing inconsistencies in my story and began to distrust me. She finally went to the Donovan Correction Facility where I had been imprisoned for twenty-five years. She was shown my rap sheet which included some information about three other women who I allegedly raped and killed."

"Did you do that Tony?" I asked.

"I did, and I told her the truth hoping that if I came clean, she would forgive me. Instead, she said she couldn't see anyone who could do such terrible things. I was devastated. I left and went back to my apartment because I didn't know where to go or what to do. I was lost. The longer I stayed there, the angrier I got so I went back to her house. I begged her to let me in just to talk. I told her I was a reformed man and would never hurt anyone ever again, so she let me in. We argued. She didn't want to see me anymore and told me never to try to contact her again. I became furious and went into an uncontrollable rage. I couldn't help myself; you see. I wanted to strangle her, to feel all the life being sucked out of her body, because that was what she had done to me. I realized if I did that, it would break the hyoid bone which wouldn't fit into what was now the plan I was concocting in my mind. I picked up a pillow from the couch and attempted to suffocate her. She struggled for a little while, and I was glad she struggled. She was getting what she deserved. She had hurt me so deeply, and I was going to get my revenge. When she finally became unconscious and I thought she was dead, I went to her studio, put on her artist's gloves and took several pairs of gloves thinking I might need them later. I got the gun she kept in the drawer of her living room desk. She was starting to revive, so I had to act fast. I cocked the hammer, placed her hand on the gun, put it in her mouth, and used her finger to pull the trigger. I then turned the gloves inside out so there was no blood on them and typed the suicide note on her computer. I wrote something like, 'Life is a deep dark cavern that I can't crawl out of. I keep sinking deeper into the blackness of the abyss. Being asked to leave my painting group was the final blow, I can't go on. There is no way out for me, and I must end this pain. Please forgive me. I love you all, Sybil.' I knew her so well. We had been writing and I was familiar with the phrases she used whenever she was feeling despondent. I then located the gold coins she told me she had been saving for many years. I managed to get her to tell me where they were hidden when I told her about the cancer. She wanted to help me with my medical bills until she found out about my background. I then wiped my fingerprints off everything else I had touched in her place and then left."

"Is Sybil's gold paying the bills for the hotel and all the dinners you've been buying?"

"I had plenty of money I took from other women long before I ever met Sybil."

"Are you aware that her daughter and grandmother are here on the island?"

"Of course, I am. Sybil had dozens of photos of them all around her house. I even went to her Celebration of Life."

"That was taking a big chance. Weren't you afraid someone might photograph you?"

"There were so many people there and I wore dark glasses and disguised myself so I wouldn't be recognized by anyone if I ran into them later."

"Why do you think Charlotte and Alice are here, Tony? I've been trying to figure it out all week. They never mentioned anything to me, and I'm sure they know who I am. They know Sybil and I were great friends. She loved you so much," I said hoping to hold his interest."

"We've talked enough." Even in the darkness I could see Tony expression change. His eyes became fixed as he moved toward me. I had to make my move now.

With every ounce of strength I had, I picked up my easel and shoved it hard into Tony's face and upper body losing my balance in the process. The force with which I shoved my easel caused Tony to stumble backward. He fell to the ground driving the knife deep into his side. He let out an unearthly howl and cursed me with a string of obscenities. I then watched as he clawed his way back to his feet and again began coming toward me. I scrambled to my feet and had no other choice but to flee down the steep embankment, my only way to escape his madness. My miner's light had fallen off and I had no way to see, but I descended the hill fleeing into the cover of darkness. All I could see on the hill was the dimly lit Chimes Tower monument, so I stumbled along on the slope slipping and falling into the blackness in my struggle to escape.

"It's no use, Annabel. You'll never get away from me. You're too small and the slope is too steep. You don't stand a chance," he wheezed.

Every second while I was trying to get away, I could hear his breathless gasping and his shoes crunching in the dry brush close behind me. I was tired and out of breath, but I had to keep going. I suddenly began slipping and sliding uncontrollably, down, down the slope cutting and scraping myself on whatever outcropping was on that hill as I fell. Then everything went black. I had fallen and slipped under something. I lay there perfectly still and in great pain without making a sound, trying not even to breathe.

"Annabel, come out, come out wherever you are. I'm going to find you," I heard as Tony sang his psycho song.

He was closer now. The wheezing and panting were growing louder. Should I get up and make a run for it or should I stay quiet and still. But I was growing terribly woozy and my muscles ceased to function.

Chapter 23: The Search for Annabel

Now aware of the dire situation Annabel was in, the police flew into action. Tom and Jim jumped into one vehicle, Corny and Ziggy in another, and Raj into his own car. The police put on their red and white flashing lights and sirens hoping they weren't too late. Tom immediately called the airport and got two choppers in the air headed for the Chimes Tower monument. When the police were nearing the scenic view where artists go to paint, they saw Tony speeding down the road in his golf cart.

"Stop, stop, I'm injured, help me, help me!" he cried as he slammed on the brakes.

"Where's Annabel," Raj demanded. "What have you done with her?"

"Please... you've got to help me. I'm bleeding to death. Help me!" he begged.

"Not until you tell us what you did with Annabel." Raj growled, getting out of his car and grabbing Tony's shirt in a rage.

"I don't know. She ran down the hill," he said as Tom slapped handcuffs on him and snarled, "Man, y'all better give your heart to Jesus now, because tonight your ass is mine."

"Jim, give me your flashlight," Raj ordered as he raced up the road to where they had found Hillary's body.

"Corny, Ziggy, go after him," Tom ordered.

By the time they caught up with Raj, he was out of his car standing by Annabel's smashed easel. Paint tubes and brushes were scattered all over the ground. It looked like the same scene he had just witnessed with Hillary's murder.

"Oh no," he grumbled. "Annabel, Annabel," he shouted repeatedly. There was no answer, not a sound. All was still until the faint sound of the choppers could be heard in the distance growing increasingly louder as they approached. Back and forth they flew with their bright lights focused on the hillside.

I see something," Raj said to Ziggy, he pointed then scrambled down the now illuminated downslope. There was a body. A pair of legs could be seen coming out from underneath a large hillside shrub.

"Oh no, Annabel," he groaned. His voice had become quiet now expecting the worst, but praying she was still alive and hopefully not horribly disfigured. From what he could see, there was blood all over the place.

*****

"Oww" I quietly moaned, putting my hand to my head. What are those loud noises and bright lights? I was confused and disoriented. Had I been unconscious? I didn't know. Then I remembered, be quiet... don't move or make a sound. Tony's coming to get you. Stay still, I thought. Then I heard a faint sound of a voice, but I couldn't make out who's voice. Oh, why am I so groggy? Who is that? Oh no... I hear his footsteps.

"Annabel, it's me," he said as he pulled me out from under the scraggly shrub that had been my hiding place. Blood was streaming down my face from a large cut in my hair, but I was alive. He gave a huge sigh of relief as he examined my head.

"Oh Raj," I said as he helped me to sit. I immediately reached for him and clung to him like a child. "Tony's the murderer," I blurted out. "He tried to kill me! It was horrible."

"We know, that's why we're here."

"How did you find out." I asked.

"We'll talk about that later; your head is bleeding badly," he said once again examining the injury. "We must get you to the hospital. Can you stand?"

"I think so." I tried and was a little dizzy at first. "I must have cut my head on something."

"I'll say you did!"

Ziggy had now joined us and was trying to help Raj get me up the embankment.

"Is she alright?" Ziggy winced as he looked at the blood covering half of my face and all down my shirt.

"I think so, heads bleed a lot," he said smiling and relieved. "I think she's just frightened and shaken. Who wouldn't be?"

"And very scraped up. I've got cuts everywhere," I said showing them my injuries. Raj just smiled with relief, but I could see his hands were trembling.

The two men helped me climb the hill to safety. When we reached the top, the area where Tony had assaulted me, I stopped and said,

"I've got to pack up my stuff." Corny had been waiting at the top of the slope and was in contact with the choppers. Now that I was safe, the choppers were told to return to the airport.

"We'll come back for everything later. We must tend to that wound." Corny demanded.

"No, you don't understand. This is my prize-winning painting. I must have it for the show, and I need my materials to do the finishing touches." I began gathering up my equipment but was too dizzy to continue.

"She's right," Raj said. You sit in the car, Sweetie. Ziggy and I will gather up all your things. Corny, find something to put on her head to stop the bleeding?"

"But Raj, I've got to put my painting in the carrier. I've got to!"

"I'll do it, but then you're going straight to the hospital... okay?"

"Okay." I said, satisfied that I would still have a chance to win the competition.

On our way to the hospital, Raj informed me that they had attained Tony's rap sheet. They learned that he had murdered his mother and probably three other women.

"The man is a psychopath, but his clinical diagnoses are antisocial and narcissistic personality disorders," Raj told me.

"That's horrible. Oh, I just remembered, I've got to call David." It's after midnight and David must be frantic. Hello, David, uh-huh, uh-huh. Yes, I'm fine now. I know he didn't explain anything to you, but there was no time to do that. I was up on Chimes Tower Road with Tony chasing me with a knife. No, I'm fine, but I hit my head on a rock or something. We're on the way to the hospital now. How are you feeling? Oh great! So you'll be able to go to the festival tomorrow then? Okay, I'll talk to you later. Bye."

"Is everything okay?" Raj asked.

"Yes, he was worried when it got this late. He called the station a few times, but they didn't know or wouldn't tell him anything. He figured I was probably with you, or he would have heard something."

It took about fifteen minutes to arrive at the hospital. When the receptionist saw the blood on my face, I was ushered immediately into the emergency room. While the doctor was examining me, he asked how I had gotten the injury. When I finished telling him an abbreviated version of the story, he told the nurses to clean up the wound on my head and prepare it for stitches. He was planning on numbing the area when I said,

"Just stitch it up. It will be over in a minute. No big deal." I saw Raj nodding his approval to the doctor.

While the doctor was stitching my head injury, he informed me that I needed to stay in the hospital that night for observation.

"That's impossible," I said. "I have to be up at the crack of dawn to put the finishing touches on my painting that I'm entering in the plein aire festival exhibition."

"You're not going anywhere tomorrow young lady. You're weak from loss of blood and you may have had a slight concussion so we can't take any chances. You'll need rest and quiet tomorrow."

"That's impossible, if I win best of show, that will make up for half my income for the entire year. I've been working like a dog all week and I'm not going to stop now that I'm on the one-yard line."

"You've experienced a great trauma tonight both physically and emotionally. After all that you've been through, it would be unwise to go anywhere until tomorrow afternoon. We really need to keep an eye on you. After that, you should take it easy for at least a few more days."

"He can't make me do that, can he, Raj?" I asked.

"Technically, no he can't, but you really should listen to him and do what he says." he said with a stern face.

"No, I can't, I must go back to the hotel tonight to get ready for the show tomorrow. You've got to help me!"

"Okay, I have a compromise, Doctor," Raj said. "What if Annabel stays here tonight, I sleep in the waiting room, and tomorrow I bring her back to her hotel. She can finish her painting quietly sitting down. Her friend David and I can carry her paintings to the Casino while she sits and watches. You have no idea how important this festival is to her, but I do. What do you say?"

"I don't think I've ever run across a more headstrong, determined young woman in all my years as a doctor, and I've met a lot. I won't be responsible if she has any complications. I'll check you out of the hospital in the morning if you promise to take it easy. Concussions can be very serious, and you can have lifelong complications if you're not careful," the doctor lectured.

"I promise to do exactly as you say, but I must be checked out of the hospital by 5:30 tomorrow morning because I've got to turn in my paintings to the organization by 9:00 am."

"I don't think you've heard a word I said, but I'm through arguing with you. I'll check you out by 5:30 tomorrow morning. She's in your hands," he said to Raj leaving the room shaking his head.

"I'll stay with you until they put you to bed, then I want to find out what's going on with Tony."

"Please don't worry about me, I'm fine... really I a.m. You go and find the others and thank you for everything. You're my hero."

"I'm hoping I'm more than that to you," he said with a smile as he lowered his voice and moved closer to me.

"You are, and so much more."

Chapter 24: Hospital Confessions

Outside Tony's hospital room, Corny and Ziggy were waiting while the medical team was giving him a transfusion because he had lost so much blood. Because his wound hadn't damaged any vital organs, and the doctor had stopped most of the bleeding, the police were then allowed into the hospital room to question Tony. Jim had brought his small tape recorder and was recording everything Tony was saying when Raj arrived.

"Tell us all about what happened the night you murdered Hillary," Sergeant Jim asked."

"It's very simple, I was hoping to get either Hillary or Karla alone Sunday night. I offered to buy a round of drinks for the women, knowing how greedy the two of them were. I had heard everything about them and knew they would try to take advantage of me, so I let them," Tony said shrugging his shoulders and smirking. "I then asked if I could buy them dinner, and of course they agreed. Nancy and Karla drank my fine wine to their heart's content, but Hillary had only a half glass. I poured drinks for myself but secretly emptied them into a planter that was next to me. I wanted everyone to think I was drinking a lot. While we were having dinner, Hillary revealed that she was going up Chimes Tower Road to do a nocturn. It couldn't have been better if I had planned it myself. Hillary left around 8:00 that evening while Karla and Nancy stayed with me till I paid the check around 9:00. The two of them then walked back to the Glenmore Hotel by themselves. I hung around for about fifteen minutes more, finishing my drink and allowing the darkness outside to set in. When no one was paying attention, I crept upstairs to my room. I was all dressed in black, and I put on a black raincoat. I stuffed a thin, plastic vegetable bag and some vinyl artists gloves into the pocket. I then went down the back entrance of Hotel Portofino to my golf cart parked at the bottom of the stairs. I climbed in and raced up Chimes Tower Road shutting off the lights of the cart before I reached the location where Hillary would be painting. I watched from the bushes for only a moment, then silently sneaked up behind her until she realized I was standing there. She was terrified when she first saw me but tried to hide it by asking what I was doing there as if nothing was wrong. I asked her 'why do you think I'm here?' That's when she saw the knife. She didn't even have time to scream before I attacked."

"Where did you get the knife?" Jim asked.

"It was a steak knife from the Portofino. That's why I kept having steaks every night," Tony said with a laugh.

"We thought it might be a steak knife, there were serrated marks on the Hillary's neck and where the knife entered," Raj said.

"Getting back to my story," Tony said casually. "I came up to her from behind and grabbed her, she struggled, but she wasn't strong, and it was easy for me to overpower her. I cut her neck, but it wasn't deep enough to kill her. She fell to the ground, knocking over her easel. I bent over her body and stabbed her in the eyes while she was still conscious. She tried hard to resist by turning her head, not wanting to lose her sight. Then I stabbed her repeatedly many times. When I finished stabbing her, I took a paintbrush of Sybil's that I had brought with me and with Hillary's black paint I painted her eyelids and eyesockets black. I then painted a smile on her face so that she looked like the Joker from the Batman movies. When I was finished, I threw Sybil's paintbrush on the ground with the other brushes."

"So why did you want to kill Hillary?" Raj asked.

"She caused Sybil, the love of my life to sink into a deep depression. Nobody treats Sybil badly and gets away with it," Tony growled.

"We noticed that one brush was a different brand than the others and that one had paint slopped all over it. All but three of the other paintbrushes Hillary had used were relatively clean," Raj added.

"Well, now you know why." Tony was smirking, proud that he had befuddled the police and obviously reveling in telling his gruesome tale.

"What does FORDS mean, Tony?" That question had been disturbing Jim from the moment he first saw Hillary's bloodstained sweatshirt.

"It's not FORDS, it's FOR DS. It means, FOR Dad and Sybil.

"So, Sybil is the main reason for these murders?" Jim asked.

"I'll get to that later." Tony was delighted to be controlling the confession.

"After I was finished with Hillary, I took off the bloody gloves and the raincoat and stuffed them in the plastic bag. I raced back down the hill and climbed the stairs to the back entrance of the Portofino carefully taking the bloody things with me to my room where I placed them in the sink. I then went down to the bar and sat talking to Henry until closing time as if I had been at the restaurant all along to give me an alibi. After that, I went up to my room and washed off the knife and stayed there till early in the morning. I then went down the back entrance stairs bringing my bag of bloody things to a dark spot by the ocean near the Yacht Club. I rinsed the blood off the raincoat and gloves and threw the raincoat in the trash. I didn't know what to do with the plastic bag and gloves but eventually decided to bury them in the sand on Descanso Beach. While I was there, I swam out deep into the water and discarded the shoes I had worn at the crime scenes. When I was having dinner with Karla and Nancy, I left the knife I had used and washed on the table and took another one to use on Karla. The busboy took it away and I'm sure it was placed in with the other steak knives." I did the same with the knife I used on Karla."

"So, some poor unsuspecting diners are using the bloody murder weapons to cut their steak," Raj whispered to Jim. "What a disgusting, dog."

"So, you admit you killed Karla too?" Ziggy, who was listening to the conversation from the doorway asked.

"Of course I did," Tony snapped. "You cops certainly are slow."

"How did you do it?" Jim asked.

"It was easy, I told nurse Charlotte I was having trouble sleeping because I was in tremendous pain at night, but she didn't have any sleeping medication. Though that bitch Karla didn't want to help me at first, Alice convinced her to give up some of her Temazepam pills. That couldn't have been better if I had planned it. Temazepam comes in capsules, so I simply opened all the pills and took out the powder. I deposited the contents into a small container I picked up at one of the little shops along Crescent Ave. The next night Nancy and Karla came back to the restaurant. It was Monday evening, and they probably were thinking they could freeload off me again, and I didn't disappoint them. I bought them drinks to start with. Nancy shared the wine with me, but Karla wanted Scotch. I kept ordering and pouring drinks throughout the night. Shortly after dinner arrived, Karla became loud and boisterous making a big drunken scene hanging spoons on her nose. Nancy tried too, but with no success. I went to the bathroom a few times and poured my drinks into the toilet knowing that what I was about to do required me to have my wits about me. I pretended to be drunk, though I was completely sober. When it was time to leave, I offered to drive the women to the hotel, but strongly suggested they go to the bathroom before we left. While they were gone, I emptied the container with the Temazepam powder into Karla's drink."

"How did you do that without anyone seeing you?" Ziggy asked.

"It was easy. Sleight of hand comes easy to me because I used to fool around with magic tricks. You distract with one hand as the other goes undetected," he explained. "Now, I'd like to get back to my story."

"Karla came back first, and I insisted she finish her drink before we left. I could tell she tasted something in the drink but was too drunk to say anything. The reason I waited till the end of the evening, was Charlotte told me Temazepam works quickly. That meant I had to get the women back to the hotel fast if I wanted Karla to make it up the stairs. Even though I was sober, I rode down the street loudly singing with the drunken women, making a big spectacle of ourselves. When we got to the hotel, I asked the desk clerk the time to be sure she knew when we came in. I slurred my words, and staggering up the stairs with the two women to make the desk clerk think I was also drunk. I put Nancy in her room first because I wanted to be alone with Karla. Karla fumbled around for her key card, so I played the gentleman and took her purse to help her find it. I let her in and handed her back the purse, but I kept the card. She didn't notice. When she had closed the door, I went to the back entrance door and unlocked it. I came down the stairs to the lobby a minute later and again asked the clerk the time, pretending I forgot what she said because I was so drunk. I wanted her to know that I was only upstairs for a couple of minutes.

I returned several hours later when everyone was asleep, climbed up the back entrance stairs and quietly sneaked in the door wearing another pair of Sybil's vinyl gloves. I used Karla's key card to enter her room again and returned it to her purse. I then went to her bed to check and see if she was dead yet. She was, so I spent some time with her. There were night lights in her room and the bathroom, so I was able to see a lipstick she had on the bathroom counter which I used to make the smile on her face and to write the word NAZI on her shirt. Everyone knew Karla was virulent antisemitic. Karla had her paint carrier in the room, so I took out a tube of her paint and smeared her eyes black. That's when I carved the smile into her face and stabbed her repeatedly. I turned the gloves inside out and silently left her room. I quietly opened the back entrance door, locked it, and left down the back stairway. You know the rest of the story," Tony said, smiling a sinister smile.

"You sexually assaulted the body?" Ziggy asked.

"What do you think? I always carry a condom, so I used it so I wouldn't leave any DNA evidence." he said grinning. Though Tony thought he was smart, he didn't realize how much he didn't know about DNA or other evidence.

"Now you asked me about Sybil. I'm tired and if you want to know how she fits into the equation, ask Annabel. I explained it all to her," Tony said, but nonetheless, he continued enjoying the limelight. "To put it briefly, those evil witches treated Sybil so badly. I loved Sybil more than I had ever loved anyone. She was the sweetest person I had ever met, and I know she loved me too. Because I feared she would leave me, I had to lie to her about my background. She caught me in some of my falsehoods and began snooping into my background at the prison. Her attitude to me changed after that and she became cold and distant. Hoping to gain her sympathy, I told her I was dying of pancreatic cancer thinking it might divert her attention, but the bitch kept snooping. When she found out about my mother and the three other women they said I raped and killed, she told me she didn't want to see me anymore."

"Did you rape and kill those three other women, Tony?" Jim asked.

Tony paused for a moment and then said,

"You'll never know how many women I've raped and killed, maybe it was just them, or maybe many more. Now, getting back to my story, I flew into a rage and tried to suffocate her. After that, I had to finish the job you see, so I staged her suicide. I typed the suicide note. Annabel can fill you in on the details. I killed Hillary and killed and raped Karla to get revenge for the horrific way they treated Sybil. I would have raped Hillary, but I didn't have enough time since I had to get back to the hotel for my alibi. I killed my mother to get revenge for the horrific way she treated me and my father. Now you understand why I did it."

"Why would you want to kill Annabel?" Raj asked.

"She was smart and knew too much. That was one reason. The other reason was, just for the thrill of doing a cute 24 year old."

"I think I'm going to be sick," Raj said, disgusted and incapable of understanding the depth of the depravity of the man.

The others kept quiet, not wanting to say something that would silence Tony.

"I had it all worked out. I planned to stage my own murder by cutting myself with a razor and leaving a bloody crime scene in my hotel room. I have a disguise with a grey wig, beard, and eyebrows that I've been wearing around the island to create another identity for myself. I was going to leave the hotel by that back entrance again wearing the disguise. I'd use my forged ID to escape back to San Diego on the Catalina Express. A forged passport would allow me to cross the Mexican border and live with an ex-convict friend who has a place in San Miguel de Allende. It almost worked, but that stupid bitch made me fall on my knife," Tony said, proud of himself and reveling in his own brilliance.

"You're going away now and you're going to die of cancer in prison, Tony. That will be the price you'll pay for everything you did to those women," Raj said, his eyes brimming with anger.

"Hey! I'm an institutional man. I do much better on the inside because woman make me lose control and do things to get revenge. And for your information, I don't have pancreatic or any other kind of cancer, that was all just a big scam to play on people's sympathy."

Saturday

Chapter 25: Art Awards Ceremony

David grumbled as he rolled over to see the clock. It was 5:30 in the morning and he still wasn't feeling great. He had been up late the night before worrying about Annabel and even after she called him to say she was alright; he still couldn't sleep. It was not quite light yet when he heard his cell phone ringing in the bathroom where he had left it charging the night before.

"Hello... Hi Annabel, how are you feeling this morning?" David asked.

"I think I'm okay, David. I need you to do me a big favor."

"After last night, my dear, anything you want," David said.

"I need to borrow your easel, mine's broken. Can you set yours up outside the hotel on the sidewalk right away? I'll explain why when I get there in about a half hour."

"You've got it! I'll see you then," he said.

After I had been released from the Catalina Island Medical Center, Raj pushed me out of the hospital in in a wheelchair. Even though Raj had been up most of the night, he was going to help carry my paintings to the Casino by the 9:00 am deadline. Raj helped me in the car and drove me to the hotel to meet David. When we arrived, David was waiting with his easel all set up and ready to go.

"How are you feeling today, my friend?" I asked.

"Much, much better. The good thing about either food poisoning or a hangover, is that you recover quickly."

I explained the situation to him, and he also offered to help deliver my paintings to the Casino. Raj piled the remnants of my equipment that he had stored in his car onto the sidewalk, and I placed the painting I had done the night before on David's easel. I completed the painting, put on the finishing touches, and David put the frame on it. There it was. This was my masterpiece. It was a great painting, and I was glad I fought for it.

"I think that's the best thing you've ever done, Annabel. It's a winner!" David exclaimed.

"I think so too. Now, let's get this and my other paintings to the Casino."

"Okay, but remember, you promised the doctor you would let David and me do all the work. You need to take it easy," Raj reminded me.

"Yes, I know you're right."

"But Annabel, you've got to do something with your hair. It's all bloodstained. Braid it and stick your pigtails up inside your hat," David suggested. I immediately complied. Though they had cleaned me up at the health center, they hadn't washed my hair.

"Wow, you've done a lot of paintings. How many did you paint?" Raj asked thinking that worrying about hair after what had happened was nonsense.

"Let me count, one, three, six, twelve, thirteen. I did thirteen paintings that are good enough to put in the show. Number thirteen could have been an unlucky painting for me considering what happened last night, but that painting turned out to be my best."

"It could have been your last painting, Annabel. You have no idea how lucky you are to still be here." Raj said.

"Oh, I'm acutely aware Raj, if I hadn't been able to lift the entire easel above my head and shove it in Tony's face, he wouldn't have fallen backward on the knife. Even though he was weak from the stab wound, I don't think I could have fought him off. He was so much larger than me. I'm happy to be standing here today," I said.

"Which two paintings have you chosen as the submissions for the awards ceremony?" David was focused on getting the paintings to the Casino on time.

"I'm entering the one I did of the Casino murals which I'm calling Deco Dreams. That's the one I was doing Sunday night while Hillary was being murdered, how macabre. Ooo I shudder just thinking about it. What shall I call this one?" I said pointing to my masterpiece. David was good at coming up with names, so I usually deferred to him to give me titles.

"How about, "I Lived to See It," David suggested half joking. Raj and I groaned.

"No, that's too dark, David. No one will want to buy a painting with that title. It will remind them of all the murders. Come up with something more up lifting."

"How about "Avalon Life," Raj suggested.

"Yes, that'll work." I looked to David, and he approved. That would be the title.

We piled my paintings into Raj's car and headed for the Casino. We were about a half hour late, but many other artists were still straggling in just as Raj had predicted. While David and Raj were carrying in my paintings, I walked around the enormous Casino ballroom and looked at the work of the other artists. There were some wonderful pieces in the show. Since "The Three Amigos" hadn't arrived with their paintings yet, I gave my vote for Artist's Choice to one of Mercy O'Reilly's paintings since Randy's weren't there for me to see. He didn't know it, but I thought he was the best plein aire artist I had ever seen, not just in California, but the entire country. If I could be only half as good as he, I would be thrilled... but every now and then, I came close.

When Raj and David were finished carrying in my paintings, they found me wandering around the exhibition. They had placed my two prize paintings on the presentation easels the art organization had provided, and they wanted me to see how they looked. By then, more paintings had arrived, and together, the three of us surveyed what was now on display. Raj was perceptive for someone who saw things in black, white, and shades of gray. We were so opposite, for with my tetrachromatic eyes, the world was a spectrum of dazzling color. I found it fascinating that he had been so oblivious to what had been so thrilling to me my entire life. I liked explaining the fundamental aspects of art to him and opening a whole new world to him which he had never been exposed.

"Are you hungry?" I asked. They both nodded.

"Good, me too. Let's go to Sally's Waffle Shop for brunch," I suggested.

David then said, "We haven't been to Sally's yet since we've been having the continental breakfast they serve at the Glenmore. We've heard Sally's is good and it would be nice to finally sit down and have a real quality breakfast. I'm so sick of those muffins."

We made our way down Crescent Avenue to Sally's, located close to the Green Pier. It was good to have the pressure of producing paintings finally removed, and for the first time since we disembarked onto the island, David and I could relax. The restaurant was still crowded even though it was late morning. The hostess seated us in a booth close to the window where I noticed the light streaming in was highlighting the beautiful bone structure of Raj's face. He would make a wonderful subject for a portrait, I thought as we sat there waiting. It took quite a while for the waitress to arrive because of the crowd, and she apologized profusely to Raj when she took our order.

"What will you have today?" she asked, still looking at him.

"What would you suggest?" I asked, still looking over the extensive menu.

"Our omelets are the best. They come with hash browns, bacon, and an English muffin," she said, still looking at Raj. He nodded, so that's what we ordered.

"Raj, aren't you going to get in trouble if you don't call in to the police station?" I asked.

He just laughed and said, "Annabel, I'm a volunteer. I set my own hours although I try to keep them somewhat regular."

"You mean they don't pay you for all the time you put into the department?" I was shocked and appalled that they would take advantage of him like that.

"No, of course not," he answered.

"That's terrible! Why don't you say something?" I asked. He just smiled and laughed. It was the first time I heard him have a good, hearty laugh.

"Annabel, I own half of Envarna. We make a lot more money in a half hour than the station commander makes in a whole year."

I sat there looking at David as he raised his eyebrows and pursed his lips. Neither of us knew quite what to say. My mind was racing attempting to grasp the impossible amount of money that would be. I was flabbergasted, but I finally blurted out,

"Well, silly me." We all laughed filling the awkward silence.

Our breakfasts arrived, and the omelets were terrific though a little cold. For a nice change David and I took our time and had a nice leisurely brunch with our host. It was getting close to the opening of the Casino to the public, so Raj paid the check, and we walked out into the sunshine.

"Thank you, that was so pleasant," I said to Raj.

"It was my pleasure, and a real treat for me. You two are so different than the people I hang around with. All we talk about is the business and the future of technical advancement. You're focused on the beautiful world that's all around you that we techies and businesspeople don't notice much. You've given me a whole new perspective on everything, a wonderful perspective, and I'm so grateful and happy to have met you." he said smiling at me.

"Do you think it would be alright to walk to the Casino?" I asked. It is such a beautiful day."

"No, we're going to ride in the car. You're going to take it easy, and David told me though he's feeling much better, he doesn't have a lot of energy. To tell you the truth, I'm tired too. I got three hours of not very sound sleep last night.

We arrived at the Casino well before the exhibition opened to the public. The anticipation of the awards ceremony was now beginning to hit me. Because I was an official artist entrant, David was my assistant, and Raj was now officially a police deputy, we all were allowed to go in early. My heart was pounding as we walked up the long ramps. As we entered the ballroom, I felt an adrenaline rush and put my hands to my face feeling the heat from the flush. Could I possibly have won Best of Show, I was about to find out. I had won some First-Place awards before, but sometimes I walked away with nothing, not even an honorable mention, but I was young and a fast learner. My work was good now, and maybe I would receive the accolades I believed I deserved and for which I had worked so hard this week.

"Annabel, Look!" David said racing toward my display. Raj and I trailed along after him unaware of what he was seeing.

I had won something; I now could see something hanging from my painting. My walk slowed as I approached, almost afraid to look. Did I win Best of Show? There were ribbons, not just one, but two. One was a red ribbon, I had won Second Place for "Avalon Life," the nocturn that almost cost me my life. The second ribbon was a white one. I had won the Artist's Choice award for my Casino murals nocturn, "Deco Dreams." It was Randy who had been awarded Best of Show for a painting called "Catalina Memories." It was a wonderful painting, and he deserved his award. Mercy O'Reilly got Third Place, and Mike and Saul each got Honorable Mention. There were lots of hugs with Raj and David, lots of congratulations with the winners, but when the elation of the moment had settled down, I found Randy and said,

"You deserved Best of Show. I study and analyze your work all the time. I'm amazed not only by your technical skill, but by your creativity, and ability to capture the spirit of whatever it is that you paint. You inspire me to strive to be a better artist."

"Annabel, that was the nicest compliment I have ever had. But what is so meaningful to me is that the accolade comes from you. I know I'm good, but you're nipping right at my heels. I considered you to be my most formidable rival at this show, and I was right. You got Second Place and Artist's Choice. You're so young and already so good. You scare me."

"Thank you, Randy, you have no idea how much what you said means to me. Oh, if you haven't heard, it was Nancy Hall who wrote those frightening notes to us."

"Yes, Tom Derringer called and told me. She's a disgusting piece of work, that woman."

"Are you going to say anything to anybody?" I asked.

"You bet I am. There must be consequences for what she did. People need to know who she is, and what she is. Are you going to say anything?" he asked.

"No, though I certainly agree with what you say. It makes perfect sense, but I'm going to leave it in God's hands, and yours too. I guess it hasn't gotten out yet, but last night they found the murderer.

"Who is it?" Randy said eager to hear more.

"I can't give you his name until Captain Derringer releases it, but last night I was the next one on his hit list. He tried to kill me when I was painting from the scenic view up Chimes Tower Road, the one that got me the second-place award. Isn't that ironic. I'm not supposed to give out information, so I need to shut up.

"What on earth were you doing alone, at night on Chimes Tower?" he asked.

"I wasn't alone, I was with the killer who fooled me into thinking he was there to protect me."

"So, it was someone you knew?"

"I can't say, but I'm lucky to be alive, Randy. You can't see it because of my hat, but I have stitches in my head where I hit it on a rock or something."

"Are you alright?" Randy asked putting his hand on my shoulder.

"I have a lot of cuts and bruises and may also have a concussion."

"When we first started talking, I noticed the bruise on your cheek and that your arms were all scraped up."

"I got all that while I was falling down the slope next to the road. The doctor told me I couldn't enter the exhibition today, but nothing and nobody was going to stop me."

"I understand. You put your heart and soul into this show. I saw it."

"I'm sure the police will announce their findings soon. The good news is, we're all safe now that they caught the killer. I wanted to put your mind at ease, but I can't say anymore."

"Oh look," Randy said as he pointed to my display. "They just put another ribbon on your painting."

While Randy and I were talking, Raj came over and interrupted us.

"Tom's going to make an announcement," he said leading me away from Randy. He knew I liked him and had a lot in common with Randy. Raj was jealous... and I liked that too.

"Okay, but I got another ribbon. I need to take a look and see what it's for. Oh Raj, it's the People's Choice Award, how wonderful. That means my painting will be on the cover of the catalogue next year."

"You're amazing, I'm so proud of you!" he said giving me a kiss on my cheek."

At that moment Tom Derringer stepped up to the podium and took the microphone.

"May I have your attention please." A lull came over the room as we all turned our attention toward Tom, awaiting the latest update on the murders. "I have good news for y'all. Last night we caught the man who murdered two of your artists. It was almost three, but by the grace of God, she is alright and here with us today. We were able to catch him in the act of the attempted murder of Annabel Adams." There were gasps and murmuring throughout the audience. "She was so close to being the third victim. The man's name is Tony Rossi, and I thank heavens, we stopped him just in time. Thank y'all for your patience during this frightening time. Now you can enjoy the rest of your festival." With that explanation, Tom stepped down from the podium and left without taking any questions.

People circled around me asking all about what happened last night and about Tony Rossi. During all the commotion, I looked over at David who was motioning for me to come back to my display area. After excusing myself, I joined David and Raj who had left me to help David tend to the people waiting to buy my paintings. I was happy to see the two mothers with their children who had posed for me. They both wanted to purchase those paintings. By 4:00 that afternoon when the show was ending for the day, I had sold all but one painting.

While David and Raj were busy finishing up the paperwork, I found Brianna Gleason and asked her if David, who wasn't a Signature Member of PAPOC, could take over my empty space and enter his work in the show. At first, she was adamant saying only Signature Members were allowed, but I explained that he was a wonderful artist and the more paintings the art organization sold, the better it was for everyone. She acquiesced when I dangled the dollar sign in front of her, but she told me to keep it quiet and not tell anyone she had given me her approval because she assured me, she would deny it.

"David, I have good news. You are going to quietly put your paintings up in my space tomorrow to sell your paintings. I framed all your best paintings yesterday when you were sick, so you'll be ready to go first thing tomorrow. But you can't tell anyone what we're doing. The show goes from 9:00 in the morning till 1:00 in the afternoon.

"Oh, Annabel, that's wonderful. Thank you so much." David was so grateful.

"I'll help you too, David." Raj said, but now I've got to go home and get some sleep before I drop."

Raj drove us to the Glenmore and promised to pick us up at 7:00 am for breakfast at Sally's and then to help set up David's paintings in the Casino. After a well needed nap, David and I awoke feeling famished around 7:00 that evening.

"Do you want to go to the Busy Bee and have our last night on the island dinner celebration for your great sales and awards?" David asked.

"We can also celebrate that after all your efforts and kindness to me, you'll get what you deserve, which is to be in this show! Karla and Hillary are the only ones who would protest, and they're gone. Nancy isn't going to cause us any trouble."

"I think that celebrating tonight is a great idea, David. Hopefully we can get a table on the patio by the water."

"Okay, let's go!" he said.

We got up and slowly took the short walk to the Busy Bee restaurant. It was crowded but the people who had arrived early were beginning to leave. Several of our friends and new acquaintances were there also wanting to enjoy the last night on the island before taking the Catalina Express back to the mainland. Charlotte and Alice stopped me as David and I were being escorted to our table and said,

"How are you, Annabel? We heard about the horrible ordeal you went through last night."

"Thank you for asking, Charlotte, I'm doing just fine. I thank God that I can say I'm happy to be alive. When Tony was getting ready to kill me, he confessed some things about Sybil to me. I know you're Sybil's grandmother, Charlotte, and you're her daughter, Alice. Sybil and I were close friends.

"Yes, she had mentioned your name with great affection many times," Charlotte said.

"I have a question for you both. Is there any particular reason why you came to this event?" The women looked at each other for a moment and Alice said,

"Neither of us believed that Sybil's death was a suicide; we could tell someone else wrote the note they found. The word choices were like the things she would say but the punctuation was wrong. Sybil was a former English teacher, a stickler for punctuation, and the note had lots of errors. We knew about her involvement with an ex-convict and were convinced he had something to do with her death but had very little to go on except an unclear photo of a man who was at Sybil's celebration of life. We were hoping he might show up here at the festival. Neither of us would have guessed it was Tony. We've just been trying to make some sense of her death since it happened."

"That's the problem, there is no sense to it. Tomorrow, the police can fill you in on all the details of Tony Rossi's confession. You can call me when we all get home, and I can spend the time you deserve discussing what I know with you. Call me soon while it's all fresh in my mind." I handed them my card.

David was seated at a wonderful table right next to the water when I caught up with him.

"Don't you love the scent of the salt water and this balmy night air, David?"

Just as I was beginning to settle into my seat, I saw Miriam and Asher Bloomberg. Miriam immediately came over to our table to offer her sympathy concerning what she called my spine-chilling ordeal and to congratulate me on my sensational win at the festival.

"Miriam, the painting that won second place was the one I was painting when Tony tried to kill me. Isn't that ironic. That's why it's called Avalon Life."

"Ironic is putting it mildly. I also heard about the terrorizing notes Nancy taped on your door and on Randy Creighton's backpack. That's just terrible," Miriam said.

"Boy, news certainly travels fast. I wasn't going to say anything about it, but others feel they must; her reputation is ruined," I said. I've enjoyed meeting you so much, Miriam. Let's exchange phone numbers and keep in touch," I suggested.

After Miriam left, I noticed Nancy sitting alone at table in a dark corner. She was pretending to read a book which was impossible because there was very little light at her table. I noticed she was deliberately not making eye contact with anyone. When the exhibition was closing for the day, I took a walk around the room wanting to see whose work had sold well and resonated with the public. When I came to Nancy's section, I could see her paintings had not sold well. There she sat now, all alone and sulking in the corner. I decided to go over to her table and speak to her.

"Hello Nancy, how are you doing?" I asked curious to see how she would react to me.

"Just fine, thanks. Congratulations on your awards," she said not making eye contact.

"Thank you... have a nice evening." I walked away thinking, who knows how this may play out. It could all blow over in a few weeks. I might have to deal with her back in San Diego, so I don't want to make her my enemy. David would say I was a hypocrite. I think I'm diplomatic. It all depends on a person's perspective. I don't need revenge; Nancy's lack of character will bring her nothing but misery."

"David, this is our last night on the island. Do you think I should call Raj and ask him to join us."

"Why don't you text him. Here, I'll show you how to do that." David said. We immediately got a response from Raj saying he would be there soon.

A few minutes later, Raj entered the patio wearing a beautiful tunic looking like some exotic Indian maharaja. He was a sight to behold. The diners all stopped their talking and watched him as he proudly strode toward us to our table.

"I'm so glad you could make it. You look wonderful, Raj," I said standing, giving him a warm, welcoming embrace. "I didn't want to call for fear of waking you, but David showed me how to text."

"I had been awake for about ten minutes when I got the text. It was such a nice surprise. I was thinking of calling you both about going to dinner to celebrate your triumph," he said looking at me.

"This is the perfect night to do that. Other than almost being murdered, I had a wonderful time here on the Island. So, let's celebrate being alive, and the happy experiences we've all had together. Meeting you, Raj was by far the highlight of this whole, remarkable adventure."

So, we spent out last night on the island, dining, drinking Arnold Palmers, and celebrating together. Misty Avalon befittingly took its name from an old Arthurian legend. Native Americans called it "the Bay of the Seven Moons," The island had been immortalized in song as "the island of romance. Others referred to Catalina as "the enchanted isle." It can't be denied that there was something magical about this place that inspired people to write poetry, sing songs, and invent special names. On my last night here, I was feeling the full measure of the island's magic.

Sunday

Chapter 26: The Final Day

It was Sunday morning, our last day, and we planned to begin the day with a nice breakfast with Raj. We met him at Sally's Waffle Shop at 7:00 am where we had breakfast and made our plans for the day. Right after breakfast, we returned to the hotel, checked out, picked up all our belongings, and piled everything into Raj's car. We would try to get most of David's paintings sold at the Casino and when the show was over, Raj would take us to the loading dock with all our effects. We would then board the Catalina Express at 4:00 that afternoon and head back to San Diego. This was the day when the greatest number of the art sales were made because most of the artists lowered their prices to avoid carrying unsold paintings back to the mainland. Unfortunately, that would mean David would have to discount his paintings. Art that wasn't sold at plein aire events frequently ended up in the artist's garage and none of us wanted that. I noticed my head was hurting more today since I wasn't focusing on my work, and the full weight of what had happened Friday night was finally beginning to sink in. As I climbed into Raj's car, I broke down and started crying. David and Raj tried to comfort me, suggesting that we go for some Big Olaf's Pistachio ice cream even though we just had a big breakfast.

"Not right now, maybe later." I said, trying to regain some composure.

"Are you sure? You know how much you love Pistachio ice cream," David said trying to entice or distract me.

No, I'm okay now, I don't know what's wrong with me, I hardly ever cry," I said sniveling and wiping my eyes.

"It's a delayed reaction. We often see it after someone has undergone a traumatic event. I was amazed that the whole horrifying experience of Friday night didn't seem to faze you at all. You took it all in stride as if that kind of thing happened to you all the time. You were so calm; it was truly astonishing. It's finally catching up to you now," Raj explained.

"Yes, I'm sure you're right. I was so focused on the festival and couldn't think about anything else. Sorry I lost it."

"Oh, I guess we can forgive you just this once," David teased.

People were lined up outside the Casino again, but this time in larger numbers hoping for bargains. David had only nine completed paintings that he felt were good enough to display in the exhibition, so we eliminated those he felt weren't adequate. It was more important for his art to show well than to present his second-rate paintings for the purpose of making sales. Right now, he needed to build his reputation as a quality artist.

Today I would focus on helping David with his sales. I told him to study the way I interacted with customers and learn some sales techniques. I wasn't supposed to exert myself for at least 48 hours, so I would remain seated as I made complimentary comments about David's paintings to potential buyers though it was better to be standing and animated. David was a good painter, but a terrible salesman. Though my friend was shy and introverted, I wasn't, so I knew I could move his work if I engaged the collectors. It's up to the artist to learn to be a closer by finding ways to ask potential customers to buy their art. I learned that by observing salespeople in art galleries.

"Oh, here they come," I said.

It was like December twenty-sixth at Macy's as the customers came running up the ramp, racing to the location where their favorite artist was located. Many headed my way; most of them immediately realized that there was a different artist now in my spot. I quickly engaged the buyers in a dialogue. I liked David's paintings, so they were easy for me to sell.

Raj helped David by keeping track of the names, email addresses, phone numbers of the purchasers, and what they had purchased so that David could develop a clientele. Though David was a bright guy, and a capable organizer, he enjoyed creating beauty so much, that he often neglected other aspects of the art business. Knowing him as I did, I suspect he probably had some form of attention deficit disorder. Despite the differences in our personalities, we worked well together though David had difficulty with some of the other artists and people in general. To me, he was a kind, considerate person and friend and that was what mattered to me.

When we had sold about two thirds of David's paintings, I encouraged him to take over sales. I left him on his own while I took a break and walked around the room so I could see what art was still available. When I passed Mike Mitchell's location, he gave me a warm hug and said,

"I'm so glad you're alright. What a horrifying ordeal that must have been for you."

"It was like a real-life version of a horror movie, Mike," I explained.

"Congratulations on your Second Place, Artist Choice, and People's Choice awards. Your paintings were wonderful. You should be so proud of yourself."

"You have no idea how much this meant to me, and congratulations on your win, as well," I said returning the compliment. I could tell by his face he wasn't pleased receiving an Honorable Mention.

Saul saw me talking with Mike and joined us. After the pleasantries, they wanted to hear the gruesome details of my previous nightmare, so I told them the story. There were lots of hugs and expressions of relief that I survived. While we were talking, I saw Officers Tom, Jim, Corny, and Ziggy coming into the room. I excused myself wanting to learn more about the details of the case.

"Hello, Annabel, how are you feeling today?" Sergeant Jim asked.

"I'm doing well, considering the circumstances. This has been quite an eventful week, hasn't it?" I commented.

"That's an understatement if I've ever heard one." Jim said.

"What did you do with Tony?" I asked.

"He's at the hospital surrounded by a phalanx of guards."

"That man should never be let out on the street; he's as crazy as a loon. It's hard to believe they let him loose on the public. How does that happen?" I asked, utterly baffled by our justice system.

"We must follow the law and sometimes we put people in places of authority that are incompetent, uninformed, or lazy. Some are ideologues who empathize more with depraved criminals than the innocent victims."

"I see," I answered thinking about what he had said.

"He made a full confession last night and I saw that insanity you're talking about. You were so right about Sybil, that was the catalyst for the murders of Hillary and Karla. You pointed us correctly in the San Diego direction. Your instincts and contributions were wonderful and probably helped save your life, but it was Raj who should get most of the credit. He did an end run around Tom and me by doing a background check on Tony. We thought Tony was sick with cancer and had a solid alibi, so we essentially ruled him out. Raj wasn't convinced, he continually rejected our conclusion and argued with us. We received Tony's background check while you were up on Chimes Tower Road with him. If that background check hadn't come in when it did, you'd probably be dead.

"Wow, Jim, I had no idea it was that close. I'm curious, did you ever get a look at Tony's timeline?"

"We finally did, but it sat on Tom's desk because we're so low on staff. Would you like to look at it? I can run to the office and get it."

"Oh yes, please! Could you also show me his rap sheet?'" I asked.

About twenty minutes later, Jim returned with his little tape recorder and began recording my findings.

"I'd like to show your conclusions to Tom. As you know, he's skeptical of handwriting analysis thinking it's not scientific and more of a parlor game."

"So I noticed, but I think I've almost changed his mind."

"This may be what it takes if you're as good at this as I think you are," Jim said handing me the timeline.

"Okay, let's see what we have here. Holy cow!" immediately, I could see danger signs all over the sample of Tony's handwriting.

"What do you see?" he asked as he stood next to me looking at the script.

"Jim, if only I had seen this sooner. At first glance I can see that this is the writing of a dreadfully sick individual. Do you see this muddy, smeary writing, this is a person who can't control his libidinal urges. It's also a sign of violence. He has extremely heavy pressure, that's an indication of intense feelings and strong reactions. This clubbing in his lower zone endings, tells me his aggression is released physically. Many of his letters are embellished indicating a maniacal, theatrical, immature person with delusions of grandeur. Con artists often embellish like he does. Here's some coiling which is the sign of a cunning, tricky person. His letters are bizarre indicating distortions in thinking. He has overinflated loops in the upper zone, a sign of delusional thinking, he's not in touch with reality."

"Boy, that's for sure," Jim said.

"Wow! Look at this. It's called the felon's claw, revealing unconscious guilt and sexual aberration. Felon's claws are common in the handwriting of criminals who are in prison. It's too bad I didn't see this with the other handwriting samples. There's no question in my mind that I would have recognized this sample as the handwriting of the probable killer," I said folding the timeline and handing it back to him.

"This is amazing, Annabel. If we had these results sooner, we might have saved Karla's life and you wouldn't have had to go through that terrible ordeal," he said. "I've never put much credence in handwriting experts. The last man we used wasn't very helpful or even very competent. Maybe the problem was with the caliber of the analyst we were using. After what you've shown me, you've changed my mind," Jim admitted. "If Tom approves, could we fax you some script samples and pay you to give us your opinions in the future?"

"Of course, I'd be glad to help you out, and I certainly could use a little extra cash. When I have all my books and articles, I can be even more precise in my analysis. When you play your recording back to Tom, I'd like to be a fly on the wall when he hears this."

"I'm sure he will find it to be very interesting. I can't wait to see his face when he hears it. Here's Tony's rap sheet," Jim said handing it to me.

I just shook my head as I read it.

"Unbelievable! I don't understand how they could ever let such a dangerous man loose on the unsuspecting public. I have a question, Jim. Why are you all here at the Casino today?"

"We're going to wait till it's almost closing time and then announce our recent findings. We'll also take some questions now that we have our murderer." Jim looked at his watch. "It's about that time now." Tom was on the podium and was motioning for Jim to join him. He stepped up to the podium taking the microphone and said,

"May I have your attention, please... Hello everyone, I'm here to give you some additional information about the capture of the murderer. We arrested Tony Rossi on Chimes Tower Road last night. He had fallen on his knife and was losing blood rapidly. We took him to the Health Center hospital where he confessed to both the murders of Hillary Applegate and Karla Streicher, and the attempted murder of Annabel Adams. He'll be removed from the island as soon as it's safe to transport him. I'll take a few questions now."

"Is he well-guarded at the hospital?

"Absolutely. There's no way he can get loose."

"What were his reasons for killing Hillary and Karla?" an artist asked.

"Revenge, he was angry at Hillary and Karla's treatment of his former girlfriend." Tom answered.

"Who was his girlfriend?"

"Her name was Sybil Halifax. I'm sure some of you knew her." There were gasps in the audience. Though there weren't many artists from San Diego at the festival, artists from many other locations were familiar with her work.

"How did he kill Hillary and Karla?"

"Hillary was stabbed, and Rossi put an overdose of sedatives in Karla's drink."

"If he was a serial killer, were there other victims?" Mercy O'Reilly asked.

"Yes, we are aware of at least two others. He murdered his former girlfriend Sybil, and his mother." There were gasps heard all around the ballroom. Sibyl's suicide was a shock to the art community, and now they had just learned she hadn't committed suicide after all... she was murdered. I felt my eyes welling up, but I somehow managed to hold back a flood of tears. I was sure Tom had informed Charlotte and Alice before he informed the public of Sybil's murder.

"Although Tony confessed to killing those two others, we suspect that there were many more.

"Can you tell us anymore about Annabel's attempted murder?" Randy asked.

"Why don't you talk to her about that. I'm sure she'll be able to fill you in on all the details much better than I could. She's quite a talker," Tom said with a wink. "Do you have any more questions?" Tom asked. No one did. All the artists were exhausted and ready to wrap things up and head home.

"Then that's all for now. Please enjoy the rest of your stay on the island." Tom and the officers then stepped down and exited the Casino.

It was time for David to gather up his few remaining paintings if we were to make it to the Catalina Express on time. It was a wonderful week. It was a terrible week. It was a week of extreme emotions and pushing physical abilities to their limit. Though I was glad to be going home, I was already feeling nostalgic wondering what my future would hold. There were still many unanswered questions concerning my relationship with Raj and what would become of us? What would happen to Nancy back in San Diego when members of our painting group learned about her note writing misconduct? Would the Bloombergs ever receive justice for their family members who were pillaged and slaughtered by the Nazis? Would Charlotte and Alice ever have any sense of closure concerning Tony's murder of Sybil? If they contacted me, how would I explain the details of his confession to me about Sybil? Reliving his words would be a nightmare for us, but we all could find solace knowing Tony's judgement would eventually be left to the highest court.

But now David, Raj, and I were hungry and decided that we would go to the Busy Bee for one last meal together. We were all physically and emotionally spent when we were escorted to our table on the patio. The afternoon sun was smiling down on us as we were seated one last time beneath one of the blue umbrellas. I looked out on the shiny white boats floating in the cobalt-blue water and closed my eyes trying to memorize the remarkable scene. Photographs never do justice to the beauty of the real vision. We ordered our lunch and tried to make conversation.

When the Arnold Palmers and Cobb salads arrived, I said, "Raj, I want to thank you and tell you how much we appreciate all you've done for us. You're the most generous, kind, impressive man I've ever met." I looked at David and said, "except for you, David, of course. Aside from almost being murdered, this was a wonderful week." We clinked our glasses and indulged. Raj was right, the Cobb salads were delicious. When we finished, we completed the afternoon with a Big Olaf's treat, then Raj drove us to the landing dock where the Catalina Express was waiting. He helped us load our suitcases and equipment into the boat storage compartment and it was time to leave.

"David, would you give me a moment so I can say goodbye to Raj?"

"Of course," he said as he walked up the ramp onto the boat.

I turned to Raj and said, "I don't want this to be the end. I don't want to leave here and never see you again. I know we live far away from each other, but let's see if we can make something work?"

"That's all I needed to hear. I can fly my plane down to San Diego to see you, or if you like, we can take off from Palomar Airport and fly here for the weekend."

"I would like that. When are you going back to San Jose?"

"I leave tomorrow. This was quite an unexpected vacation, but it ended well for us. I'm so glad you're okay. I'll call you when I get home."

"I'll be waiting," and with that, he kissed me goodbye.

David had found us our seats on the boat, but before I was seated, I waved to Raj who was still standing on the dock below. As the Catalina Express pulled away, I found David and took my seat.

For a moment I sat quietly and thought about the past week and wondered what my future would bring... grateful that I would even have a future. I wondered why it was me who survived? I thought about this island and the people who came here a hundred years ago. How they must have marveled at its unspoiled beauty. I thought about the lovers who cruised here to dance to the music of their era, dreaming they might experience a night of pleasure and romance. We come and we go, dancing and loving throughout the ages during that brief period of time we have when we're young and beautiful. How fragile we are, and yet we live as if our lives will last forever reveling in our glory days. We press on, like little boats beating against the current, forever tainted by the echoes of the past.

David looked at me wondering what I was thinking and why I was so quiet. With hopeful anticipation he asked, "Well, how did it go?"

"Beautifully!" I said.

THE END

Made in the USA
Monee, IL
25 October 2025

0935984e-41da-4045-8bf6-03242295e053R01